The BLUE & the GRAY

THE CONFLICT BETWEEN NORTH & SOUTH

MARTIN F. GRAHAM
RICHARD A. SAUERS, PH.D.
GEORGE SKOCH

CONSULTANT: WILLIAM C. DAVIS

PUBLICATIONS INTERNATIONAL, LTD.

Louis Weber, C.E.O.
Publications International, Ltd.
7373 North Cicero Avenue
Lincolnwood, Illinois 60646

Manufactured in U.S.A.

8 7 6 5 4 3 2 1

ISBN: 0-7853-1707-4

Library of Congress Catalog Card No.: 96-68490

Martin F. Graham is the coauthor of several Civil War books including *The James E. Taylor Sketchbook, Mine Run: A Campaign of Lost Opportunities, Great Battles of the Civil War,* and *The Civil War Wall Chart.* He specializes in Civil War and World War II history and is a frequent contributor to *Civil War Quarterly, Civil War Times Illustrated,* and *America's Civil War.* He frequently lectures on Civil War figures such as Stonewall Jackson and James E. Taylor and is past president of the Cleveland Civil War Round Table.

Richard A. Sauers, Ph.D., earned his doctorate in American history from Pennsylvania State University. He is the author of more than a dozen Civil War books, including *The Gettysburg Campaign, A Caspian Sea of Ink: The Meade-Sickles Controversy,* the two-volume set *Advance the Colors! Pennsylvania Civil War Battleflags,* and *A Succession of Honorable Victories: The Burnside Expedition in North Carolina.* His articles and reviews appear regularly in a variety of Civil War publications.

George Skoch, associate editor for *Blue & Gray* magazine, has written and edited numerous articles and books about the Civil War. He is coauthor of *The James E. Taylor Sketchbook, Mine Run: A Campaign of Lost Opportunities, Great Battles of the Civil War,* and *The Civil War Wall Chart.* He is a regular contributor to *Civil War Times Illustrated, America's Civil War,* and *Civil War Book Exchange & Collector's Newspaper.*

William C. Davis is an award-winning historian who has written and edited many Civil War titles, including *A Way Through the Wilderness, A Government of Our Own: The Making of the Confederacy,* the six-volume series *The Image of War,* and *Touched by Fire.* He is a Pulitzer Prize nominee for *Breckinridge: Statesman, Soldier, Symbol* and *Battle at Bull Run.* A frequent lecturer and consultant on the Civil War, Mr. Davis was editor and publisher for 20 years at *Civil War Times* magazine.

Research assistance: Desdra E. Horwitz

Photo tinting artist: Cheryl Winser

Flags courtesy Todd Fisher, Emperor's Headquarters, Chicago, Illinois

Contents

INTRODUCTION
LOOKING BACK ✴ 6

CHAPTER 1
CLOUDS OF WAR ✴ 10

The North: Bustle and Industry • The South: An Agrarian Land • A Race
Apart • The Backbone of the Cotton Crop • Surrender of Fort Sumter •
Victory at Fort Sumter • The Call to Enlistment • The Flush of Victory

CHAPTER 2
WARTIME POLITICS ✴ 40

Abraham Lincoln • Jefferson Davis • Northern Governors •
Southern Governors • Lincoln and Congress • The Confederate Congress •
Lincoln's Cabinet • Davis's Cabinet

CHAPTER 3
THE ECONOMICS OF WAR ✴ 66

Funny Money • Financing the War • The Demise of Cotton • The Sanitary
Fairs • The Blockade • The Importance of Transportation • An Inadequate
Rail System • The Hum of Machinery • Tredegar Iron Works

CHAPTER 4
THE ARMIES ✴ 86

The Search for a Leader • The Confederate Forces • Ulysses S. Grant •
Robert E. Lee • The Union Plan • The Strategy of the South • The Northern
Army • The Southern Army • A Powerful Ally • Slaves and Soldiers •
Northern Prisons • Southern Prisons

CHAPTER 5
THE COMMON SOLDIER ✴ 128

Billy Yank • Johnny Reb • Northern Uniforms • Southern Uniforms •
Union Camp Life • Confederate Camp Life

CHAPTER 6

THE NEW SCIENCES OF WAR ✷ 150

Northern Ironclad Ships • Southern Ironclad Ships • The Henry Rifle •
Southern Weaponry • Northern Weapons Technologies • Southern Weapons
Technologies • Northern Trench Warfare • Southern Trench Warfare

CHAPTER 7

MEDICAL CARE ✷ 182

Medical Care in the Union Army • Confederate Medical Care •
The U.S. Sanitary Commission • Chimborazo Hospital •
Northern Casualties • Southern Casualties

CHAPTER 8

THE MEDIA ✷ 206

Newspapers of the North • Southern Newspapers • Newspaper Suppression •
The Wandering Newspaper • Northern Photographers • Confederate
Photographers • Artists of the North • Southern Artists

CHAPTER 9

THE HOME FRONT ✷ 232

Food Shortages in the South • The Expansion of the Northern Economy •
The Confederate Draft • The Draft in the North • Richmond Food Riot •
New York City Draft Riot • The North Grew Tired • Facing the End

CHAPTER 10

WOMEN IN THE WAR ✷ 254

Union Spies • Confederate Spies • Mary Todd Lincoln • Varina Howell Davis •
Women in Blue • Women in Gray • Angels of the Battlefield • Confederate
Women • Union Women of Valor • Working Women

CHAPTER 11

LEGACY OF THE WAR ✷ 280

Lincoln's Assassination • Lee's Surrender at Appomattox • The North:
Prosperity • The South: Desolation • An America Transformed •
Reconstruction • Union Veterans • Confederate Veterans

CIVIL WAR TIME LINE ✷ 300

INDEX ✷ 308

LOOKING BACK

*W*e cannot escape history."
That is what Abraham Lincoln said. In the 130 years since he
spoke, millions of Americans have been unable to escape the
Civil War that spawned those words. Nor have they had any
desire to escape. The Civil War experience remains a part of
the air we breathe, a tangible sight, sound, even taste, of
American life and culture. It remains, and forever will be, a
part of our definition as a people.

Year after year we reexamine, redefine, revise, and rein-
terpret the story and meaning of the events of 1861–1865, but
one thing we do not do is resist it. In a country with a lively
mythology, our greatest body of myth comes from the War Between the States. We part with the myth reluctantly, if at all.
We cherish even what we know to be wrong.

Every few years it is time to take a broad overlook, though,
to seek to remind ourselves of what is fact and what is fiction
and what constitutes the latest thinking about what happened
and what it meant. Thus a book like *The Blue & the Gray* appears. There have been uncounted illustrated histories of the

Opposite: *"Fight for the Standard" (artist
unknown)*

Ulysses Grant Monument, Vicksburg National Military Park

war. Most of them have strayed little if at all from the battlefields to look at the people themselves. Most, too, have simply put a new gloss on hoary old generalizations, recounted time-honored anecdotes, passed on a fair bit of misinformation through carelessness, and assumed the reader was satisfied.

The Blue & the Gray is a different sort of book. It is an illustrated history aimed at the general reader that truly covers the war and its people in all their shades and aspects. Moreover, even with the full benefit of the latest in Civil War scholarship, this book does not adopt an academic tone. It

Antietam National Battlefield

recognizes differences of opinion and allows the reader to make choices. For each subject—government, the home front, women and minorities, finance, diplomacy, and more—this book compares the North and the South to see differences and similarities. In fact, the pages of the book are bordered in blue or gray depending on which region is being discussed. Well-chosen illustrations accompany the text, giving us a chance to see firsthand the people who fought and suffered and to evaluate the gains and losses that made up the balance sheet of the Civil War.

Lookout Mountain, Chickamauga and Chattanooga National Military Park

It is a portrait that is at once inspiring, terrifying, and in some indefinable way humbling. Different as we think we are from our ancestors of those times, still we would be like them if we could, for they responded to an unimaginable ordeal. And perhaps we are more like them than we think, if only we knew them better. *The Blue & the Gray* gives us a perfect opportunity to get acquainted.

William C. Davis

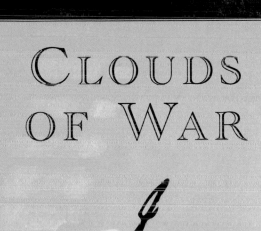

CLOUDS
OF WAR

*I*n 1787 the founding fathers gave each state the right to choose its stance on the issue of slavery. For more than 70 years afterward, slavery and states' rights were heatedly debated in the halls of Congress, with some discussions turning into physical confrontations between politicians. No grounds for final compromise could be found, and in retrospect, it seemed inevitable that the issue could not be permanently resolved in any other way than on the battlefield.

✴

"Richmond Slave Market Auction," by Eyre Crowe

THE NORTH: BUSTLE AND INDUSTRY

✳

To a Southern friend in Louisiana, Ohio native William Tecumseh Sherman spoke bluntly on Christmas Eve of 1860. Just four days earlier, South Carolina had become the first state to secede from the Union, and now Sherman was certain that the United States stood on the eve of civil war. "The North," Sherman said, "can make a steam engine, locomotive, or railway car; hardly a yard of cloth or a pair of shoes can you make. You are rushing into war with one of the most powerful, industriously mechanical, and determined people on Earth. . . . You are bound to fail."

Sherman's words were more than just rhetoric. By 1860 the North possessed all the tools to build a formidable war machine. In population alone, Northerners outnumbered Southerners better than two to one.

In contrast to the rural society of the South, the North had been developing an economy largely based on manufactured goods. Its success could be attributed to a large pool of immigrants willing to both work for low wages and live in the congested cities of the North. To transport these goods to market,

The Seth Thomas Clock Company, organized in 1853, was one of the growing number of Northern businesses producing consumer goods.

Artificial waterways such as the Erie Canal, shown in this 1832 drawing, helped to widen Northern territories for expansion and production.

By the early 1860s, when this photograph of the New York harbor district was taken, New York was a major world port. It remained busy throughout the war.

This 1830s sketch of wooden-masted ships depicts the bustling port of the Long and Central wharves in Boston Harbor.

Iron casting plants like this one produced the thousands of tons of steel needed to supply the Northern war effort with weapons and machinery. While a few large plants like this existed at the beginning of the war in Southern cities such as Chattanooga and Richmond, the resources necessary to produce quality steel were exhausted by 1865.

an effective network of rails and canals crossed the Northern terrain. Eighty-five percent of the factories and 70 percent of the nation's railroad mileage lay north of the Mason-Dixon line. Meanwhile, over the previous decade, manufacturers had increasingly turned to specialized machinery to mass-produce everything from nuts and bolts to railroad spikes to revolvers. "There is nothing," New England industrialist Samuel Colt had claimed, "that cannot be produced by machinery."

During the first months of the war, the Northern economy suffered setbacks. "Never before perhaps in the history of this country," trumpeted the New York *Tribune,* "has such feeling of uncertainty, of alternate hope and fear, prevailed in the business community." Northern investors lost $300 million in Southern debts, trade with the South came to an abrupt end, and 6,000 businesses failed throughout the North. These hardships were short-lived, however. The effort required by Northern industry to win the conflict simply propelled the economy forward. Speaking about the war, New York Congressman Roscoe Conkling said, "It is not regulated by the laws of honor, but by the laws of trade. I understand [that] the practical problem to be solved in crushing the rebellion . . . is who can throw the most projectiles."

This print shows women working in a doubling room in a cotton manufacturing plant. Throughout the first half of the 19th century, cotton was the major product for Southern planters and Northern manufacturers.

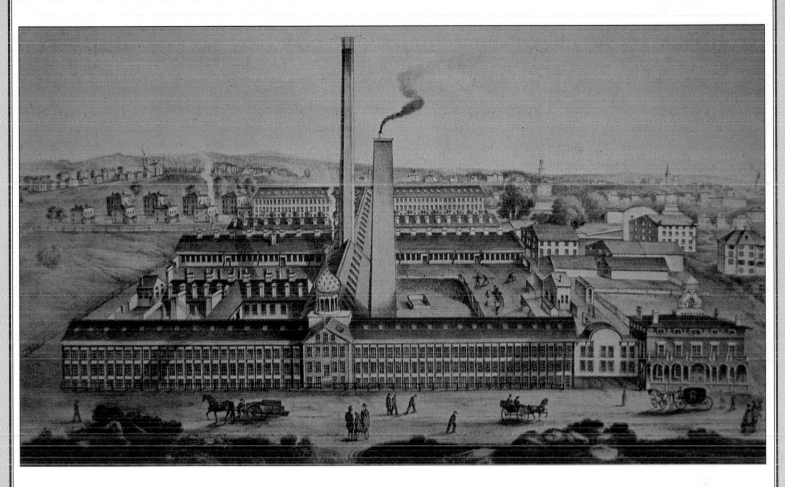

As the war lengthened and expanded, so too did the Northern economy. Men who flocked to the army and navy by the hundreds of thousands had to be fed, clothed, equipped, and sheltered. And all this came at a time when labor-saving machinery was revolutionizing American manufacturing. By the second year of the war, Northern industry turned out bullets as easily as it turned out biscuits.

President Abraham Lincoln's annual message to Congress on December 6, 1864, reflected the impact the war had had on the Northern economy. With a million men in uniform and better than 600 ships in the navy, Lincoln still could claim that Northern resources "are unexhausted and, as we believe, inexhaustible." Even more chilling to Southern ears was his boast that "we are gaining strength and may, if need be, maintain the contest indefinitely."

The Samuel Colt Factory, the world's largest privately owned armory, was built in 1854 in Hartford, Connecticut. More than 1,500 persons were employed in it. Colt supplied the Federal government with more than 40 percent of the revolvers used during the war. Prior to the first battle of Bull Run, Colt also sold revolvers to the Confederacy.

THE SOUTH: AN AGRARIAN LAND

✴

Southern emotions and hopes ran high with the start of war. "The capacity of the establishment is almost without limit," wrote New Orleans journalist James D. B. De Bow. "Every branch of manufacturing is springing up." Another journalist reported hearing about "new schemes and designs—manufacturers, arts, sciences. We shall soon be able to produce every cannon and gun, every pistol and sabre, every rifle and spear." These were assessments based on passion, not fact.

From the beginning, the balance sheet lay heavily on the side of the North. Southern society was primarily agrarian, rooted in generations of genteel values. It was headed by landed gentry who depended on the labors of the large class of poor, landless whites as well as black slaves. Forty percent of the population were slaves.

The economy of the South was built on the production of staple crops. Tobacco thrived in Virginia and Kentucky, rice was a major crop in South Car-

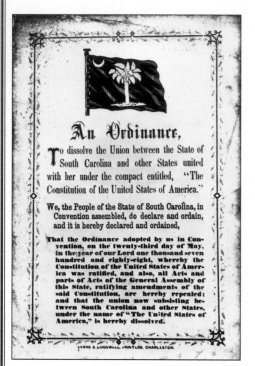

By a vote of 169 to zero, the secession convention meeting in Charleston, South Carolina, voted to leave the United States on December 20, 1860. "The cheers of the whole assembly continued for some minutes," wrote a delegate, "while every man waved or threw up his hat, and every lady waved her handkerchief." Six more Southern states followed South Carolina's lead by February 1, 1861.

Prior to the invention of the cotton gin, one slave typically took more than ten hours to manually remove one pound of cotton lint from the plant's seed. With the new gin, planters could easily produce 300 to 1,000 pounds of cotton each day.

olina, and sugarcane was the dominant crop in Louisiana. With the invention of the cotton gin in 1793, the South's dependence on that crop dramatically increased. Within two years the South was exporting 8,000 tons of cotton per year. From 1800 to 1860, the spread of cotton fields throughout the South made it the major crop of the region. As cotton fields increased, the demand for field laborers increased, further entrenching the institution of slavery in the South.

The Rosedown Plantation is still standing in St. Francisville, Louisiana, along the Mississippi River. Many old plantation houses have been restored as museums to show the antebellum way of life.

COTTON GIN

Although Northern textile mills increasingly demanded cotton, the manual resources required in preparing it made it uneconomical to grow. After harvest, it took a slave as many as ten hours to remove one pound of cotton lint from the sticky seed. Due to lack of adequate manpower, cotton crops would often decay in the fields.

Eli Whitney, a Northern tutor and amateur inventor, learned of this problem in 1793 while in Georgia. Whitney later wrote, "...All agreed that if a machine could be invented...it would be a great thing, both to the Country and the inventor."

Within ten days Whitney developed the cotton gin, a device that used toothed cylinders to separate the cotton fiber from the seed through wire screens. With the gin, planters could produce 300 to 1,000 pounds of cotton per day. Cotton production dramatically expanded throughout the South.

The impact of cotton's growth also helped fuel the growing textile manufacturing industry of the North, creating a strong economic bond between the two regions. By the start of the Civil War, the South had heavily invested in the production of cotton, while the North had developed a strong manufacturing base. The South grew the cotton, but Northern manufacturers grew rich on it. "Every day [the North] grows more wealthy and densely populated," a French visitor observed, "while the South is stationary or growing poor." While Southerners envied the growth of the Northern region, they despised "the filthy, crowded, licentious factories . . . of the North."

Maintaining an agrarian society in an industrial age proved costly to the Southern economy and its war effort. The North had little trouble shifting its manufacturing resources to supporting the war effort. The South, however, with its plantation base, had relatively few factories to transform. Moreover, many Southern mills had been forced into bankruptcy due to the success of their Northern competition.

Once the Southern manufacturing war machine finally got into gear, the biggest difficulty it faced was delivering products to the armies and civilians alike. Although "the railroad is our backbone," as one Southern diarist observed, only 9,000 miles of track were in place throughout the South. Worse,

Slaves wrestle with bales of cotton along the New Orleans levee. More cotton was shipped out of New Orleans than any other Southern port.

this system was divided among more than 100 separate companies of varying quality that used various track widths. This created transportation nightmares for Southern manufacturers and accounted for significant delays in the delivery of manufactured or grown products. By the end of 1864, the rail system had broken down to the point that it was practically nonexistent. No other means of transportation ever surfaced to replace the crippled railroads.

The effect of the Union blockade along the Southern coast eventually strangled trade with Europe, crippling the Southern economy even more. It didn't take long for the shortage of supply to affect the economy of the South. Inflation ran rampant when demand for all products far exceeded supply. The Confederate armies were forced to fight without adequate weaponry or supplies. A new class appeared on the Southern scene: the speculators who grew wealthy at the expense of the helpless. "So much we owe the speculators," the Richmond *Dispatch* printed, "who have stayed at home to prey upon the necessities."

Bales of cotton are piled as high as possible on the deck of the Mississippi steamer Henry Frank. Because of the number of ships laden with cotton that left New Orleans for Northern industrial ports, the city was called King Cotton's capital.

A RACE APART

✦

When President Abraham Lincoln took the podium to deliver his annual message to Congress on December 1, 1862, he spoke for a nation that had been bitterly divided for generations. "Among the friends of the Union," he declared, "there is a great diversity of sentiment and policy in regard to slavery and the African race amongst us. Some would perpetuate slavery; some would abolish it suddenly and without compensation; some would remove the Freed people from us; and some would retain them with us. . . . Because of these diversities, we waste much strength in struggles among ourselves."

SCENES FROM UNCLE TOM'S CABIN. № 1.

PERILOUS ESCAPE OF ELIZA AND CHILD.

Originally appearing as a serial in the Washington National Era *in 1851,* Uncle Tom's Cabin *was published in book form in 1852. More than 300,000 copies of the book were sold within the first year of its publication. It was even more popular in England, where 1 million copies were sold within a year.*

While incidents of slave uprisings were relatively rare, isolated incidents of rebellion added to the establishment of strict controls over slaves. The most publicized episode was the massacre of more than 50 whites in Virginia by a band of slaves led by Nat Turner. This drawing depicts Turner's arrest in October 1831.

Even before the Constitutional Convention of 1787, many Northerners embraced the antislavery movement. In 1817 the American Colonization Society was founded to send free blacks from the United States to the colony of Liberia on the western coast of Africa. Though largely unsuccessful, the Society's efforts helped to promote antislavery ideals.

In 1831 activist William Lloyd Garrison began publication of *The Liberator,* an abolitionist journal that favored immediate emancipation of the slaves without compensation to their owners. By 1836 "safe houses," or well-established networks of "stations," were operating in the North to aid runaway slaves in their escape to Canada. The so-called Underground Railroad assisted an estimated 75,000 blacks in finding freedom between the War of 1812 and the Civil War.

As the 1860s dawned, less than one percent of the Northern population was black. Those blacks who lived in the North were commonly segregated and resided in substandard conditions. Several states, in-

Situated in Manhattan's Greenwich Village, this house served as a headquarters for the Underground Railroad. Created as a means to assist escaped slaves to freedom in the North and Canada, the Underground Railroad was a series of Abolitionist-owned "stations." "Conductors" guided the runaways by night from one station to another along a preestablished path.

The calm, bespectacled expression of William Lloyd Garrison (1805–1879) belied his fanatic abolitionist sentiment. Refusing to compromise on the issue of slavery, Garrison once burned a copy of the Constitution in protest. He called it "a covenant with death and an agreement with hell."

HENRY WARD BEECHER

Henry Ward Beecher, brother to Harriet Beecher Stowe (who wrote *Uncle Tom's Cabin*), was himself an outspoken critic of slavery. However, Beecher, a minister, was equally critical of radical and fanatic abolitionists. Beecher called John Brown's disastrous raid on the Federal arsenal at Harpers Ferry the "act of a crazy old man."

Born in Litchfield, Connecticut, in 1813, Beecher had a knack for oratory and theatrics that helped attract public attention to his antislavery message. A gifted writer, Beecher continued to encourage an end to slavery. After the end of the Civil War, Beecher supported readmitting the Southern states quickly. Until his death in 1887, Beecher championed humanitarian causes.

cluding President Lincoln's own state of Illinois, had enacted "Black Laws" that discouraged or prevented blacks from settling within their borders. Only four states allowed blacks to vote, and in no states could they serve on juries. "The truth is," a foreign visitor observed, "the Negroes, slave and free, are a race apart, in both North and South."

Abolitionists, though firm in their convictions and loud and relentless in their appeal, nevertheless managed to attract only a small active following among Northerners. At the same time that many Northerners opposed slavery, few wanted to have millions of freed slaves mixing with white society and competing for white jobs. "We cannot afford to let the abolitionists succeed," a New York merchant wrote. "It is not a matter of principle with us. It is a matter of business necessity."

Abolitionist principles generally ran to extremes. They ranged from the radical doctrines of outspoken journalist Garrison to the more moderate sentiments of Reverend Henry Ward Beecher, both of whose impassioned pleas combined to emblazon the plight of slaves on the nation's conscience. Their voices helped to chart a new course for the nation.

Too often the voices of protest had led to violence and bloodshed. On a chilly November night in 1837, a proslavery mob of men 200 strong, wielding torches and firearms, surged along the bank of the Mississippi River to Alton, Illinois, to the warehouse office of a weekly abolitionist newspaper, the *Observer*. The editor, Reverend Elijah P. Lovejoy, was infamous in the region for his bitter denouncements of slavery, and the mob aimed to silence him. Shouts, then shots, were exchanged between the mob and Lovejoy and several of his supporters in the warehouse. Finally, flushed from the building, Lovejoy died in a blaze of gunfire.

Reaction across the North to Lovejoy's death was swift and strong. "Thousands of our citizens who lately believed that they had nothing to do with slavery," an abolitionist wrote, "now begin to discover their error." During one protest meeting at a church in Ohio, the minister challenged his congregation, saying, "Are we free, or are we slaves under mob law?" From the back of

The spirit of abolitionist John Brown dominates this dramatic depiction of the many symbols of the Civil War. With a Bible in one hand and a gun in the other, Brown towers above the living and dead victims of the war. Some in the North saw Brown as a martyr, but he really was a secondary figure in the events that led to war.

the church, a grim figure rose, raised his right arm, and cried, "Here, before God, in the presence of these witnesses, I consecrate my life to the destruction of slavery." The man was John Brown.

For the next 21 years, Brown attempted to make good on his pledge. Though he failed at the businesses he tried, Brown maintained his abolitionist zeal. Violence flared from his hand at Pottawatomie Creek, Kansas, where he led antislavery forces fighting to bring the Kansas Territory into the United States as a free state. There in May 1856, he and four of his sons hacked five unarmed proslavery men to death.

Three years later, Brown devised a grandiose scheme to ignite an armed slave uprising and establish a stronghold for escaped slaves in the Appalachian Mountains. His plot failed miserably when he and about 20 followers captured the Federal arsenal at Harpers Ferry, Virginia. Ten of Brown's men died in a shootout with local militia and Federal troops. Brown and six of his followers were tried for treason and sentenced to hang. From the scaffold, Brown stood as grim and defiant as he had in the church two decades earlier and handed one of his guards a note. It read: "I, John Brown, am now quite certain that the crimes of this guilty land will never be purged away but with blood."

THE BACKBONE OF THE COTTON CROP

✦

"Cotton is king," reflected Senator James Henry Hammond of South Carolina, "and the African must be a slave, or there's an end of all things, and soon."

Sprawling plantations built adjacent to massive fields of cotton sprang up across the South during the decades before the war. The spread of cotton as a staple crop created a small group of landed gentry, less than 25 percent of the Southern white population, who controlled large groups of black slaves. The cost of purchasing the large number of slaves necessary to work the fields was often greater than the cost of the plantation and the land. The price of a single strong field hand in 1860 was as high as $1,800. Since purchasing and maintaining a large slave population was so costly, the plantation owners could not afford to invest in development of devices that could reduce their dependence on slavery.

VALUABLE GANG OF YOUNG NEGROES

By JOS. A. BEARD.

Will be sold at Auction,

ON WEDNESDAY, 25TH INST.

At 12 o'clock, at Banks' Arcade,

17 Valuable Young Negroes, Men and Women, Field Hands. Sold for no fault; with the best city guarantees.

Sale Positive and without reserve!

☞ TERMS CASH.

New Orleans, March 24, 1840.

This 1840 slave auction poster was typical in the major slave markets throughout the South. The importation of slaves from other countries was banned by Congress in 1808 and made punishable by death in 1820. Blacks were sold openly in auctions prior to the Civil War. Individual slaves of exceptional value could be sold for as much as $2,500.

One of the North's most skilled propagandists, artist Thomas Nast drew this cartoon for Harper's Weekly *in 1861. Hailed by President Lincoln as "our best recruiting sergeant," Nast here parodies the strength of the South built on the oppression of the black slave.*

This painting depicts plantation life along the Mississippi River. The cotton crop was planted in the spring. Harvesting and preparing the crop for sale normally extended into the early winter months.

Slaves planting sweet potatoes at the Pope Plantation near Hilton Head, South Carolina. Although staged for the photographer, the picture presents a view of various tasks assigned to slaves on a typical plantation.

This serene image of blacks waiting to be placed on the auction block is far from typical. Although owners made sure their slaves were scrubbed and well dressed, the blacks themselves were rarely as relaxed as those depicted here, particularly when loved ones accompanied them to the block. Faced with separation and an uncertain future, they found auction a terrifying experience.

With the growth of the abolition movement in the North, slaveholders found it necessary to develop arguments for retaining the "peculiar institution." They portrayed themselves as benefactors who treated their blacks much better than the industrial barons of the North treated their "hired hands." Other arguments plantation owners gave for retaining slavery included these: Adult slaves were like children, lacking in intelligence and therefore unable to care for themselves; and the cotton industry would collapse without slave labor. This collapse would throw the American economy into turmoil, since the vast textile industry of the Northeast was dependent on the production of the crop.

Although the life of a slave on most plantations was not as severe as typically depicted in the Northern press, blacks were treated more as property than human beings. Masters intervened directly into the lives of their slaves. The Louisiana code of 1806 stated: "The condition of the slave being merely a passive one, his subordination to his master and to all who represent him is not susceptible of modification or restriction. . . . He owes to his master, and to all his family, a respect without bounds, and an absolute obedience, and he is consequently to execute all the orders which he receives from him, his master, or from them."

Slaves had few civil rights. They were denied legal standing in court and were prohibited from testifying against whites. They were even required by law to step off a sidewalk when a white approached. Teaching slaves to read or write was prohibited. Marriages and divorces were not a matter of legal record and required the master's permission.

Some laws existed to protect personal rights of slaves. Limits were set on the number of hours per day

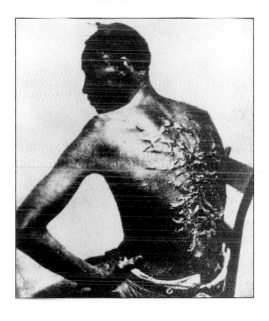

This escaped slave shows the extent of plantation justice to a photographer in 1863. The master had power of complete discipline over his slaves.

FREDERICK DOUGLASS

The son of a slave and a white man, Frederick Douglass escaped to the North in 1838. Self-educated, he became an eloquent spokesman for abolition.

"In thinking of America," Douglass wrote, "I sometimes find myself admiring her bright blue sky —her grand old woods. . . . But my rapture is soon checked when I remember that all is cursed with the infernal spirit of slaveholding and wrong; When I remember that with the waters of her noblest rivers, the tears of my brethren are borne to the ocean, disregarded and forgotten; That her most fertile fields drink daily of the warm blood of my outraged sisters, I am filled with unutterable loathing."

Douglass traveled to Europe, where he wrote his autobiography to silence skeptics and raised $600 to purchase his freedom. Returning to the United States, he published a weekly abolitionist newspaper, the *North Star,* and assisted the Federal government in raising black regiments throughout the war. He served as United States Minister to Haiti from 1889 to 1891.

Before being brought out to the auction block to face their uncertain future, slaves often waited in pens like these. Slave pens were frequently no better than common jails.

The outside of the building with the slave pens depicted above right. This structure stood in Alexandria, Virginia, across the Potomac from the nation's capital in Washington.

masters could force them to work, and slave owners were required to give adequate care. Penalties up to hanging were provided for a slaveholder who killed a slave. While the laws were relatively harsh, the actual practice of the law was at the discretion of the master. Some slave owners taught their slaves to read and write and allowed them to choose their own mates as well.

Masters developed their own set of regulations for the plantation, and—if the estate was large enough—an overseer would be hired to ensure obedience. Slave drivers were chosen from among the more responsible and educated slaves to issue daily orders and to be held responsible for the performance of those under their control. Once they were old enough, children were put to work as quarter-hands and gradually advanced to full-time field worker status. They stayed in the fields until they were too old or physically unable to continue.

Slaves generally lived in windowless log cabins that served primarily as sleeping quarters, since they were fed in common dining rooms. Those children too young to work in the fields were cared for in large nurseries.

Two fears plagued the minds of slaveholders: violence on the part of their slaves and the loss of their investments if their slaves ran away. Although incidents of violence toward whites were isolated and rare, much publicity was given to each episode. In 1831 a rebellious slave, Nat Turner, recruited about 60 followers who killed more than 50 whites in Southampton County, Virginia. The group was hunted down and killed, but the fear of further uprisings haunted plantation owners for decades.

Most discontented blacks did not turn to violence, however. They were satisfied with nonviolent acts of disobedience, such as malingering, petty theft, or running away. The plight of the slave was best described by the most famous runaway, Frederick Douglass. "I appear this evening as a thief and robber," he told Northern audiences. "I stole this head, these limbs, this body from my master, and ran off with them."

In a ritual repeated at hundreds of plantations across the South, blacks near Charleston, South Carolina, carry bundles of harvested cotton to the mill in this post-war photograph. Even though the war was over and they were no longer slaves when this photograph was taken, working in the fields was still the primary occupation of Southern blacks.

The job of picking cotton in the field was rigorous for the unfortunate laborers. Because cotton grew relatively low to the ground, overseers on horses could easily supervise the work.

SURRENDER OF FORT SUMTER

✳

On December 26, 1860, Major Robert Anderson and more than 70 Federals under his command rowed from their garrison at Fort Moultrie to the safety of Fort Sumter in the middle of Charleston Harbor. Since the secession of South Carolina from the Union six days earlier, Anderson felt that the move from the mainland was necessary to ensure the safety of his men. Federal President James Buchanan had decided to hold Sumter at all cost.

Although newly inaugurated President Abraham Lincoln had sworn to defend all Federal property within the boundaries of the seceded states, he also pledged that he would not be the one to fire the first shot. The stalemate continued until the early hours of April 12, 1861, when four Confederate emissaries rowed to Fort Sumter, demanding its surrender. When negotiations failed, Confederates opened fire at 4:30 A.M.

After 34 hours of shelling, Anderson realized that further resistance was futile. He agreed to evacuate the fort on the 14th only if his men were permitted to fire a 50-gun salute to the Federal flag.

At 2:00 P.M. on the 14th, the salute began. Halfway into the salute, a cartridge bag prematurely ignited, killing one man and wounding five others, one mortally. Anderson cut short the salute. By 4:00 P.M., the Federals filed out of the fort carrying the flag that had flown throughout the bombardment. The same flag would once again be triumphantly raised over the fort four years later.

Charleston Harbor, showing the position of Fort Sumter and Confederate troops on shore.

Charleston Harbor

Cooper River

Mount Pleasant

Charleston

Castle Pinckney

Charleston Harbor

Ashley River

SULLIVANS ISLAND

Fort Moultrie

Fort Johnson

JAMES ISLAND

Fort Sumter

Cummings Point

Atlantic Ocean

MORRIS ISLAND

N
W   E
S

— Confederate positions

VICTORY AT FORT SUMTER

✻

*A*ll the pent-up hatred of the past months and years is voiced in the thunder of these cannon," one civilian observed, "and the people seem almost beside themselves in the exultation of a freedom they deem already won." The exhilaration felt by all observers as they watched shells fly across Charleston Harbor, plowing into Fort Sumter, stemmed from months of anticipation. Southerners saw the transfer of the Federal garrison of Fort Moultrie to Sumter on December 26, 1860, as an act of aggression.

The Confederate Stars and Bars flag waves in the breeze above Fort Sumter. The Union garrison surrendered the fort to Confederate forces on April 13, 1861, after 34 hours of bombardment. Not until April 14, 1865, did the U.S. flag once again fly over the fort.

When the *Star of the West* attempted to bring supplies and troops to Fort Sumter, it was fired on by batteries lining Charleston Harbor. The stalemate continued for three more months before the newly elected president of the Confederate provisional government, Jefferson Davis, felt it was time to act.

Davis sent word to General Pierre G. T. Beauregard to demand the surrender of the fort. If refused, he was to attack it. When the Federal commander, Major Robert Anderson (Beauregard's artillery instructor at West Point), refused to surrender on April 12, the Confederate gunners opened fire.

The bombardment had been watched with delight by the citizens of Charleston. Upon hearing the first shot, diarist Mary Chesnut wrote, "I sprang out of bed. And on my knees—prostrate—I prayed as I never prayed before." This was among the first of many prayers this war generated over the following four years.

THE CALL TO ENLISTMENT

✳

W ar!" Word had reached Jonathan Upson's Indiana farm while he and his young son, Theodore, were preparing for spring planting. A neighbor had delivered the news that the Rebels had fired upon and taken Fort Sumter. Their neighbor announced: "The President will soon fix them. He has called for 75,000 men. . . . And just as soon as those fellows find out that the North means business, they will get down off their high horse."

Though differing in circumstances, this was a scene repeated countless times across the North as the nation was plunged headlong into civil war. The public reacted swiftly and in overwhelming numbers.

"Everywhere the drum and fife thrilled the air with their stirring call," wrote Mary Livermore, a Chicago minister's wife who later devoted herself full-time to care for Union soldiers. She continued:

> Recruiting offices were opened in every city, town and village. . . . Hastily formed companies marched to camps of rendezvous . . . the streets echoing the measured tread of soldiers. Flags floated from the roofs of houses, were flying to the breeze from chambers of commerce and boards of trade, spanned the surging streets, decorated the private parlor, glorified the schoolroom, festooned the church walls and pulpit, and blossomed everywhere. All normal habits of life were suspended, and business and pleasure alike were forgotten. . . .

The suspense was over. Decades of politics and oratory had stirred passions of North and South to a flash point. A Confederate cannon in Charleston Harbor had sparked the conflict. Now eager but untested armies of young men, naive and unfamiliar with the horrors of the battlefield, hospital, and prison pen, hurriedly prepared to do combat, where results would be measured in blood.

"Civil war is actually upon us," wrote U.S. Senator John Sherman, "and strange to say, it brings feelings of relief." Within days of learning the news from Charleston, 100,000 patriotic spectators assembled at Union Square in New York City to view the tattered flag that had flown above Fort Sumter. The scene was bedlam. The crowd cried for vengeance.

Recruiting posters like this sprang up throughout the North immediately after the fall of Fort Sumter.

Irish and German immigrants enlisting on the Battery in New York. More than 500,000 foreign-born soldiers served during the Civil War, mostly for the Union. The majority of them welcomed the chance to show patriotism for their adopted nation. Prejudice against immigrants often clouded their performance in battle.

"Their Country's Call," by J.L.G. Ferris, depicts the sacrifices made by families whose young men went off to the war.

Cadets of the West Point class of 1862 relax for the camera. The young man standing to the left is Ranald Mackenzie, who would rise to the rank of general within two years of graduation and go on to greater fame as an Indian fighter. Ulysses Grant stated in his memoirs, "I regarded Mackenzie as the most promising young officer in the army."

By April 15, President Lincoln had called for 75,000 volunteers to serve for 90 days. Soon he called for 200,000 more. "One thing, as regards this matter," 57-year-old author Nathaniel Hawthorne lamented, "I regret . . . that I am too old to shoulder a musket." Then with the same stroke: " . . . and joyful thing is that [my son] Julian is too young."

The conflict would become a young man's war, however. Youths in their teens and 20s flocked to recruiters. "War! and volunteers are the only topics of conversation or thought," wrote an Ohio college student. "I cannot study. I cannot sleep, and I don't know how I can write." After joining the army, a young enlistee recalled his mother having said, "My son, other mothers must make sacrifices, and why should not I? If you feel that it is your duty to enlist, I will give my consent."

In some places across the country, the number of volunteers exceeded the government's ability to clothe, feed, and arm them, and the men went home to wait for another call-up. "We thought the rebel-

The Union and Confederate states. Missouri, Kentucky, and Maryland were slave states that did not secede from the Union.

North
South
Border states
— Mason-Dixon line

Me.
Minn.
Western Territories
Wis.
Vt.
N.H.
Mass.
N.Y.
Mich.
R.I.
Conn.
Iowa
Penn.
Ill.
Ind.
Ohio
N.J.
Md.
Del.
Mo.
Ky.
Virginia
Kansas
N.C.
Tenn.
Ark.
S.C.
Atlantic Ocean
Miss.
Ala.
Ga.
Texas
La.
Fla.
Gulf of Mexico

N
W
E
S

Private Arnold of the 22nd Regiment New York National Guard Infantry strikes a heroic pose.

ELMER ELLSWORTH

This Union soldier displays the crisp new uniform and equipment typical of volunteers early in the war. Their natty attire soon gave way to standard-issue Union blue once the soldiers were mustered into Federal service.

Called by his friend Abraham Lincoln "the greatest little man I ever met," Ellsworth became the North's first martyr soon after he responded to the call for volunteers.

Before the war, Ellsworth was celebrated for leading a national championship drill team called the U.S. Zouave Cadets. At the outbreak of hostilities, he recruited a regiment largely from New York City's fire department that he patterned after his drill team. Said Ellsworth, "I want men who can go into a fight now."

Clothed in colorful Zouave uniforms that were based on a French army design, his regiment was among the first to reach Washington. On May 24, 1861, the day after Virginia officially seceded from the Union, Ellsworth led his men to seize Alexandria, Virginia. Spying a Rebel flag flying atop a hotel, he entered the build-

ing, climbed to the roof, and tore the flag down. Descending the stairs, he was shot to death by the innkeeper, who in turn was killed by one of Ellsworth's men. The Union martyr's body lay in state at the White House, where a grieving Lincoln led the nation in mourning.

lion would be over before our chance would come," wrote one despondent recruit from Madison, Wisconsin. Meanwhile, in Cincinnati, Ohio, a 39-year-old lawyer determined he would go to war no matter what. "I would prefer to go into it if I knew I was to die, or be killed in the course of it," wrote Rutherford B. Hayes, who later became the 19th president of the United States, "than to live through and after it without taking any part in it."

In the spring of 1861, Hayes was only one of tens of thousands of Northerners who responded to the call to arms. "Recruiting officers were filled with men eager to enroll their names as defenders of their country," observed one young lady, "and women were busily engaged in preparing all the comforts that love and patriotism could suggest for those who were so soon to go forth to victory or death, while the clash of arms and strains of martial music almost drowned the hum of industry, and war became the theme of every tongue."

THE FLUSH OF VICTORY

✳

he streets of Charleston present some such aspect as those of Paris in the last revolution," a reporter for the London *Times* observed after the fall of Federal Fort Sumter. "Crowds of armed men singing and promenading the streets, the battle blood running through their veins—that hot oxygen which is called 'the flush of victory' on the cheek. . . . Sumter has set them distraught; never such a victory. It is a bloodless Waterloo."

The surrender of Fort Sumter on April 13, 1861, spurred great celebration across the South. Finally, after decades of political and social conflict, the Southern states had struck their first major blow for independence. South Carolina once again took the lead in setting the course of Confederate history, just as it took the first step in breaking ties with the United States when it seceded from the Union on December 20, 1860. In its Declaration of Secession, delegates from that state declared that nonslaveholding states

> have denounced as sinful the institution of slavery; they have permitted open establishment among them of societies, whose avowed object is to disturb the peace and to eloign the property of the citizens of other States. They have encouraged and assisted thousands of our slaves to leave their homes; and those who remain have been incited by emissaries, books and pictures to servile insurrection.

Similar sentiments led to the secession of six other Southern states by February 1, 1861. On February 4, 1861, delegates from these states met in Montgomery, Alabama, to form the provisional government of the Confederate States of America, electing Jefferson Davis as their president. In his inaugural address, Davis expressed his wish that the Federal government allow the Confederate states to peacefully set their own course. He followed up, however, with a warning to Federal President Abraham Lincoln. "If the Northern states . . . desire to inflict injury upon us . . . a terrible responsibility will rest upon it, and the suffering of millions will bear testimony to the folly and wickedness of our aggressors." Later he said to an emergency session of Congress: "All we ask is to be left alone."

Marcellus N. Moorman's resplendent uniform as a member of the graduating class of 1856 from the Virginia Military Institute is a long way from the more practical garb he would wear later as a member of a Virginia artillery unit.

This painting by James Massalon shows the inauguration of Jefferson Davis as president of the Confederacy on February 18, 1861. The ceremony took place on the portico of the Alabama State House in Montgomery, then the Confederacy's capital.

Early in the war men rushed to join the Confederate army. Expecting a short war, many feared they would miss the fighting. "So impatient did I become for starting," recalled a Confederate volunteer; "that I felt like ten thousand pins were pricking me in every part of the body, and started off a week in advance of my brothers."

This cartoon shows Jefferson Davis attempting to sneak out of the Union carrying the armaments of Fort Sumter with him. Uncle Sam is in the doorway asking Davis where he is going with Federal property. As this cartoon illustrates, the South relied heavily on weapons and equipment seized from the United States to supply its own armed forces.

News of Sumter's fall came as a great relief to many. The die had been cast, and everyone now realized that war was inevitable. "The intelligence that Fort Sumter has surrendered to the Confederate forces," recorded the editor of the *Montgomery Advertiser,* " . . . sent a thrill of joy to the heart of every true friend of the South. The face of every southern man was brighter, his step lighter, and his bearing prouder than it had been before."

On April 15, Lincoln called for 75,000 men to put down the rebellion. This was followed two days later by a Virginia state convention decision to join the Confederacy.

The preparation for war was on, but not everyone in the South felt that the firing on Fort Sumter was the best step in the interest of the new republic. "The firing on that fort will inaugurate a civil war greater than any the world has ever seen," predicted Confederate Secretary of State Robert Toombs. "It is unnecessary; it puts us in the wrong; it is fatal."

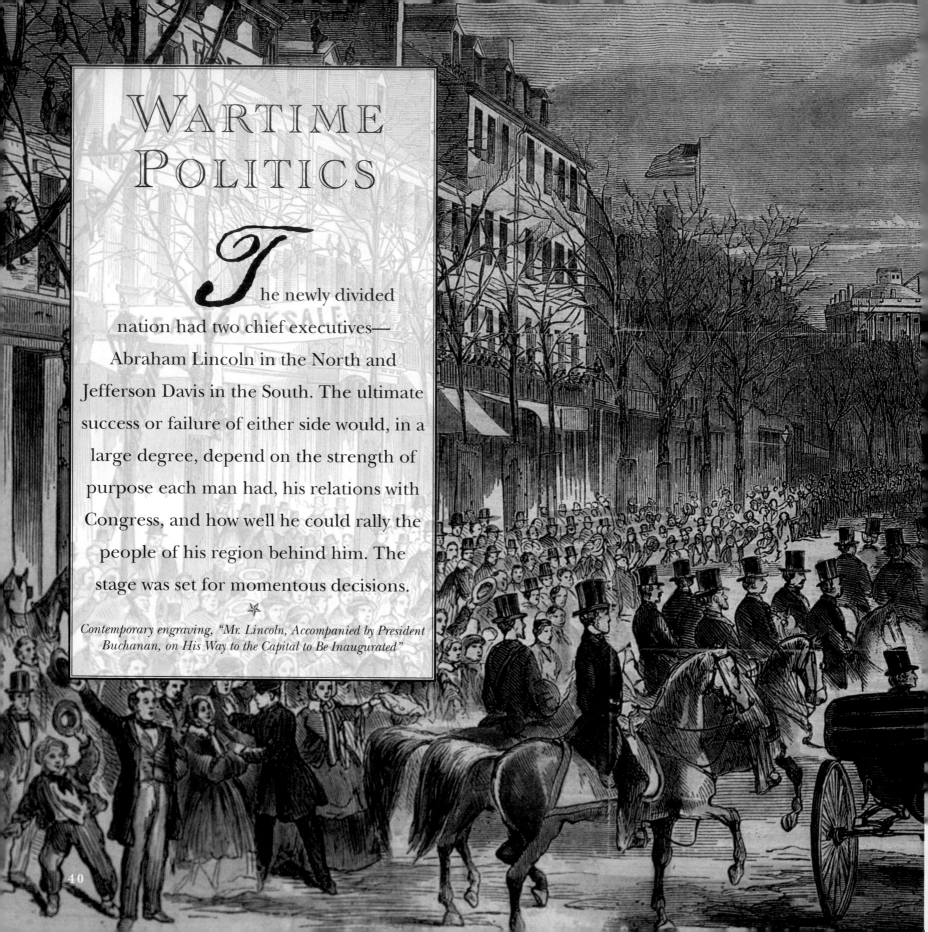

WARTIME POLITICS

*T*he newly divided nation had two chief executives—Abraham Lincoln in the North and Jefferson Davis in the South. The ultimate success or failure of either side would, in a large degree, depend on the strength of purpose each man had, his relations with Congress, and how well he could rally the people of his region behind him. The stage was set for momentous decisions.

✳

Contemporary engraving, "Mr. Lincoln, Accompanied by President Buchanan, on His Way to the Capital to Be Inaugurated"

ABRAHAM LINCOLN

✱

*A*braham Lincoln approached his March 1861 inaugural as a minority president. He had garnered only 39 percent of the popular vote; his three Democratic rivals, Douglas, Breckinridge, and Bell, accounted for the rest. The states of the Deep South had already left the Union, and the remaining Southern states were waiting to see how the new president would handle this deepening crisis.

At the time Lincoln was not considered a good candidate for the presidency. He had served four terms in the Illinois state legislature and a single term in the U.S. House of Representatives. Opponents viewed him as an uncouth frontiersman. In actuality, Lincoln was a consummate politician. If he

"Abe Lincoln, the Rail-splitter," one of many such depictions from the period of the 1860 presidential election. To garner support for Lincoln, Republican delegates came up with tales of his humble beginnings, which have since grown into legend. One of the most popular stories was Lincoln's splitting rails to make fences in rural Illinois.

On March 4, 1861, Chief Justice Roger B. Taney swore Lincoln in as the 16th president of the United States. Lincoln, in his inaugural address, tried to allay Southern fears that the government would move to end slavery. He also denied the right of secession and maintained that "we are not enemies, but friends."

had not had the political skills now associated with him, the Union would not have survived.

The new president had not even been his party's first choice as presidential nominee. Simon Cameron, Salmon P. Chase, and William H. Seward were more likely candidates, but each man had had problems attracting the necessary voters to even hope for a Republican victory. As a result, Lincoln became the party's choice because of his moderate views on the slavery question.

POLITICAL OPPOSITION

Many people viewed the Republican party with distrust. It symbolized a stance against the spread of slavery that completely alienated the South and also made many Northerners uneasy. The single unifying strand in the Republican party was that its members opposed extending slavery. The group known as the Radical Republicans wanted to eliminate slavery immediately, while moderates like Lincoln wished only to stop it from spreading into new territories. They theorized that by containing it, slavery would eventually die of itself without the need to attack it head-on. Throughout the war, Lincoln had to work hard to appease the broad spectrum of Republican opinions about slavery without alienating most of the party.

HON. ABRAHAM LINCOLN, OF ILLINOIS.

HON. HANNIBAL HAMLIN, OF MAINE.

FOR PRESIDENT.

FOR VICE PRESIDENT.

This 1860 election banner for the Republican party shows Lincoln and his running mate, Hannibal Hamlin (1809–1891) from Maine. Hamlin was a representative, a senator, and governor prior to becoming vice president. He was not a powerful vice president and apparently bore Lincoln no ill will when he was dropped from the ticket in 1864.

Lincoln also had to work with Northern Democrats who remained committed to the Union. These "War Democrats" supported Lincoln's efforts against the Confederacy but opposed Radical Republican plans to free the slaves. "Peace Democrats," on the other hand, opposed both Lincoln's pursuance of the war effort and the Republican policies against slavery. Led by Clement L. Vallandigham of Ohio, this faction of the party included many Midwesterners born in the South but now living in Northern states.

CLEMENT L. VALLANDIGHAM

The most famous thorn in the side of the Lincoln administration, Vallandigham was an Ohio member of the House of Representatives until defeated in 1862. He consistently opposed Lincoln and the war against the South. After giving an especially antiwar speech, he was arrested for treason by General Ambrose E. Burnside and confined in a Cincinnati prison. Lincoln and his Cabinet, embarrassed by Burnside's action, decided to banish Vallandigham to the Confederacy.

Unwanted in the South, Vallandigham made his way to Canada and conducted the Ohio gubernatorial campaign from exile. After losing, Vallandigham returned to Ohio in mid-1864 but was officially ignored by Lincoln, who nevertheless had the Democrat watched closely. Vallandigham took part in the 1864 Democratic party convention in Chicago, then returned to his law practice after the war.

Foes of Lincoln also included a clandestine group called the Knights of the Golden Circle. Formed in 1854 to promote American expansion into Mexico and the Caribbean, the KGC—although not really the huge threat believed by many—helped create a climate of fear across the Midwest. Fear of KGC activities led to restraint of civil rights as Federal troops cracked down on dissenters.

MILITARY APPOINTMENTS

The need to appease the major political factions in the North also influenced Lincoln's policies as commander in chief. Lincoln had practically no military experience. He had served in a volunteer militia company during the Black Hawk War in Illinois in 1831 but thought little of his brief call to arms and on more than one occasion used his militia experience as humorous color for other stories.

Instead of depending solely on professional military officers who were West Point graduates, Lincoln relied also on the so-called political generals for help in the war effort. This method of appointing politicians without military experience as generals was a weak feature of Union military strategy, but in 1861 it was necessary for success on the political front.

Lincoln visited officers of the Army of the Potomac at the battlefield at Antietam, October 3, 1862. Major General George B. McClellan is facing Lincoln. Captain George A. Custer, who in 1876 would be killed at Little Bighorn by Sioux Indians, is at the far right.

On Friday, October 2, 1862, Alexander Gardner photographed the President in front of a tent. On the left of this scene is Allan Pinkerton, the famous detective, and Major General John M. McClernand is on the right.

This cartoon pokes fun at the Copperheads' overly conciliatory approach to reuniting the nation.

COPPERHEADS

The term *Copperheads,* used to identify Democrats opposed to the war policy of President Abraham Lincoln, first appeared in the July 20, 1861, edition of the New York *Tribune.* Copperheads, or "Peace Democrats," desired a negotiated settlement with the Confederacy. The word itself originated with Republicans who likened antiwar Democrats to the poisonous snake—the copperhead. The nickname also derived from Peace Democrats who wore copper pennies to identify themselves.

Though especially strong in Ohio, Indiana, and Illinois, opposition to the war was widespread. Democratic Congressman Clement L. Vallandigham of Ohio, chief spokesman of the Copperheads, was among prominent antiwar leaders who were arrested for what many considered their treasonable behavior. Vallandigham was banished from the country from May 1863 to June 1864.

THE SOLDIER VOTE IN THE 1864 ELECTION

The 1864 presidential election occurred in the midst of the Civil War. A major question prior to the election was how Union soldiers would be able to vote. Most states—California, Iowa, Kentucky, Maine, Maryland, Michigan, New Hampshire, New York, Pennsylvania, Rhode Island, Vermont, and Wisconsin—allowed their soldiers to cast votes from wherever their units were stationed or from hospitals where they were convalescing. In other states, such as Illinois and Connecticut, any soldiers who voted went home to do so, and their ballots were tallied along with their fellow citizens'.

Charges of voting irregularities were lodged against the administration. New York Democratic commissioners were thrown in prison, and only Republicans visited the regiments in the field. In Ohio camps, there were shortages of Democratic ballots. In the end, more than 116,000 soldiers voted for Lincoln; only 33,748 votes went to his Democratic opponent, George B. McClellan.

The appointments Lincoln made revealed the need for broad-based support for the preservation of the Union. To the end of the conflict, Lincoln never lost sight of the war's goal—the reunification of the United States. Everything he did during the war was subordinated to this goal, and the appointments of politicians to military command were part of Lincoln's early strategy to unify the war effort.

Carl Schurz, one of the leading German Americans in 1860, was given a brigadier generalship in early 1862, in part to help sway German-American opinion. Likewise, Thomas F. Meagher, commander of the celebrated Irish Brigade, owed his appointment to politics as well. Democrats such as Benjamin F. Butler and Daniel E. Sickles also received commissions to help rally support for the Lincoln administration's war policy. With few exceptions, these political generals were indifferent as leaders of soldiers, and most were no longer serving by 1865.

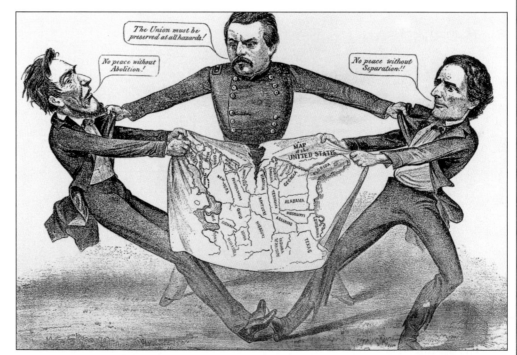

This August 1864 political cartoon shows General George B. McClellan, the Democratic candidate, trying to compromise with the warring North and South and their uncompromising presidents. McClellan advocated peace with union.

As commander in chief, Lincoln grew in stature as the war progressed. Early in the conflict, he interfered too much with his field commanders, especially when they were slow to advance and when they seemingly did not understand Lincoln's policies. Popular opinion linked the success of the Lincoln administration with battlefield victories. Consequently, the President often quarreled with some of his generals over the slow pace of their movements. Lincoln's impatience with George B. McClellan is well known, as is his disappointment with George G. Meade's failure to aggressively pursue Robert E. Lee's beaten army after Gettysburg. In Ulysses S. Grant, Lincoln found a general who agreed with his policy of targeting an advance on the enemy army itself rather than Richmond or another geographical objective. Lincoln allowed Grant free rein in his plans and rarely interfered.

WARTIME ELECTIONS

The military successes—or lack thereof—influenced the several wartime elections held throughout

THE EMANCIPATION PROCLAMATION

Five days after the bloody battle of Antietam in September 1862, President Abraham Lincoln issued a preliminary Emancipation Proclamation to his Cabinet. For any state that had not returned to the Union by January 1, 1863, he stated, all slaves living therein would be forever free. Lincoln's plan produced disappointment everywhere. Radicals believed he had not gone far enough because the proclamation referred only to states then in rebellion. Antigovernment and foreign presses lambasted the President, saying that Lincoln freed slaves only in areas where the Federal government had no power.

But Lincoln acted within his powers to seize enemy resources (slaves) and at the same time acted within his constitutional powers by not acting against slavery in loyal areas. The President knew he had to wait for legislation to end slavery; his proclamation, however, turned the war into one of liberation for the slaves and helped to doom Confederate hopes for foreign recognition. The January 1863 version also authorized the government to enlist black soldiers and sailors. "In giving freedom to the slave, we assure freedom to the free," Lincoln averred. "We must disenthrall ourselves, and then we shall save our country."

Union General William T. Sherman defeated Confederate General John Hood in bitter fighting on the outskirts of Atlanta in July 1864. By September, Atlanta had fallen, and Sherman telegraphed to Lincoln: "Atlanta is ours, and fairly won." The news helped turn Lincoln's election fortunes.

the North. The fall 1862 elections centered on six gubernatorial races as well as some Congressional seats. Although Democrats won only two of these races for governor (New York and New Jersey), they managed to secure a majority of House seats in five states that had voted for Lincoln in 1860. Republican defeats were attributed to recent military defeats, reaction to the Emancipation Proclamation, and general war weariness. The Republicans recouped some of their losses in the spring 1863 races, however, primarily because radical Democrats were now tending toward disloyalty and scared away moderates, who voted Republican.

Lincoln faced his greatest challenge as the parties geared up for the presidential election of November 1864. Radical Republicans were dissatisfied with Lincoln's conciliatory attitude toward the South; behind the scenes more than one attempt was made to replace Lincoln with another candidate. Chase and John C. Frémont were two of the potential nominees. In the end Lincoln was the unanimous choice for a second term.

"Jeff Davis's November Nightmare" was Abraham Lincoln being elected for a second term. Southerners hoped that Democratic candidate George B. McClellan, who might extend the olive branch to the South, would defeat Lincoln in the 1864 election. However, Lincoln won an overwhelming victory and continued to press for total victory.

Battlefield news was not encouraging to the administration. In Virginia, Grant was nicknamed "The Butcher" for the enormous casualty lists incurred in the constant fighting against Lee's army. In Georgia, William T. Sherman was stalled before Atlanta, while Jubal Early's small Confederate army had dared to approach Washington before retiring to the Shenandoah Valley. Late that summer, even Lincoln did not expect himself to be reelected.

Events soon turned the tide. Sherman captured Atlanta on September 2, 1864, and Early's men were routed at Cedar Creek on October 19. These victories ensured Lincoln's reelection. His opponent, former general McClellan, carried only three states. Lincoln won 55 percent of the vote. Several states allowed their soldiers in the field to vote in absentia; the men in blue voted three to one in favor of Lincoln.

JEFFERSON DAVIS

✳

*J*efferson Davis was the Confederacy's only president during the four-year period of the Civil War. He managed to create a viable government, ably direct the Confederacy's military effort, and try to hold together a diverse population whose dedication to secession was questionable to a large extent. He was courageous, dedicated, intelligent, a tireless worker, and devoted to friends. But he also was stubborn, was unable to delegate authority properly, and never forgot an insult.

When the end came, Davis was not able to establish a separate Southern Confederacy. Throughout the war he had a legion of critics who castigated his every move. Newspaper editors repeatedly insulted him, and some of his top generals hated him. As a result, Davis has received a mixture of praise and damnation from historians ever since.

DAVIS'S EXPERIENCE

Certainly Davis was the best available choice for president of the Confederacy. Although born in Kentucky in 1808, Davis regarded Mississippi as his

Criticized throughout the Civil War, Jefferson Davis aged greatly from the effect of four years of warfare and two years of postwar imprisonment. Defiant to the end, he never sought to regain the citizenship stripped from him—Congressional action in 1978 posthumously restored it.

The "White House of the Confederacy" was Jefferson Davis's residence. The Confederate Congress purchased the Brockenbrough House at the corner of Clay and 12th streets in Richmond for an executive mansion. Although Davis, a tireless worker, had an office in the Capitol, he also had a small private office in this house's second floor.

home state because his family moved there when he was quite young. After entering Transylvania College, Davis received an appointment to West Point and graduated 23rd in the 32-man class of 1828. After seven years of boring army service, Davis married, but his wife died of disease soon thereafter. Davis then went into self-imposed exile on his plantation, emerging to marry again in 1845.

In February 1861 delegates from the seceded states named Davis as provisional president of the new Confederate States of America. On receiving the news, he was stunned and disappointed. "[He] looked so grieved," recalled his wife, Varina, "that I feared some evil had befallen our family."

Only weeks before, Davis had resigned from the U.S. Senate after his home state of Mississippi voted to leave the Union. Returning to his plantation, Davis was named commander of the Mississippi State Militia and fully expected to receive a high command in the Confederate army. After all, he was a graduate of West Point, had served seven years in the U.S. army, and had distinguished himself in action at the battle of Buena Vista during the Mexican War. Between serving terms in the U.S. Congress and Senate, his reputation had grown during four years as secretary of war during the Pierce ad-

President and Mrs. Jefferson Davis greeting guests at a reception in Richmond. This engraving centers on Varina Howell Davis, the lovely and charming wife who was Davis's best friend and confidant.

ministration. He took measures to modernize and increase the size of the army, strengthen frontier outposts, and chart routes for a transcontinental railroad. It was no surprise then when Davis admitted, "I thought myself better adapted to command in the field."

RALLYING THE CONFEDERACY

But Davis accepted the unexpected office. As a moderate, he commanded more respect than most other Southern politicians, who were by far more radical. He took the oath of office on February 18, 1861, in Montgomery, Alabama. Alexander H. Stephens of Georgia was his vice president, also chosen by the secession convention. By the time the capital was transferred to Richmond, Davis had selected his Cabinet.

The new president faced a nightmare. The Northern states had more people, military supplies, ships, and industrial might than the South. However, Davis quickly developed a strategy to defend the new nation. Southern armies would defend the borders of the Confederacy and try to prevent Union forces from penetrating into Southern territory and disrupting the South's agricultural and industrial areas.

The South stood for states' rights, limited government, an agrarian society, and a belief that blacks and whites could coexist only in a slave-based society. By 1865 Davis had challenged every one of these fundamental beliefs. In his 1862 inaugural address as president under the permanent Confederate constitution, Davis had deplored Lincoln's suspension of the writ of habeas corpus; yet five days later, Davis supported a new law that allowed him to do the same.

"Jeff Sees the Elephant," an early war political satire aimed at the new Confederacy and its president. Already the Republicans were being depicted as elephants and Democrats as donkeys. In this drawing, with constitutional authority, the North is moving to subdue the rebellious South.

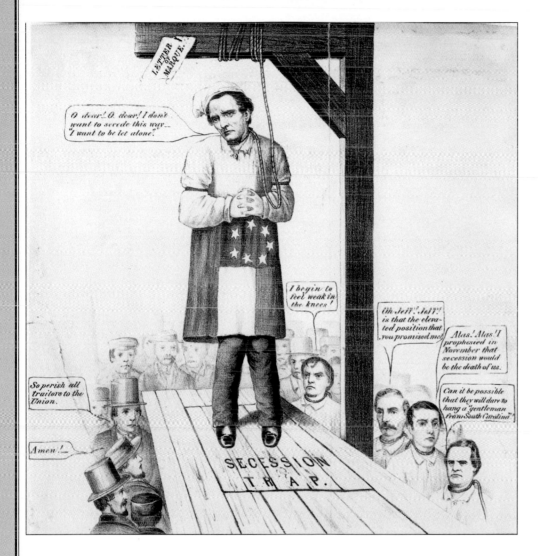

This Northern political cartoon shows Jefferson Davis about to be hanged in a secession trap. Supporters of the Confederacy on the right—Robert Toombs, P.G.T. Beauregard, Alexander H. Stephens, and Francis Pickens (governor of South Carolina)—all quake in fear as Davis whines on the scaffold. The letter of marque above Davis's head is a reminder to Northerners that the Confederacy granted permission to privateers to seize U.S. merchant ships as prizes of war.

In April 1862, acting on a suggestion from Davis, the Confederate Congress passed the first American conscription law. It gave Davis the power to call to arms all white males between 18 and 35 and extended the enlistments of troops from a year to three years without consent of the men in uniform.

All in all, Davis worked hard to centralize the government and the war effort. The conscription law encroached upon state recruitment rights. Davis saw to it that the War Department took partial control of Southern telegraph lines and railroads and even set up new manufacturing establishments that were deemed important to the war effort.

This undated painting shows a slave auction. Abolitionists, outraged at reports of black families being divided up at such auctions, capitalized on sensational stories and their effect on Northern opinion. When Abraham Lincoln finally met Harriet Beecher Stowe, author of Uncle Tom's Cabin, *he reputedly said, "So this is the little lady who made this big war."*

The main task that Davis faced was to rally Southerners to the war effort. Many Southerners agreed that the North's aim in fighting the war was to free their slaves and invade their territory, but they agreed on little else. Davis sought to advance the idea that the Southern Confederacy better embodied the ideals of America—limited government and states' rights. The North was the section that had drifted away from the ideals of the founding fathers, not the South.

Frank Leslie's Illustrated Newspaper *printed this cartoon of a fugitive Jefferson Davis running off with the Confederacy's gold. When Davis left Richmond in 1865, he fled south with some of his cabinet members and was captured in Georgia in May. Northern papers made political hay with their satires of Davis, who was rumored to have been taken while wearing women's clothes as a disguise.*

Many Southern firebrands called the slavery issue the main cause of the sundering of the Union. Most Southerners knew that the institution of slavery had led to secession, but only one of four Southerners owned slaves. The dirt farmers of the South resented fighting to protect slavery for the wealthy landowners. They also feared social problems resulting from emancipation. Davis couldn't pander to that fear and had to rally his people by other means.

Like Lincoln, Davis had his success and failure measured on the battlefield. As Union troops moved deeper into Southern territory, Davis lost support. He was never able to engender a Confederate nationalism. As Yankee invaders became more successful, desertions crippled the Southern armies. Men went home to see to the safety of their loved ones. By 1865 the South had lost the will to continue the war.

NORTHERN GOVERNORS

✦

President Abraham Lincoln faced a challenge throughout the war from state governors. Generally, Northern governors gave wholehearted support to the war effort, but Washington decided to take over more and more responsibilities that had once been left to the states. This made several governors uneasy and led to minor quarrels throughout the war.

When Lincoln announced that the government wanted 75,000 three-month militiamen to suppress the rebellion, the government left it up to the states to raise the troops and send them to the front lines. Soon Lincoln and the war department decided it was better for the government to take over the responsibility of paying and equipping the troops. This left governors out of the decision-making process and allowed the government, not state officials, to appoint generals. Lincoln permitted governors to appoint colonels and lesser officers only. Many of these officers were elected by their men.

Woodcut of a recruiting detail in Philadelphia in August 1862. Major Roy Stone of the famous Pennsylvania Bucktails (13th Pennsylvania Reserves) had obtained permission to recruit a full brigade of Pennsylvania marksmen. The recruiters urge men to enlist and avoid the draft by entering one of the state's most famous units.

On the whole, most governors supported Lincoln. Andrew G. Curtin (Pennsylvania), John A. Andrew (Massachusetts), Oliver P. Morton (Indiana), and Richard Yates (Illinois) were among Lincoln's strongest advocates. New York's midwar governor, Horatio Seymour, exemplified Democratic opposition to Lincoln's policies. Seymour, although he supported the war effort against the South, opposed centralized federal power. He was a proponent of states' rights, opposing conscription of soldiers, suspension of the writ of habeas corpus, and emancipation. In spite of these differences with Lincoln, Seymour continued to raise troops for the Union army and generally supported other administration policies.

SOUTHERN GOVERNORS

✦

*J*efferson Davis's military strategy led to clashes with Southern governors. Because the Union had a navy and established a blockade, seacoast states were vulnerable to attack at any time. Most Southern states had a coastline that needed defending. As a result, the Richmond government was constantly inundated with requests—even demands—from governors and other officials seeking troops and supplies to defend their coasts from Yankee invaders.

Indeed, part of Union General George B. McClellan's strategy for 1862 was to send amphibious expeditions against vulnerable points along the Southern coast to seize vital points, interrupt rail traffic, and draw off Southern troops from the main armies. The Carolinas, Georgia, and Louisiana all felt the sting of Union attacks in late 1861 and early 1862 as McClellan's strategy developed.

A contemporary illustration shows General Ambrose E. Burnside's troops landing at Slocum's Creek prior to their march toward New Bern, North Carolina, in March 1862.

The Union forays resulted in a flood of telegrams, letters, and denunciations of Davis by Southern governors. When Union General Ambrose E. Burnside's expedition attacked and seized a foothold on the North Carolina coast in early 1862, the Confederate government failed to provide adequate protection to the coast. Local citizens and officials believed that they had been abandoned. Eastern North Carolina became a no-man's-land, sandwiched between garrisons of Union soldiers in coastal towns and Confederates defending railroads farther inland.

Davis rightly realized that he could not send troops and weapons to every governor who called for help. Instead, he sought to strengthen the main armies for the inevitable defense against Northern offensive operations. Davis, like many other Southerners, hoped that by a staunch defense, the North would quickly weary of the war and allow the South to go its own way.

LINCOLN AND CONGRESS

✦

*W*hen the Confederacy opened fire on Fort Sumter on April 12, 1861, and effectively started the Civil War, President Abraham Lincoln responded swiftly. He called for 75,000 three-month militiamen to suppress the rebellion, proclaimed a blockade of the Southern coastline, and declared martial law in certain areas deemed important to the war effort. At the time, Congress was not in session. By the time Congress convened for a special session on July 4, it had an army to suppress the insurrection as well as a general strategy already in place.

Lincoln's executive action without Congress symbolized the President's independence and dedication to the preservation of the Union. Congress ratified Lincoln's actions and before adjourning issued a call for 500,000 troops for three years.

Charles Sumner (1811–1874), the Radical Republican senator from Massachusetts, caricatured here in 1872, staunchly opposed reconciliation with the Confederacy, advocated immediate abolition, and, after the war, opposed Andrew Johnson's soft stance toward the defeated South.

"The 'Rail Splitter' at Work Repairing the Union," a political cartoon produced after Abraham Lincoln and Andrew Johnson were nominated by Republicans for the 1864 election. Johnson, a tailor by trade, is shown sewing up the nation while Lincoln uses a rail to assist.

OPPOSITION AND SUPPORT

Throughout the war, the Congress generally sided with Lincoln's plans and provided few instances of intense opposition. The Democrats comprised only a quarter of the members, and most of these men were War Democrats who supported Lincoln in his policies toward the South. Moderate Republicans also supported the President, as did the Radical Republicans most of the time. Moderates and Democrats often banded together to oppose Radical demands on abolition and punishment of the South.

Indeed, the Radical demands for harsh treatment of Southern states and people, as well as their increasingly hostile stance on abolition, led to conflict between Radicals and the President. Lincoln preferred to ignore any formal recognition that the Southern states had seceded; he instead advocated that they were in rebellion. Radicals, on the other hand, sponsored bills that would have torn apart the existing state structure and created new states as punishment for the South. Lincoln consistently opposed such extreme measures, and his lenient attitude often brought him into opposition with Radical demands.

For example, Lincoln appointed Edward Stanly as military governor of North Carolina in the spring of 1862. Stanly was to uphold state laws and try to entice the state's population to repudiate secession and return to the Union. As civil authority in the state, Stanly upheld existing laws to the point that he returned runaway slaves to their owners if they resided within Union-held territory. Such actions brought him, and Lincoln, into conflict with Radicals, who denounced Stanly's policies and attacked Lincoln at the same time.

OTHER LEGISLATION

Congress allowed Lincoln to centralize the war effort at state expense, and with the absence of Democratic opposition, passed a number of Republican-sponsored acts that had been defeated prior to 1861. Among the progressive legislation passed was the Morrill Act establishing land-grant colleges, the Homestead Act, the Railroad Act, the Legal Tender Act, and the creation of the Department of Agriculture.

Benjamin F. Wade

RADICAL REPUBLICANS

Radical Republicans were members of the party who advocated immediate and full emancipation of all slaves without compensation to owners. They pressed Lincoln from the beginning for quick action on this issue and were never satisfied with Lincoln's more gradual approach. The Emancipation Proclamation, which applied only to the rebel states, did not go far enough for them because it did not cover the entire slavery system. The slave states Kentucky, Missouri, Maryland, and Delaware stayed loyal to the Union. Radicals continued to advocate more extreme measures.

Radical leaders included Senators Zachariah Chandler (Michigan), Benjamin F. Wade (Ohio), and Charles Sumner (Massachusetts). In the House, Thaddeus Stevens (Pennsylvania), Henry Winter Davis (Maryland), and Owen Lovejoy (Illinois) were among the most militant of the Radical Republicans.

THE CONFEDERATE CONGRESS

✳

From the start, President Jefferson Davis's centralizing schemes brought him into conflict with the Confederate Congress. Composed of 26 senators and 106 representatives, the two-house legislature was modeled after the U.S. Congress. A unicameral provisional Congress was followed by two regularly elected bicameral sessions, in November 1861 and 1863.

The provisional Congress probably contained the best men, but the attraction of military service enticed many into active service. Of the 267 men who were Confederate congressmen, only 27 served in all three Congresses. Many of the newcomers to the Second Congress were elected after the defeats at Gettysburg and Vicksburg. Several of these men were former Whigs and Unionists who represented a discouraged constituency and, as a result, opposed the Davis administration.

FACTIONS IN CONGRESS

Relations between Davis and Congress were at first harmonious. The legislature promoted unity for the war effort by approving most of Davis's emer-

Benjamin Harvey Hill (1823–1882) was a Georgia lawyer who changed his political affiliations as the situation warranted. He was a member of both sessions of the Confederate Congress, serving as a senator and chairman of the Judiciary Committee. Generally, he was one of Jefferson Davis's strongest supporters.

This woodcut shows delegates from the seceded states in open session in Montgomery. Howell Cobb was elected president of the convention, but he soon left politics to serve as colonel of the 16th Georgia infantry. He was later promoted to brigadier and then major general and commanded the District of Georgia and Florida.

gency measures. The Congress passed laws on army enlistments, monetary appropriations, suspension of habeas corpus, and other such measures.

However, relations deteriorated as Davis moved to centralize government and infringed on states' rights. The absence of political parties meant that Congress divided into pro- and anti-Davis factions. He soon had several foes in Congress. Chief among them was Henry S. Foote, who had defeated Davis for governor of Mississippi before the war. Foote, representing Tennessee, constantly argued with Davis and sought investigative committees to search out governmental wrongdoing and fraud.

The Alabama state capitol in Montgomery. Here, on February 18, 1861, Jefferson Davis was sworn in as president of the Confederate States of America. For all his faults, Davis was the best man for the position.

HOT TEMPERS

Much congressional business was conducted behind closed doors. As a result, newspapermen presented the legislators to the public in an unfavorable light. Personal misconduct also clouded the Congress. In one heated debate, Senator William L. Yancey of Alabama accused Georgian Benjamin H. Hill of lying. Hill tossed an inkstand at Yancey, cutting his face and drawing blood. Representative Foote told Alabamian E. S. Dargan that he was a "damned fool." In a fit of rage, Dargan drew a knife and rushed Foote, only to be wrestled to the floor by other members.

William L. Yancey (1814–1863) was an Alabama politician who advocated extreme Southern nationalism. His faction of the Democratic Party nominated John C. Breckinridge as a presidential candidate in 1860. As a member of the Confederate Congress, Yancey fought against Davis, calling him a "conceited, wrong-headed, wranglesome, and obstinate" traitor.

LINCOLN'S CABINET

✳

*P*resident Abraham Lincoln was beholden to a number of politicians, and this colored his choices for his Cabinet. But Lincoln was also boss of his Cabinet. Throughout the war, 13 men served in the seven Cabinet positions. Lincoln usually allowed each Cabinet officer to run his own department with a minimum of interference, but he made the crucial decisions without seeking Cabinet approval. By using patience and humor, Lincoln managed to control the disparate personalities within the Cabinet without losing control, although three of his Cabinet members gave Lincoln trouble.

SIMON CAMERON

Simon Cameron of Pennsylvania was his first secretary of war. Cameron owed his appointment to the Cabinet to his influential role in state politics and his deliverance of the state to Lincoln in 1860. Cameron's flagrant dispensation of patronage, as well as charges of corruption and general lack of expertise, embarrassed Lincoln. In January 1862 the President accepted Cameron's resignation and named him minister to Russia.

Cameron's replacement was Edwin Stanton, a War Democrat who initially had no admiration for Lincoln but who ran the department competently for the rest of the war. Stanton eventually came to admire Lincoln, but his earlier remarks seemed to be the base for later groundless charges that he had a hand in Lincoln's assassination.

Edwin M. Stanton (1814–1869), Lincoln's secretary of war from 1862 to 1865, was one of the War Democrats. Stanton once remarked that Lincoln was "the original gorilla," but Lincoln stood behind this extremely capable secretary and admired his capacity for hard work.

SALMON P. CHASE

Erstwhile Republican opponent Salmon P. Chase was named secretary of the treasury. Although short on financial experience, Chase proved a competent secretary. However, as the most radical of Lincoln's Cabinet, Chase often found himself at odds with Secretary of State William H. Seward and the President himself. In 1864 opponents of Lincoln secretly drafted Chase to run for president. The bid failed when word of it was leaked to the press. Although Chase apologized for such conduct, Lincoln accepted his resignation in June. Then, still valuing Chase's ability, the President appointed Chase chief justice of the United States.

Salmon P. Chase (1808–1873) was Lincoln's secretary of the treasury. Tall, square-jawed, and dignified, he remained in the cabinet until June 1864, when he resigned under a cloud as a surreptitious candidate against Lincoln for the presidential nomination.

WILLIAM H. SEWARD

Secretary of State Seward hailed from New York. Although he blundered early in the administration when he proposed to provoke a war with France and Spain in an effort to unite the country, Seward was a very effective secretary. His astute maneuvering kept European nations from intervening in the war. Seward was the man responsible for the purchase of Alaska from Russia in 1867 for a mere $7.2 million.

William H. Seward (1801–1872), secretary of state in the Lincoln administration, performed his duties well and came to admire the President. Later, while still serving in the same capacity in Johnson's administration, Seward endured harsh criticism when he purchased the Alaska territory ("Seward's Folly") from Russia.

DAVIS'S CABINET

✴

Jefferson Davis and his cabinet with General Robert E. Lee. From left to right: Judah P. Benjamin (attorney general), Stephen R. Mallory (navy), Leroy P. Walker (standing, war), Davis, Lee, John H. Reagan (postmaster general), Christopher C. Memminger (treasury), Alexander H. Stephens (seated, vice president), and Robert A. Toombs (state).

*R*elations between Jefferson Davis and his Cabinet were surprisingly good considering the heavy turnover rate and position shifts. Fourteen men served in the six Cabinet positions over the course of the war. Davis had five attorneys general, six secretaries of war, and four secretaries of state. Davis held frequent informal meetings and steadfastly defended his Cabinet from ever-increasing public and congressional criticism. Judah P. Benjamin's role as secretary of state and Stephen Mallory's direction of the navy were especially noteworthy.

Benjamin started as attorney general, then replaced an ineffectual Leroy P. Walker as secretary of war. However, Benjamin had the misfortune to preside over the department during a period of Southern defeats—Port Royal, Roanoke Island, Fort Donelson—and public clamor led to Benjamin's transfer to the State Department, which he led with competence for the rest of the war.

Secretary Mallory had been a senator from Florida who served on naval committees and appreciated naval power very fully. He tried to build a navy from scratch, supplementing limited resources by purchasing and outfitting commerce raiders in English ports. He also advocated ironclad warships, submarines, and mines.

ALEXANDER H. STEPHENS

From the start, Jefferson Davis faced a number of problems. First was his vice president, Alexander H. Stephens of Georgia. Although both were chosen by the secession convention, Stephens and Davis eventually came to distrust each other. Stephens wished to start peace negotiations with the North—not because he wanted peace without independence, but because he believed that by doing so there would be antiwar sentiment stirred up in the North.

Upset with his lack of clout within the administration, Stephens spent much of the war at his Georgia plantation, venturing to Richmond only three times. Although he was supposed to be the presiding officer of the Senate, Stephens's absence led to the appointment of Senator Robert M. T. Hunter to the post.

Stephens was arrested at war's end and spent a few months in prison before being released. After writing his two-volume apologia, he was elected governor of Georgia in 1882. Stephens died of an intestinal illness three months later.

JUDAH P. BENJAMIN

A former U.S. senator, Benjamin served the Confederacy as attorney general, secretary of war, and secretary of state. Born in the Virgin Islands in 1811, Benjamin was a product of English-Jewish parents and entered Yale at age 14. Though he didn't graduate, he later studied law with a firm in New Orleans and built a very successful practice of his own.

An eloquent orator, Benjamin was elected to the U.S. Senate in 1852, serving there until Louisiana seceded. Jefferson Davis made him the Confederacy's first attorney general soon afterward. Benjamin shook off anti-Semite brands to become Davis's closest advisor. After the war, Benjamin fled the country to become one of England's finest lawyers. He died in Paris in 1884.

THE ECONOMICS OF WAR

*T*he resources available to the North and South in April 1861 were far from equal. More than 85 percent of the nation's manufacturing industry and more than 50 percent of the food crops were produced in the North. The North had twice as many railroad miles. The South's wealth lay in land, cash crops, and its slave population, none of which proved of much value in the ensuing war. "In all history," William T. Sherman wrote in 1860, "no nation of mere agriculturists ever made successful war against a nation of mechanics."

✳

"Cotton Plantation on the Mississippi," by William Aiken Walter

FUNNY MONEY

✳

*T*he greatest problem facing the Confederate government at the start of the war was not its lack of mills, but its lack of finances. When Christopher G. Memminger assumed the office of Confederate secretary of the treasury in 1861, he had to use his own money to furnish his office. The Confederacy relied on loans from the states of Alabama and Louisiana to begin the war in a state of solvency.

TAXATION

On the advice of the major financial minds of the South, Memminger first decided on four principal methods to finance the war: taxation, loans, treasury notes, and import duties. The Confederate Congress was reluctant to impose taxes on the citizenry. Most civilians felt that they shouldn't have to shoulder the responsibility of both fighting and paying for the war. "The burden of taxation, State and Confederate," the editor of the Wilmington *Journal* wrote, "should be laid as lightly as possible on our suffering people. We of today are paying the price of our righteous war of defense in blood and wounds and death." Taxes were eventually levied but were never great enough to cover the mounting expenses.

At the start of the war, import taxes brought more than $3 million to the Confederate coffers, but as the Federal blockade tightened, little commerce

This $1,000 bond was issued by the Confederate government in 1863. The sale of bonds was brisk at the start of the war and amounted to about $15 million by the end of 1861. As money became tighter throughout the South, bond sales drastically decreased.

Unsupported by gold and with few printing restrictions, paper money flowed from national, state, and local presses. Banks, railroads, and private businesses often issued their own currency.

arrived from Europe. Loans from various sources eventually totaled more than $700 million, yet that amounted to only about 39 percent of total revenues. The sale of bonds amounted to about $15 million by the end of 1861 but soon fell off as money became tighter. With revenues drying up, Memminger was forced to look to other sources for financing. Since he was unable to collect enough money, he decided to produce it.

SHINPLASTERS

Memminger felt that printing it was "the most dangerous of all methods of raising money," but he realized it was necessary for two reasons: The populace needed some form of circulating currency other than Federal "greenbacks," and the Confederate Congress was more willing to approve printing currency than taxing citizens. From the beginning, these treasury notes were not backed by gold. The government agreed to pay the specified amount to the bearer from six months to two years "after the ratification of a treaty of peace between the Confederate States and the United States." Individual states, private companies, banks, and railroads were also authorized to print their own currency. Rampant counterfeiting dropped the value of currency even more.

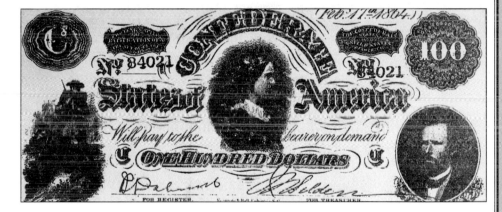

This $100 Confederate note was issued in February 1864. In an attempt to bolster its sagging economy, the Confederate government permitted the circulation of state, city, and private-business notes. The Confederacy issued more than $1.5 billion in notes by the end of the war.

The lack of die cutters for coins necessitated the printing of small paper currency in denominations of 5 to 50 cents. These were called shinplasters and were the most widely counterfeited notes. Realizing that it could not stop the creation of forged notes, Congress eventually legitimized them, creating an even greater problem. By the end of the war, the Confederacy had issued more than $1.5 billion in notes, but the value of a one-dollar note was worth only 1.7 cents, and it was not accepted by most businesses. "Today Mrs. McCord exchanged 16,000 dollars, Confederate bills, for gold—300 dollars," Southern diarist Mary Chesnut recorded in 1865. "Sixteen thousand—for three hundred."

FINANCING THE WAR

✳

During the third week in July 1861, some members of the U.S. Congress abandoned their debate about a novel way to help pay for the war in order to go and see the war for themselves. With picnic baskets packed, in the company of wives and friends, they traveled toward Manassas Junction to see what many expected would be the decisive battle to end the war near a stream called Bull Run.

In a matter of hours, their world was turned upside down. The Union army suffered a beating and staggered back to Washington to lick its wounds. In its wake, Congress reconvened to struggle with the grim prospect of a long and costly war. "War is not a question of valor," claimed New York Congressman Roscoe Conkling, "but a question of money. Who can afford the most iron or lead?"

THE FIRST INCOME TAX

Congress resumed its debate and, in a matter of weeks following the defeat at Bull Run, enacted the nation's first income tax. Other revenue measures soon followed. Appropriations included $10 million to buy and manufacture weapons, $1.2 million for naval vessels, and another $20 million for organizing and equipping new recruits.

Lincoln had chosen Salmon P. Chase, a man with strong Republican ties but little financial experience, as his secretary of treasury. Chase's value to the

Salmon Portland Chase (1808–1873), a stately, refined man, served as U.S. senator and then governor of Ohio before being selected secretary of the treasury by President Lincoln. Chase's ambition to be president often led him into conflict with Lincoln and others in the administration. In 1864 Chase resigned as treasury secretary. Lincoln, however, valued Chase's abilities and soon appointed him chief justice of the United States, a post he held until his death in 1873.

A portrait of President Abraham Lincoln's first secretary of the treasury, Salmon P. Chase, adorns the first one-dollar paper bill issued.

To assist in financing the war, Congress passed an act on August 5, 1861, authorizing the issue of $140 million in three-year treasury notes with an interest of 7.3 percent. The interest rate of 7.3 percent was chosen out of convenience, since it amounted to an even 2 cents per day on a $100 note. The United States government accrued a total debt of more than $2.5 billion during the course of the war.

President lay more in his ability to steer finance bills through Congress than in his financial expertise. When Congress adjourned on August 6, members had passed 74 bills in 29 days to give the President broad war powers. Included was the sum of $400 million to continue the fight.

By the end of 1862, the North was spending $2.5 million per day on the war. To raise this money, the Federal government relied on several more unique and innovative measures. In addition to the income tax, excise taxes were increased on products ranging from yachts to billiard balls. Also included were inheritance taxes, license taxes, and revenue taxes that someone commented were taxes on "everything."

GOVERNMENT BONDS

Meanwhile, financier Jay Cooke was employed to conduct an aggressive national campaign to sell long- and short-term government bonds. Also, a National Bank Act was passed in 1863 that strengthened and standardized U.S. currency.

The battle for funding was, at times, as intense in the halls of Congress as on the battlefield. "The army and the Treasury," warned Secretary Chase, "must stand or fall together."

GREENBACKS

To help pay for the Union war effort, Congress passed the Legal Tender Act in February 1862. The act established a standard form of paper money, though it was not backed by the gold reserve. Nicknamed greenbacks for their distinctive color, this currency was good for "payment of all taxes, internal duties, excises, debts, and demands of every kind due the United States." Though this was unpopular with the financial community, Congress authorized circulation of about $450 million in greenbacks. By 1910, the cost of the war—including pensions and burial of veterans—had reached $11.5 billion.

Financier Jay Cooke (1821–1905) approached Secretary of the Treasury Salmon Chase in 1861, when the Federal government had an $80 million deficit, with a plan to sell government bonds on commission. His agency sold more than $1 billion in bonds. Some consider his company's bond sales to have contributed as much to the Union's success in the war as any victory in battle.

THE DEMISE OF COTTON

MARY CHESNUT

One of the best-known Southern diarists of the Civil War, Chesnut was born Mary Boykin Miller on a South Carolina plantation in 1823. Her father became governor of South Carolina and later served in the U.S. Senate. Well educated, she married lawyer James Chesnut when she was 17 and followed her husband to Washington when he served in the Senate.

When South Carolina seceded, they returned home, he to serve in the Confederate Congress and army, she to roam the inner circles of Southern high society. It was either "distraction or death," she claimed. Chesnut coupled her access to important people and events with her keen powers of observation to compose an insightful, 400,000-word journal of her wartime experiences. Mary Chesnut died in 1886, almost 20 years before an abridged edition of her diary was published.

Cotton had been the largest cash crop in the United States at the start of the Civil War. Many planters hoped to make a fortune on the market by continuing to grow cotton after the conflict began. With the Northern market cut off, however, and the European market drying up due to the blockade, cotton was no longer a profitable cash crop.

Early in the war, the Confederate government realized the importance of a transition from staple to food crops. A campaign was initiated to convince planters to convert to grains to feed the army as well as the citizens. "Plant corn and be free, or plant cotton and be whipped," became a popular plea.

Many farmers complied with the government's request; cotton production dropped by 66 percent from 1861 to 1862. A large number of farmers continued to grow cotton, however, speculating that in the near future the war would end or the blockade would be lifted, allowing them to make a killing. As the war continued, those who chose cotton over food crops grew poorer. "Cotton pays everybody who handles it, sells it, manufactures it, &c&c," wrote Mary Chesnut, "rarely pays the men who make it. Secondhanded, they received the wages of slavery."

Before the Civil War, cotton was the South's major money crop and spawned a society almost exclusively dependent upon its cultivation and marketing for its livelihood. In 1860 the South produced more than 2 billion pounds of cotton, an amount that would not be matched by the region for almost 20 years.

Much of the cotton grown by speculators wound up being burned in order to keep it out of the hands of the invading Northern troops. By the end of the war, cotton was far from being king. It fell to an eighth of its prewar level.

THE SANITARY FAIRS

✦

By October 1862, the United States Sanitary Commission was in dire need of money to continue its relief efforts on the battlefield and in army camps and hospitals. Otherwise, this privately funded civilian aid society would have to consider disbanding.

In response, Commission members Mary Livermore and Jane Hoge of Chicago conceived

the idea of a sanitary fair. Through newspaper ads and church bulletins, the two women solicited goods and "battle relics and mementoes of the war" to be sold or displayed for charity. They offered a gold watch for the largest contribution. In return, they hoped to raise $25,000.

The 1863 fair opened after a tumultuous parade in downtown Chicago. Schools, businesses, and courts shut down for the event. It was a huge success, averaging more than 5,000 spectators a day for 20 days at 75 cents admission. In came a flood of donations, from a steam engine to a "curious tooth pick." By the end of the spectacle, organizers had netted close to $100,000. President Abraham Lincoln won the gold watch for donating his copy of the Emancipation Proclamation, sold at auction for $3,000. "I had some desire to retain the paper," Lincoln admitted, "but if it shall contribute to the relief and comfort of the soldiers, that will be better."

Due to its success, the sanitary fair in Chicago became a model for similar fund-raisers held in cities and small towns throughout the North. The largest fair, held in New York City in spring 1864, raised over $1 million. By the end of the Civil War, sanitary fairs had generated nearly $5 million in donations.

The main building at the 1865 Great North Western Sanitary Fair in Chicago. For a small admission, visitors were treated to elaborate exhibits of military relics and other goods for display or sale. The money raised was used by the United States Sanitary Commission to aid sick and wounded soldiers and their families.

Potholders sold at the 1865 Sanitary Fair in Chicago

THE BLOCKADE

✳

*W*ithin one week of the firing on Fort Sumter, Abraham Lincoln declared a blockade of Southern ports extending from South Carolina to the Mexican border. Once Virginia and North Carolina joined the Confederacy, the blockade was extended to Chesapeake Bay.

The initial reaction of Southerners to the blockade was one of ridicule and scorn. Most felt the power of "King Cotton" would draw England, a major buyer of the crop, into the war. The common belief was that without cotton, the English mills would be forced to close, throwing their economy into turmoil. In fact, many Southern cotton brokers called for a cotton embargo on Europe in order to accelerate British intervention. Although promoted by many throughout the South, the embargo was never officially declared by the Confederate Congress. Even if an effective embargo had been imposed, its effect would have been negligible. European cotton speculators had surpluses

Parisian women's fashions like these were readily available in New York's finer shops, but the blockade reduced the amount of luxury goods coming into Southern ports from Europe.

This sleek, dual-stack sidewheeler served the Confederacy as a blockade runner under the name CSS Robert E. Lee. *The game of cat and mouse on the high seas could be very profitable for the blockade runners who managed to elude their guards. A successful captain could make as much as $5,000 on a single trip.*

from recent bumper crops. Furthermore, new and cheaper sources had opened up in India and Egypt.

Not everyone felt that a cotton embargo would be effective. Confederate Attorney General Judah Benjamin advised sending large amounts of cotton to Europe before the Federal blockade tightened in order to secure as much credit in Europe as possible to cover future purchases of military supplies. His plea was ignored, however, which proved to be a costly mistake when the blockade tightened and the Confederate treasury dissipated.

THE EFFECT OF THE BLOCKADE

In the beginning the blockade was ineffective at best. In April 1862 Lincoln had fewer than 60 ships to cover the Southern coast. "You have heard, no

The CSS Sumter ran the Union blockade into the Gulf of Mexico. Commanded by Raphael Semmes, who was instructed "to do the enemy's commerce the greatest injury in the shortest time," the Sumter captured or destroyed 18 Union vessels in six months. Mechanical trouble forced its sale to a British buyer in January 1862.

Minnesota Wisconsin Michigan N.Y. Conn.

Pennsylvania

Iowa N.J.

Ohio Md.

Illinois Del.

Indiana

Virginia

Kansas

Missouri Kentucky

North Carolina

Arkansas Tennessee

South Carolina

Alabama

Mississippi

Georgia

Texas

Louisiana

Florida

Atlantic Ocean

Gulf of Mexico

N
W E
S

········· **Railroads**

Federal blockade

The Confederate blockade runner Colonel Lamb *was one of an estimated 1,650 ships attempting to evade the Northern blockade of Southern ports. About 16 percent of the ships were captured or destroyed by the Federal navy. By war's end the blockade runners succeeded in bringing into the South goods worth more than $200 million.*

doubt, Old Abe has blockaded our port," wrote one citizen of Charleston. "A nice blockade indeed! On the second day, a British ship, the A and A, ran the gauntlet with a snug freight of $30,000. . . . Don't you wish you had a hundred ships for one voyage?"

Lincoln's secretary of navy, Gideon Welles, an excellent administrator with no naval experience, aggressively increased the size of his navy. From July to December 1861, he more than tripled the number of Federal ships. Nevertheless, two obstacles stood in the way of the blockade's success: the lack of land bases in the South and the increasing number of fast, effective blockade runners.

Lacking an effective naval presence at the start of the war and the inability to establish one after it began, the South turned to blockade running as the primary method for combating the blockade. Although vast quantities of arms, food, and clothing were carried through the Federal ring, the volume of goods smuggled in by these ships was never enough to bolster the sagging Confederate economy. Still, the success of these ships against the hated Yankees did much to bolster the likewise sagging Confederate morale.

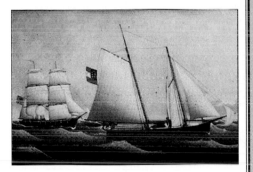

BLOCKADE RUNNERS

With 3,500 miles of coastline containing nearly 200 harbors and inlets, the South stretched the Union blockade to the limit. Through the gaps in this Yankee seawall slipped more than 1,650 Confederate vessels bound on an estimated 8,000 round trips during the Civil War. Hundreds of these Southern blockade runners were captured or destroyed in the attempt, but the potential rewards were worth the risks.

These sleek, low-profile craft carried out cotton and returned filled with weapons, munitions, medical supplies, and other scarce items that fetched huge profits. However, an influx of luxury goods, such as fine silks and satins, in place of vital war supplies drew the ire of the Confederate Congress. A law was passed in February 1864 requiring a permit for blockade runners and restricting imports to necessities.

Opposite: *The map shows the extent of Union blockades against Southern ports. It also illustrates the North's superiority in railroad miles.*

Not only troops, but wartime matériel as well, could be brought to the front with railroads.

THE IMPORTANCE OF TRANSPORTATION

✳

They came by railroad from the Union army in Virginia, 1,233 miles away, to help break the Confederate siege at Chattanooga in 1863. Twenty-three thousand men, with artillery and baggage plus hundreds of horses, arrived in only 11 days. It was the longest and fastest movement of troops by rail in military history up to that time.

THE NORTH'S RAILROADS

The Civil War saw the first wide-scale use of railroads for military purposes. In fact, military campaigns were often planned and staged with the location and capacity of railroads in mind.

Laced with 22,000 miles of track and a vast, well-equipped supply of locomotives and rolling stock, the North clearly held the upper hand in railroads during the war. In addition, President Abraham Lincoln, a former lawyer for the railroads, quickly grasped their military value. Three days after the war began, he authorized government control over certain railroads for military

General Haupt, the man and the locomotive, attend to a railroad work site. An aggressive, experienced railroad administrator, bearded Herman Haupt stands at the upper right corner, wearing a long, dark coat, slouch hat, and boots. He served as head of U.S. military rail transportation and construction.

The James River Terminal was home for the U.S. Military Railroad at City Point, Virginia. An engine house, water tanks, and three locomotives are pictured here. City Point was the site of a huge supply depot to support the Union siege of Petersburg. Each day, 18 trains ran from City Point to the battlefront over a 21-mile-long railroad built especially for that purpose.

The locomotive General Haupt pictured here was named in honor of Brigadier General Herman Haupt. In 1864 and 1865, the Union's 365 engines and more than 4,000 cars transported more than 5 million tons of supplies.

With 500 new horses and mules coming to the Union army each day—aside from the thousands of mounts already with the army requiring maintenance—soldier-blacksmiths like the ones pictured here were kept very busy.

Confederate Fort Donelson was perched atop a bluff on the west bank of the Cumberland River. The earthen fort guarded the approach to Nashville and helped to hold western Kentucky and Tennessee for the Confederacy. In mid-February 1862, a combined Union army and navy force under Brigadier General Ulysses S. Grant battered the fort. Its capture helped the Union control the Cumberland River.

use. Then early in 1862, the President ordered the creation of the United States Military Railroad Service. Directed by Colonel (later Brigadier General) Daniel C. McCallum, the Military Railroad Service ran all trains in support of the army, built and maintained all equipment, and constructed and repaired tracks and bridges to provide excellent rail transportation throughout the war.

The army had also benefited from a government policy dating from 1837 whereby officers were loaned to railroad companies to conduct scientific studies of their use to the military. During the Civil War, many officers had the chance to put their studies to the test.

PACK ANIMALS

For all the importance of railroads during the war, the army horse and mule were still the mainstay for transportation. More than 650,000 horses and 450,000 mules served with the Union armies. Each animal had its special task. "The horse," observed one soldier, "was the sole reliance of the artillery and cavalry. . . . The mule replaced him for the most part in the wagon trains. . . . In the ambulance train, horses were retained because they were steadier." Four-legged transportation was indispensable in camp, on campaign, and across the battlefield. To quote a veteran, "Horses under fire behaved far better than men did."

WATERWAYS

Water transportation also played a crucial role during the war. Numerous amphibious operations—combining naval and land forces—were conducted along the coastlines and inland waterways. Major rivers and seaports were often the focus of military planners and frequently became the sites of important battles. The capture of Fort Henry and Fort Donelson in February 1862 to win control of the Tennessee and Cumberland rivers, the successful siege of Vicksburg in July 1863 on the Mississippi, and the capture of the port city of Savannah in December 1864 rank among the decisive Union victories of the war.

The free flow of men and supplies over the railroads and waterways provided the lifeblood of the Union armies and were key elements in helping to make the final victory possible.

AN INADEQUATE RAIL SYSTEM

✤

ailroads," observed Confederate Brigadier General James H. Trapier, "are at one and the same time the legs and the stomach of an army." Although there were some visionaries like Trapier, from the start of the war few Southern officials realized the importance of a good rail system. The Confederacy started out with an inadequate system that deteriorated even further during the course of the war.

The Southern rail system at best was just a network of more than 100 locally owned companies, many of which required entirely different equipment between the connecting lines. Vested interests, rather than military strategy, played the main role in determining policies and functions of the South's rail system.

THE SOUTH'S DIFFICULTIES

Four major problems made the rail system insufficient to meet military and civilian needs. The first was the inadequacy of rail service throughout the South; the Northern rail system was more than twice as large. This lack of rail service between major cities often necessitated long, roundabout journeys. Bridges washed out by January 1861 rains and the lack of a rail link between Selma and Montgomery, Alabama, required Jefferson Davis to travel more than 250 miles farther by rail to attend his inauguration in Montgomery.

The lack of uniformity between local rail companies posed a major problem for civilian and military transportation. The gauges of the tracks—the distances between the rails—were not constant, which often necessitated changing trains during the course of a relatively short trip. Since different rail companies served major cities throughout the South, transporting goods by rail often required unloading a train and transporting goods across the city in wagons, only to be loaded onto another train.

Another problem was the inability to properly maintain the rail system as the war progressed. Unable to keep up with either natural wear or the destruction of the lines by advancing Union armies, the South let conditions slowly

Because they were important to the military for moving troops and supplies, railroads were often marked for destruction by enemy forces. Here the tangled ruins of a bridge over the North Anna River smoulder after being demolished in May 1864. This bridge, along the Richmond, Fredericksburg & Potomac Railroad, fell victim to both Union and Confederate torches.

Railroad laborers, called gandy dancers, mending tracks of the Nashville & Chattanooga Railroad.

deteriorate to the point that the railroads were no more than "a right-of-way and two streaks of rust," as one Southerner quipped.

Perhaps the greatest problem with the Confederate strategy in utilizing the railroads was that there was no strategy. Concerned about the reaction of states'-rightists to centralized control of the rails, the government assumed a hands-off policy until too late into the war. In December 1862, Davis appointed William M. Wadley to act as an intermediary between individual rail companies and the Confederacy's military interests. Frustrated by the lack of governmental support, he resigned seven months later. His replacement, Captain (later Lieutenant Colonel) Frederick W. Sims, had little more success. With the war coming to an unsuccessful conclusion, Sims reported in February 1865, two months before the end, that "not a single bar of railroad iron has been rolled in the Confederacy since [the beginning of] the war, nor can we hope to do any better during the continuance."

THE HUM OF MACHINERY

In contrast to its Confederate opponent, the Union increased ordnance production throughout the war. In fiscal 1864 alone, the Federal government spent $38.5 million on military supplies, including more than 800,000 small arms, 8 million pounds of powder, 1.7 million cannon shells, and more than 169 million rounds of small arms ammunition.

Industries like the Assabet Manufacturing Company in Massachusetts, pictured here, flourished in the North. Textiles, lumber, shoes, clothing, iron, and machinery were among the leading industries. The burgeoning cities of the North satisfied the need for labor and capital to develop and operate its factories, mills, and mines.

News of the battle of Gettysburg, and especially the ferocious artillery barrage preceding Pickett's charge, stirred imaginations in Pittsburgh. Citizens there were sure they had heard the cannon fire, like distant thunder, even though the battlefield was 140 miles away. The irony may have escaped them, but it's likely many of those same cannon had been manufactured right in their own backyard.

In the decade preceding the Civil War, Northern industries had enjoyed phenomenal growth. Scores of labor-saving machines had been introduced to help increase production in almost every industry. By 1860 more than four out of every five American factories were located in the North.

MANUFACTURING CENTERS

Drawing on vast supplies of raw materials from the Great Lakes region, Pittsburgh became a center for iron and steel production, turning out cannon, mortars, and a wide array of other steel products. Pennsylvania, in fact, had more industry than the entire South.

Pennsylvania was not alone in its productivity, however, as the North geared itself totally for the war effort. "The hum of machinery is heard on every hand," reported a newspaper in Lynn, Massachusetts, where a factory was assembling several hundred pairs of shoes each day. In Norwich, Connecticut, one enterprising textile manufacturer converted his mill to produce 1,200 muskets a week. Northern industries of all kinds prospered as they raced to supply the vast needs of the Union army and navy. "It may well surprise ourselves and all other nations," commented an article in *Scientific American* for January 17, 1863, "that during a year of the greatest civil war on record, our country has been wonderfully prosperous."

TREDEGAR IRON WORKS

✳

ames D. B. De Bow, in *De Bow's Review*, described the marvels of the Tredegar Iron Works in Richmond: "The capacity of the establishment is almost without limit," he wrote. "It seems like a special providence that it exists." The North may have had six times the number of factories as the South, but very few held the capacity of this great mill.

The Tredegar Iron Works produced a number of items important to the Confederacy's war effort, including all forms of projectiles, cannon, gun carriages, wheels and axles for rail cars, armor plates for ironclad ships, and smaller furnaces for other factories throughout the South.

A transplanted Pennsylvanian, Josiah Gorgas, was chosen as the head of the Confederate Ordnance Bureau with the unenviable task of keeping the Confederate armies armed. As the war progressed, Southern factories expanded and met most of his military needs. "I have succeeded beyond my utmost expectations," he wrote in his diary early in 1864. "Where three years ago we were not making a gun, pistol nor a sabre, no shot nor shell . . . we now make all these in quantities to meet the demands of our large armies." During the next year, however, he saw his manufacturing base quickly decline, as mills and the rail lines supplying them throughout the South were captured by invading Union troops.

This mighty cannon, called "Whistling Dick" because of the distinctive sound of its missiles, was mounted in Confederate batteries at Vicksburg. It was a product of the Tredegar Iron Works.

Situated on the banks of the James River in Richmond, the Tredegar Iron Works was the largest factory in the South.

THE ARMIES

During the first few months of the war, thousands of aspiring soldiers streamed into the opposing capitals of Washington and Richmond. The task facing both the Union and the Confederate governments was to find the men capable of forming these raw, untrained recruits into an efficient fighting machine. It took Abraham Lincoln three years and several generals to find the man who would lead the North to victory, Ulysses S. Grant. Jefferson Davis was fortunate in finding the man who would set a standard for military excellence, Robert E. Lee.

✦

"The Battle of Bull Run," lithograph by Kurz & Allison

THE SEARCH FOR A LEADER

✶

*a*lthough the North was a strong manufacturing nation with all the resources necessary to wage a successful war, it lacked the one military resource essential to victory: tested field leadership. In April of 1861, eight of the nine highest-ranking Northern officers were veterans of the War of 1812.

The general-in-chief for the previous 20 years, Winfield Scott, was 75 years old and frequently bedridden. His mind was sharp, however, and he proved valuable in directing the development of the initial Federal strategy. But Scott and his fellow commanders were not up to the rigors of raising and training a large army. Younger generals were promoted and brought to Washington to perform that task.

GENERAL IRVIN McDOWELL

The first general chosen for the job of subduing the Confederate forces was 43-year-old Brigadier General Irvin McDowell (West Point, 1838). Never having commanded anything larger than a squad in the field, McDowell was asked to assemble the young men who were streaming into Washington into a viable fighting unit. After only two months, he was pressured to send his ill-prepared force against an equally green Confederate army. Although his plan of attack was well developed, his officers and troops were not experienced enough to carry it out. The first battle of Bull Run (First Manassas), Virginia, on July 21, 1861, ended with the rout of his army.

GENERAL GEORGE B. McCLELLAN

Fresh from military success in western Virginia, 34-year-old Major General George B. McClellan (West Point, 1846) was brought to Washington to establish order in the midst of the chaos after Bull Run. An excellent administrator, McClellan quickly instilled discipline and organized the troops into a presentable army. He impressed Lincoln and the administration with his ability and was named general-in-chief of the Union army after Scott's resignation.

Although McClellan was not convinced that his army was ready to resume the offensive in the spring of 1862, he was ordered to do so by Lincoln. Mc-

Fond of comparing himself to Napoleon, General George B. McClellan (1826–1885) is shown striking a pose reminiscent of the French leader. McClellan's tenure as commander of the Army of the Potomac was marked by repeated incidents of uncertainty and overcaution on the battlefield.

Clellan's plan was to attack Richmond from the east, moving up the James River Peninsula. The campaign began on March 17, 1862, with his troops landing at Fort Monroe. The progress of his 118,000 men up the peninsula was marked by a snail's-pace advance. He was consistently stymied by numerically inferior troops. Although McClellan's army finally reached the suburbs of the Southern capital, it was thrown back after a series of strategic counterstrokes by the Confederate commander, Robert E. Lee. McClellan abandoned his campaign at the beginning of July of 1862.

While the war in the East faltered, Union generals were meeting with success in the West. A series of victories in Tennessee, including the taking of Fort Henry (February 6, 1862) and Fort Donelson (February 16) as well as a deci-

The tenure of Ambrose E. Burnside (1824–1881) as commander of the Army of the Potomac lasted less than three months, primarily due to his devastating defeat at Fredericksburg, Virginia. "It was plain, that he felt he had led us to a great disaster," one subordinate later wrote, "and one knowing him . . . could see he wished his body was also lying in front of Marye's Heights."

sive victory at Shiloh (April 6 and 7), led Lincoln to look in that direction for a general who could firmly lead his armies. He chose the 47-year-old commander of the Federal troops in the West, Major General Henry W. Halleck (West Point, 1839), as his general-in-chief, replacing McClellan. McClellan was named commander of the Army of the Potomac, and he and Halleck were almost immediately at odds.

The conflict was short-lived, though, as the advance of the Confederate army into Maryland caused McClellan to send his troops in pursuit. After a series of blunders and delays, McClellan finally confronted the army in a small town in Maryland called Sharpsburg. Although the Union was victorious in this battle of Antietam (September 17, 1862), McClellan's failure to decisively deploy his troops allowed the Confederates the opportunity to escape to Virginia. Fed up with his general's excuses and delays, Lincoln finally relieved McClellan of command on November 7. "McClellan was not conspicuous for his energy and skill in handling large bodies of troops," a Confederate officer later wrote.

GENERAL AMBROSE E. BURNSIDE

Lincoln chose 38-year-old Major General Ambrose E. Burnside (West Point, 1847) as McClellan's successor. Although Burnside was a capable subordinate general, Lincoln soon learned that he was not competent to command the Army of the Potomac. Realizing the importance of following up the victory at Antietam as soon as possible, Burnside devised a plan to cross the Rappahannock River at Fredericksburg, Virginia, in an attempt to take Lee's army by surprise. But a series of delays allowed Lee to entrench his troops and await a Federal attack.

Though realizing surprise was no longer a factor, Burnside still decided to attack (December 13, 1862), a mistake that cost his command more than 12,000 casualties. In an attempt to redeem himself, Burnside devised a plan to steal a march on Lee along the Rappahannock and attack the Confederate flank. The march became bogged down in mud and was nicknamed Burnside's "Mud March." "Men, horses, artillery, pontoons and wagons were stuck," one

Union officer wrote, "The wagons began to turn over and mules actually drowned in the mud and water. . . . The Rebels put up a sign marked 'Burnside stuck in mud.'" The fiasco cost Burnside his command—little more than two months after relieving McClellan.

GENERAL JOSEPH HOOKER

Lincoln chose 48-year-old Major General Joseph Hooker (West Point, 1837) as Burnside's successor, as much for his political connections as for his military ability. "Fighting Joe" Hooker reorganized the army and did much to salvage its sinking morale. He abandoned any plan to strike Lee's front at Fredericksburg. Instead he decided to leave a small force in front of Lee's forces and, copying a page from Burnside's failed "Mud March," rapidly march up the Rappahannock, cross it, and strike the rear of Lee's line.

The plan was executed to perfection, with the Union troops approaching the exposed Confederate rear. Once Lee discovered Hooker's intentions and attacked, however, Hooker lost his nerve and immediately halted the advance. Lee took advantage of his opponent as he did McClellan and Burnside, and after four days of fighting around Chancellorsville (May 1–4, 1863), Lee drove

After replacing Ambrose Burnside in January 1863, Joseph Hooker (1814–1879) devised a brilliant plan to steal a march on Robert E. Lee. He was at the brink of success when his courage failed him. Turning the initiative over to Lee, Hooker's army was decisively defeated. "To tell the truth," Hooker later wrote, "I just lost confidence in Joe Hooker."

Though outnumbered better than two to one by the Union Army of the Potomac at the battle of Chancellorsville, May 1–4, 1863, Confederate General Robert E. Lee boldly divided his Army of Northern Virginia to win a crushing victory. Tragically, Lee lost his most able subordinate when Thomas "Stonewall" Jackson was accidently shot by his own men. Informed of Jackson's death, Lee said, "I have lost my right arm."

Above, left: *Headquarters encampment of Union Major General George Gordon Meade. Appointed to command of the Army of the Potomac on June 27, 1863, Meade guided the force until its final victory in April 1865.*

Above, right: *Within days of assuming command, George Gordon Meade (1815–1872) defeated Robert E. Lee at Gettysburg, Pennsylvania. He was later criticized for his less-than-aggressive pursuit of Lee's defeated army after the battle.*

Right: *In their push south following the battle of Spotsylvania Court House, Virginia, in 1864, Ulysses Grant and George Meade and their staffs stopped at Massaponax Church. Grant had the pews brought into the yard under two shade trees. In this photo, Grant leans over Meade's right shoulder, pointing out a position on an open map.*

the defeated Federal force back across the Rappahannock. Not receiving the subsequent support from Halleck that he felt he needed to face Lee, Hooker—after six months of command—resigned on June 28.

GENERAL GEORGE G. MEADE

The Confederate army was in the process of invading Pennsylvania as Lincoln pondered the choice for his next commander. He chose 47-year-old Major General George G. Meade (West Point, 1835). Three days after Meade assumed command, before he had had time to develop his own campaign strategy, the Army of the Potomac stumbled on the enemy at the Pennsylvania town of Gettysburg. After three days of some of the fiercest fighting of the war (July 1–3, 1863), the Confederates withdrew from the field back into Virginia.

GENERAL ULYSSES S. GRANT

Ulysses S. Grant (1822–1885) was named general-in-chief of Union armies with the rank of lieutenant general on March 9, 1864. In this portrait, Grant stands in front of his tent at Cold Harbor, Virginia, in June 1864.

Although he was praised for the victory, Meade was also criticized for allowing the Confederate army to escape after retreating from Gettysburg. The postbattle decisions by Meade led Lincoln to believe that he had not yet found the man who could lead the Federal armies to ultimate victory. "General Meade was an officer of great merit," Ulysses Grant recorded in his memoirs, "with drawbacks to his usefulness that were beyond his control." Having focused primarily on the East for most of the war, Lincoln finally turned to the Western battlegrounds to find his general. The choice seemed obvious, for one man had surfaced as a winner in practically every engagement in which he fought.

Pickett's Charge

THE BATTLE OF GETTYSBURG

Considered by some as a turning point of the Civil War, the battle of Gettysburg was fought from July 1 to July 3, 1863, in and around the small crossroads community in southern Pennsylvania. The battle marked the farthest invasion of the North by a Confederate army.

For three days, nearly 170,000 soldiers in both armies fought desperately to destroy their enemy. The battle climaxed with the final Confederate attempt to pierce the Union line, Pickett's Charge. "In every direction among the bodies was the debris of battle," recalled a witness, "haversacks, canteens, hats, caps . . . blankets . . . bayonets, cartridge boxes. . . . Corpses strewed the ground at every step."

This romanticized view of Ulysses S. Grant galloping along with other prominent Union officers existed only in the imagination of the artist, Ole Peter Hansen Balling. Grant, hatless in this painting, and the officers pictured with him never appeared together on or off the battlefield.

Vicksburg, called the Gibraltar of the Confederacy, was the South's major bastion on the Mississippi River. Beginning in November 1862, Union General Ulysses S. Grant launched a series of maneuvers and assaults to take the Confederate stronghold. The city and its garrison, near starvation, finally surrendered on July 4, 1863, after a 47-day siege.

At a ceremony in the White House on March 9, 1864, Ulysses S. Grant received his commission as lieutenant general from President Abraham Lincoln. "[T]he nation's appreciation of what you have done," said Lincoln, "and its reliance upon you for what remains to be done in the existing great struggle, are now presented, with this commission. . . ."

Lincoln brought 41-year-old Major General Ulysses S. Grant (West Point, 1843) to Washington.

Grant's stature as a competent commander had steadily grown from one engagement to the next in the West. He had turned certain defeat into victory at Shiloh, had successfully captured Vicksburg, Mississippi, after a long siege (May 18–July 4, 1863), and had not only raised the Confederate siege of Chattanooga but had decisively defeated them there (November 23–25, 1863).

Lincoln promoted Grant to the rank of lieutenant general and made him the general-in-chief of all Federal armies. Realizing that the most effective way to defeat the Confederates was to conduct a war of attrition, Grant's aim was not only to fight the enemy, but to destroy its will to continue. He chose 44-year-old Major General William T. Sherman (West Point, 1840) to command the Federal armies in the West and kept Meade as the commander of the Army of the Potomac. Unlike Halleck, his predecessor, Grant desired to avoid Washington and its multitude of politicians. He therefore decided to remain with the Army of the Potomac. Although Meade was the army's commander, Grant was the strategist in the battle of wits against Lee.

Abraham Lincoln named Henry Halleck (1815–1872) general-in-chief of all Union armies as much for his reputation as a military genius as his successes in the Western theater. While he was a good administrator, he was not up to the task of designing and implementing a successful military strategy. In March 1864 he was displaced by one-time subordinate Ulysses S. Grant.

In September 1863 Union General George Meade made his headquarters at Culpeper, Virginia. "[T]he best country . . . we have yet been in," wrote Meade. Seated in the middle, Meade is surrounded by his staff.

When William Tecumseh Sherman (1820–1891) assumed command of the Army of the Tennessee in the spring of 1864, he realized that his objective was not limited to the military force opposing his vast army. "War is cruelty . . . ," he stated, "and those who brought war . . . deserve all the curses and maledictions a people can pour out."

As Sherman cut through Georgia in his campaign for Atlanta (May 7–September 2, 1864), Lee was brilliantly utilizing his inferior army to block Grant's attempts to capture Richmond. After bloody engagements in the Wilderness (May 5–7, 1864), at Spotsylvania (May 8–18), and at Cold Harbor (June 1–3), the Virginia campaign bogged down at Petersburg, south of Richmond. Following ten months of trench warfare, the Confederates abandoned Petersburg, thereby opening the way to Richmond. Seven days after the fall of Petersburg, Lee surrendered his command to Grant at Appomattox Court House, Virginia (April 9, 1865). The commander of the Confederate Army of the Tennessee, Joseph Johnston, surrendered his army to Sherman at Durham Station, North Carolina, on April 26, 1865.

Many men wore the uniform of general officers in the Federal army throughout the war. Few would have chosen Grant as the savior of the Union when the war began. From a position as a simple clerk in a tannery, Grant rose to become the hero of the great conflict.

Fierce fighting raged around Spotsylvania Court House, Virginia, for nearly two weeks in May 1864. One of the most ferocious attacks of the entire war took place on May 12, when thousands of Union troops launched a massive surprise assault near the center of the Confederate line. The action resulted in thousands of casualties and became known as the Bloody Angle.

A soldier who fought in the Wilderness May 5–6, 1864, wrote: "[I]t was a blind and bloody hunt to the death, in bewildering thickets, rather than a battle." Another survivor called it "simply bushwacking on a grand scale." The bloody two-day battle between the forces of Ulysses Grant and Robert E. Lee inflicted about 18,000 Union and 10,000 Confederate casualties.

THE CONFEDERATE FORCES

*Although the North was not prepared for war in April 1861, the South was at an even greater disadvantage. There was no standing army with a general staff. The only weapons widely available to the Confederate army were those that would be seized from captured Federal arsenals. In all, about 135,000 weapons were confiscated by the South, but of that number, only 10,000 were modern rifles. The Southern states were reluctant to form a strong central government, so any attempt to nationalize troops was met with sectional opposition. On top of all these shortcomings, the only variable the South had in common with the North was a lack of experienced, capable field commanders.

Uniform coat attributed to Beauregard

Pierre Gustave Toutant Beauregard (1818–1893) earned renown early in the war by directing Confederate victories at Fort Sumter and First Bull Run. His reputation faded soon after his defeat at the battle of Shiloh in April 1862. Afterward, he directed the defense of Charleston, South Carolina, and finished the war in command of the Department of North Carolina and southeastern Virginia.

With the fall of Fort Sumter, Confederate President Jefferson Davis turned to 42-year-old Brigadier General Pierre G. T. Beauregard (West Point, 1838), the hero of that event, to lead the army being formed in northern Virginia. Coming from the Shenandoah Valley, 54-year-old Brigadier General Joseph E. Johnston (West Point, 1829) joined Beauregard to decisively defeat the Union army at Bull Run (First Manassas) in July 1861. Conflicts with Davis resulted in Beauregard's transfer to the Western Theater. Johnston remained to command the troops at Manassas Junction, Virginia.

GENERAL ROBERT E. LEE

Promoted to the rank of full general, Johnston spent the winter of 1861 training and equipping his army. With the start of George McClellan's Virginia Peninsula campaign, Johnston moved most of his force south to defend against the Federal offensive. When Johnston was severely wounded at the battle of Seven Pines (May 31, 1862), Davis was forced to replace his field commander in the middle of the campaign. He turned to 55-year-old General Robert E. Lee to save Richmond.

This fanciful illustration shows Confederate General Robert E. Lee at center surrounded by other prominent officers. Many of the Confederacy's high-ranking officers were trained and experienced soldiers who had graduated from the United States Military Academy at West Point. Many others came from militia units and owed their rank to election or government appointments.

Following the unsuccessful defense of western Virginia, Lee's appointment to command the army defending Richmond was met with mixed emotions. He had been nicknamed "Old Granny Lee" by some. Even McClellan greatly underestimated the abilities of his opponent. "I prefer Lee to Johnston," McClellan stated. "[Lee] is too cautious and weak under grave responsibility. Personally brave and energetic to a fault, he yet is wanting in moral firmness when pressed by heavy responsibility and is likely to be timid and irresolute in action." Perhaps no other observation of the war was so off the mark. Lee immediately seized the initiative and rarely relinquished it for the next three years. His ability to take advantage of his enemy's weaknesses led to the majority of his successes.

THE WESTERN FRONT

Once Lee's army drove the Federals from the outskirts of Richmond, Davis realized his general had the campaign in the East well in hand. Early in 1862 the Confederate President focused more attention on the war in the West.

THE SIEGE AND BATTLE OF VICKSBURG

Union General Ulysses S. Grant's campaign to capture Vicksburg, Mississippi, was conducted between October 1862 and July 1863, ultimately for control of the Mississippi River. Located on the steep, rugged eastern bluff of the river, the city of Vicksburg was well "fortified and defended at all points," wrote Charles Dana, U.S. assistant secretary of war, "impregnable against any force that could be brought against its front."

For months, Confederate troops commanded by General John Pemberton held off the combined might of Union army and navy forces directed by Grant and Admiral David Porter. Soldiers and civilians alike suffered through numerous assaults, bombardments, and deprivations of food and other goods. Finally, on July 4, 1863, the day after Lee's defeat at Gettysburg, Pennsylvania, Vicksburg surrendered. The defeat cost the South more than 30,000 soldiers and almost 200 cannon. The Confederacy also lost control of the mighty Mississippi River.

In an effort to stem the Federal advance through Tennessee, 59-year-old Confederate General Albert S. Johnston (West Point, 1826) launched a surprise attack on the enemy at Pittsburg Landing, Tennessee, in the battle of Shiloh (April 6–7, 1862). While leading an attack on a pocket of resistance, Johnston was fatally wounded. General Beauregard assumed command and failed to defeat the temporarily staggered Union army. After retreating from Corinth, Mississippi (May 30, 1862), Beauregard went on sick leave and relinquished command to 45-year-old General Braxton Bragg (West Point, 1837). Davis took this as the opportunity to permanently replace Beauregard with Bragg, a personal friend.

Bragg remained in command of the Confederate Army of Tennessee for the next 17 months. While achieving mixed success throughout most of 1863, Bragg gained his most significant victory at Chickamauga, Georgia (September 19–20, 1863). Driving the Federals back to Chattanooga, Bragg suffered his most humiliating defeat at the battle of Missionary Ridge, Tennessee, (November 25, 1863) and resigned by December. He was replaced by Joseph Johnston, who was himself relieved on

A great-nephew of Patrick Henry, Virginian Joseph E. Johnston (1807–1891) was a West Point graduate and Mexican War veteran. Johnston was called "Uncle Joe" by his soldiers, though he could be a stern disciplinarian. At different times during the war, he commanded the main Confederate armies in the Eastern and Western theaters of operations.

July 17, 1864, when he consistently refused to take the initiative against the advancing Union army of William T. Sherman. Davis chose 33-year-old General John Bell Hood (West Point, 1853) to save Atlanta. Failing in that effort and suffering disastrous defeats at Franklin, Tennessee, (November 30, 1864) and

Nashville (December 16), Hood was replaced by Joseph Johnston, who was recalled to active duty on February 23, 1865.

LEE'S SURRENDER

Although he was the Confederacy's most consistent and successful commander, it wasn't until February 6, 1865, that Robert E. Lee was named commander of all Confederate armies, far too late to have any impact on the final outcome. Little more than two months later, Lee surrendered to Grant at Appomattox Court House, Virginia.

Chickamauga Creek, an Indian term meaning River of Death, lived up to its name September 19–20, 1863. During a two-day battle in the Georgia woodlands between the Union Army of the Cumberland and the Confederate Army of the Tennessee, one out of every four soldiers became a casualty. Only the last-ditch stand by troops under General George H. Thomas prevented the complete rout of the Union army.

ULYSSES S. GRANT

✵

*T*he impact of war often changes the fortunes of those who participate in it. There is no better example of this than the military career of Ulysses S. Grant. In April 1861 he was a 39-year-old clerk in his father's tannery. A graduate of West Point, he had won citations for gallantry during the Mexican War and later served in various outposts on the West Coast. But boredom and loneliness caused him to turn to the bottle. "I don't know whether I am like other men or not," Grant later admitted, "but when I have nothing to do, I get blue and depressed."

Facing court-martial for neglect of duty, he resigned from military service in 1854 and returned home only to fail in a number of business ventures.

Grant received the Republican nomination for president in 1868 and won the election against Democrat Horatio Seymour. Reelected in 1872, Grant attempted to follow a Reconstruction policy lenient toward the former Confederacy. Unfortunately his inexperience in politics worked to his disadvantage; his administration was tainted with corruption. After leaving office he wrote his memoirs. He died of throat cancer in 1885.

When the war began, he left his father's tannery and sought a commission in the Union army. The only position offered him was as a mustering officer. Using political contacts, he became a colonel of an Illinois regiment in June 1861. Two months later, he was made a brigadier general.

Grant attained national recognition with the captures of Fort Henry and Fort Donelson in February 1862. His demand for "unconditional and immediate surrender" of Fort Donelson gained him the nickname "Unconditional Surrender" Grant. After successive victories in the West over the next two years, President Abraham Lincoln called him to Washington in March 1864 to command all the Union armies. "Grant is my man," Lincoln proclaimed, "and I am his the rest of the war."

Grant determined that the only way to defeat the enemy was by using the superiority of Northern resources to exhaust those of the Confederates. His war strategy resulted in many casualties on both sides but also wore the Confederacy into submission within a year.

ROBERT E. LEE

✴

*T*he son of the Revolutionary War hero Light-Horse Harry Lee, young Robert grew up in military tradition. Graduating from West Point in 1829, he served in the Corps of Engineers and received three brevets for gallantry during the Mexican War. Lee's distinguished peacetime military career led Abraham Lincoln to offer him command of the Union army in Washington. Torn between his love for the Union and his beloved Virginia, Lee chose the latter and resigned from the U.S. Army. "I cannot raise my hand against my birthplace, my home, my children," he wrote in his letter of resignation.

On April 23, 1861, Lee accepted command of Virginia's defenses. Despite early failures, Confederate President Jefferson Davis never lost confidence in Lee and placed him in command of those troops attempting to stop Federal General George McClellan's troops, who had pushed to the outskirts of Richmond. Lee assured Davis that Richmond would not fall, and he proceeded to push the larger Union army back to the James River. A string of successes, seldom matched in military history, created a feeling of invincibility for Lee and his army. Lincoln went through a succession of generals looking for the man who was a match for the Confederate general.

After bloody struggles through the Virginia Wilderness, Lee learned that the latest and last of the Federal generals he would face, Ulysses S. Grant, was not as easily intimidated as the others. Less than a year later, with resources depleted and his men spent, Lee surrendered his army. "There is nothing left for me to do but to go and see General Grant," he said, "and I would rather die a thousand deaths." "Boys," he told his exhausted troops, "I have done the best I could for you. Go home now, and if you make as good citizens as you have soldiers, you will do well, and I shall always be proud of you. Goodbye, and God bless you all."

Following the Civil War, Robert E. Lee returned to his family and civilian life. Declining several lucrative job offers, Lee accepted the post of president of Washington College (later named Washington and Lee University) in Lexington, Virginia. His salary was $1,500 per year. He died in Lexington on October 12, 1870, at the age of 63.

THE UNION PLAN

✴

*F*ederal General Winfield Scott was not eager for war, unlike most people in the North. "Old Fuss and Feathers," nicknamed by troops he commanded during the Mexican War because of his demand for "exactness in military procedure," was the highest-ranking officer in the U.S. Army at the time. Scott had seen plenty of action in his day, dating back to the War of 1812, and he knew what he was talking about. But now that he was 74, rotund, infirm, and unable to mount a horse, Scott's plan to defeat the South was being scoffed at.

Suffering from dropsy, vertigo, and obesity, Winfield Scott (1786–1866) was not up to the task of crushing the rebellion. However, the plan he devised before his retirement in November 1861, calling for the blockade of Confederate ports and the control of the Mississippi River, contributed to the Federal success.

SCOTT'S PLAN

A majority of the Northern public and its leaders had a romantic notion of what the war would be like. They foresaw a short conflict. A quick, decisive strike to defeat the upstart Confederate army and capture the enemy's capital at Richmond would bring the rebellion to a speedy close.

Not so, Scott insisted, and he communicated his ideas to President Abraham Lincoln. To begin with, the aged general proposed to strengthen the naval blockade of the 3,500 miles of Southern coastline. This would cut off the Confederacy from the outside world. "In connection with such a blockade," Scott continued, "we propose a powerful movement down the Mississippi to the ocean." In the meantime, months would be required to properly train and equip the thousands of raw recruits that had flocked into the army.

Once these preparations were completed, the army would invade the South along the paths dictated by the geography of the region, in particular the Mississippi, Cumberland, Tennessee, and Shenandoah rivers. A separate thrust, overland from Washington, would be directed at the Confederate capital in Richmond. Thus, the strategy was to surround, divide, and conquer— the classic Napoleonic style that dominated military instruction of the era. Scott claimed his scheme would win the war "with less bloodshed than any other plan. . . . 300,000 men under an able general might carry the business through in two or three years." Scott predicted that "the greatest obstacle in

the way of the plan" was "the impatience of our patriotic and loyal Union friends. They will urge instant and vigorous action, regardless, I fear, of consequences." And so they did.

PUBLIC REACTION

When word of his plan leaked to the Northern press, it was dubbed the "Anaconda Plan," after the slow, methodical death grip the snake applied to its victims. "Let us make quick work," wrote the editor of *The New York Times*. "A strong active pull together will do our work effectively in thirty days. We have only to send a column of 25,000 to Richmond, and burn out the rats there. . . ."

Turning the thousands of raw recruits into soldiers and fusing them into an efficient army was the first task for the Union. These smartly marching troops from the 26th New York regiment saw intense action during the war.

105

Answering to cries from the press and the public of "on to Richmond," the army, commanded by Brigadier General Irvin McDowell, advanced against Rebel forces located near Manassas, Virginia, and was whipped at the first battle of Bull Run (First Manassas). The optimistic notion of a short war quickly vanished. "Every order was a blunder," wrote a Union soldier, "and every movement a failure."

DELAYS AND INEXPERIENCE

In the aftermath of defeat, Northern military planners began to employ the sound and thoughtful concepts of Scott's strategy. Scott himself retired in November 1861, and into his place stepped Major

Lieutenant General Ulysses S. Grant, at center, is flanked on his right by staff officer General John A. Rawlins and on his left by Lieutenant Colonel Theodore S. Bowers. When Grant was put in charge of all Union armies, he developed a coherent Northern strategy for winning the war.

General George B. McClellan. The young general understood the need to build and train the army before sending it into battle against the enemy. "I am getting my ideas pretty well arranged in regard to the strength of my army," McClellan wrote his wife. "It will be a very large one. I have been employed in trying to get the right kind of officers."

McClellan succeeded admirably in rebuilding the Army of the Potomac, the main Union army in the East, but he failed to take action. Frustrated by the delay, President Lincoln attempted to prod some activity from McClellan, but to no avail. It was a trait that characterized McClellan until he was dismissed from command in November 1862. Elsewhere, the blockade was growing steadily more effective, and success was being achieved along the Mississippi and Tennessee rivers.

What the North lacked early in the war, however, was a general staff capable of coordinating the activities of all the armed forces on all fronts. The U.S. Army numbered only 15,000 at the start of the Civil War, and these soldiers were scattered in outposts across the frontier. Few of the officers had experience commanding large numbers of troops. Nor were these officers necessarily familiar with the military applications of new technologies of warfare, such as the telegraph and railroads. Trial and error as well as experience played large roles in shaping strategy during the Civil War.

GRANT'S CONSOLIDATION

It wasn't until 1864, when Ulysses S. Grant emerged as general-in-chief of all Union armies, that a well-coordinated Northern strategy was developed. In the past, Grant noted, Northern armies had "acted independently and without concert, like a balky team, no two ever pulling together."

Grant aimed to destroy the South's ability to make war. "Lee's army will be your objective point," Grant instructed Major General George Meade, com-

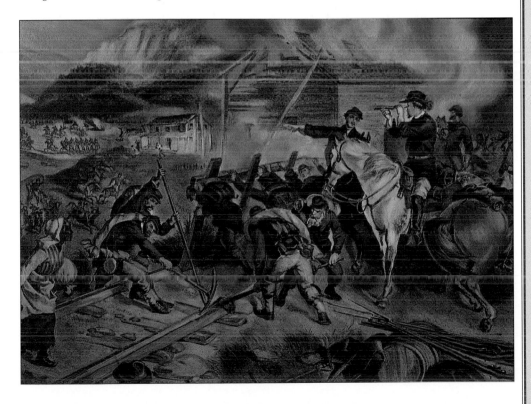

With Atlanta in flames behind him, Union General William T. Sherman embarked on November 15, 1864, on his famous march to the sea. Intent on destroying the deep South's ability to wage war, Sherman's army left in its wake a trail of wreckage 60 miles wide.

manding the Army of the Potomac. "Wherever Lee goes, there will you go also." At the same time, Grant ordered Major General William T. Sherman to lead his force "against Johnston's army, to break it up, and to get into the interior of the enemies [*sic*] country as far as you can, inflicting all the damage you can against their war resources."

In the end, probably no one was more pleased with the final victory than an aging warrior who lived in retirement at West Point, New York, and whose troopers had once called him "Old Fuss and Feathers."

THE STRATEGY OF THE SOUTH

✳

*J*efferson Davis's military roots were the foundation and fate of Southern military strategy during the Civil War. Davis often cast himself in the role of military leader and assumed a knowledge of military matters superior to that of his field commanders. This, when coupled with his stubborn, prideful, and uncompromising nature, often led to conflict and dissension in the government and on the battlefield. Subordinates, at times, found his interference intolerable. The Confederate War Department, for example, saw six secretaries come and go in four years. "He did not know the arts of the politician," Varina Davis confessed of her husband, "and would not practice them if understood."

THE QUEST FOR EUROPEAN SUPPORT

As the Confederacy's principal strategist, Davis developed what he termed the "offensive-defensive." This concept was rooted in his knowledge that the South lacked the arms, supplies, and manpower to compete evenly with the North. Confederate forces, he felt, must preserve their strength and counterattack only when opportunities and supplies permitted.

Political considerations, foreign and domestic, dictated Confederate strategy as well. Many Southerners were confident that abundant supplies of Southern cotton would bring in abundant supplies of European arms and munitions in return, if not outright military assistance. The Army of Northern Virginia's Maryland campaign in 1862—the Confederacy's first great invasion of the North—was partly driven by the

Stockpiles of Confederate torpedoes like these were common wherever Federal ships posed a threat. They were generally of two types: torpedoes detonated by contact with enemy ships or those ignited by electrical current from shore.

Quaker guns, logs fashioned to look like cannons to distant observers, were often used by Confederates to delay enemy advances.

quest for European aid and recognition. It ended in a bloody stalemate. The second invasion of the North a year later ended with great losses on the slopes around Gettysburg, Pennsylvania.

Meanwhile, the ever-powerful Union blockade curtailed the Confederacy's commercial access to the rest of the world. Europe succeeded in finding new sources for cotton from its colonies, thus neutralizing "King Cotton" as a diplomatic bargaining chip.

DAVIS'S PLAN

At home Davis was determined to protect the Confederacy's extensive borders. Military departments were created along geographical lines, and troops were parceled out among them. Each was "a separate nation for military purposes," wrote a government official, adding grimly, "without . . . cooperation or concert." Though smaller in numbers and weaker in weapons and equipment, Southern armies would have the advantage of fighting on defense and on interior lines. Thus, soldiers and supplies could be concentrated more quickly at threatened points.

Railroads played a key role in military operations on both sides. Campaigns were often staged along rail lines to take advantage of them for moving troops, munitions, food, and other military necessities. Several times the arrival of reinforcements by rail helped determine the outcome of a battle. Their importance made railroads prime targets for destruction by every raiding party.

Armies required an immense amount of supplies. The standard army wagon, pulled by four horses or six mules, was the primary means of transport. From 40 to 60 wagons were required for every 1,000 soldiers.

Although sound in theory, in practice these concepts handicapped Davis's strategy. As Union forces penetrated Confederate borders, communication lines crumbled. Roads and rivers were cut off, and railroads—fragile and disorganized from the start—were captured or destroyed. Travel between the widely scattered military departments gradually collapsed. Reinforcements were idled. Food, equipment, and other supplies destined for the armies rotted on railroad sidings. Davis confessed to a friend:

> I acknowledge the error of my attempt to defend all the frontier, seaboard and inland; but will say in justification that if we had received the arms and munitions which we had good reason to expect, that the attempt would have been successful and the battlefields would have been on the enemy's soil. . . . Without military stores, without workshops to create them, without the power to import them, necessity not choice has compelled us . . . to confront the enemy without reserves.

In the last months of the war, the strength and determination of leaders like Davis and General Robert E. Lee sustained the Confederacy more than any strategy. "There has been no country for a year or more," one of Lee's officers told him just before he surrendered at Appomattox Court House. "You are the country for these men."

Opposite: The map shows the locations of many places important in the Civil War.

THE NORTHERN ARMY

✳

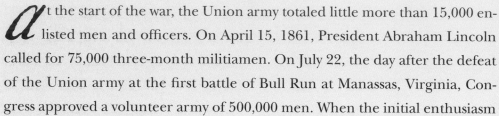

*a*t the start of the war, the Union army totaled little more than 15,000 enlisted men and officers. On April 15, 1861, President Abraham Lincoln called for 75,000 three-month militiamen. On July 22, the day after the defeat of the Union army at the first battle of Bull Run at Manassas, Virginia, Congress approved a volunteer army of 500,000 men. When the initial enthusiasm for the war subsided and the number of volunteers began to fall below the number needed to continue the war, the Enrollment Act of March 3, 1863, was passed by Congress. Conscription proved to be a public relations nightmare for the Federal government.

Draft riots broke out across the North, the most serious occurring in New York City (July 13–16, 1863). About 13 percent of the 292,441 men drafted for service failed to report. Of those reporting, 65 percent received exemptions. Of the 35,000 men eventually entering the service as a result of the draft, more than 25,000 were paid substitutes, lending credence to the assertion that this was a poor man's army.

Although the draft was not successful in filling the ranks depleted by death, injury, and desertion, more than 1 million men volunteered for service during the last two years of the war. Of more than 2 million enlistments in the Union army, 110,100 were killed or mortally wounded in battle, 199,720 died of disease, 24,866 died in Confederate prisons, 9,058 died from accidents or drowning, and 15,784 died from other causes.

This Northern volunteer of 1861 displays a spit-and-polish militia uniform that was soon replaced with standard Union blue. For most recruits, the novelty of military life soon wore off, too.

THE SOUTHERN ARMY

✳

On March 6, 1861, the Confederate Provisional Congress established the Provisional Army of the Confederate States of America. In the first call for troops, states provided up to 100,000 equipped volunteers to the Confederate army for a year. In May 1861, the Confederate Congress extended enlistments for the duration of the war. In April 1862 President Jefferson Davis approved the congressional act establishing a draft of every white male between 18 and 35 years of age.

This first draft in American history met with much criticism. "From this time on till the end of the war," one Southerner observed, "a soldier was simply a machine, a conscript. . . . All our pride and valor had gone, and we were sick of war and cursed the Southern Confederacy." The Confederate conscription act was no more successful than its counterpart in the North. Less than half of those eligible for the draft bothered to sign up.

Due to the lack of accurate records, the enrolled strength of the Confederate army has been placed between 600,000 and 1.5 million men. It is widely accepted that the actual number of enlistees was nearly 1 million men. It is estimated that about 250,000 men were killed, mortally wounded, or died of other causes. Only 174,223 men were recorded as having surrendered to Union forces in 1865.

A young victim of the war, Confederate Private Edwin Francis Jennison of Georgia was only sixteen years old when he was killed at the Battle of Malvern Hill in July 1862.

A POWERFUL ALLY

✴

$\mathcal{T}$he dead lay in heaps, their blue uniforms saturated with blood. Many men had been ripped open with bayonets. Others had their skulls crushed with musket butts. Some had been shot. Most of the dead soldiers were black casualties of the first important battle of the Civil War in which soldiers of African descent had fought.

"The bravery of the blacks at Milliken's Bend," wrote a Union officer who had witnessed the gory aftermath of the June 7, 1863, battle along the banks of the Mississippi River in Louisiana, "completely revolutionized the sentiment of the army with regard to the employment of Negro troops. I heard prominent officers who formerly had sneered . . . at the idea of the Negroes fighting, express themselves after that, as heartily in favor of it."

PREJUDICE

It wasn't until July 1862 that Congress first authorized the use of blacks in the army, and not until after the Emancipation Proclamation, on January 1, 1863, were large numbers of blacks recruited into the Federal army. Before

Andrew Scott, a black who served with the Federal army

Before they were officially accepted into the military, many blacks served the army as laborers. Called contrabands, these fugitive slaves performed as teamsters and cooks as well as other behind-the-line workers. In March 1865 Congress created the Freedmen's Bureau to assist former slaves.

then, widespread prejudice in the North had kept blacks from serving. "I have had the question put to me often," said General William T. Sherman, "'Is not a Negro as good as a white man to stop a bullet?' Yes! and a sand-bag is better; but can a Negro do our skirmishing and picket duty? Can they improvise bridges, sorties, flank movements, etc., like the white man? I say no."

Sherman could not have been more wrong. From the firing line to service behind the lines—as well as in the navy—blacks saw action in 449 engagements

These soldiers are pictured at Camp William Penn in Pennsylvania. Each black regiment had all white officers. "The officers and men are both carefully picked," wrote Governor John Andrews concerning the formation of the 54th Massachusetts. "We have arrived at getting officers of high character, making careful selections out of many candidates.

The 54th Massachusetts Infantry was the most famous of the many black regiments that served in the war. Led by Colonel Robert Gould Shaw, who died in the assault, the 54th attacked Fort Wagner near Charleston on July 18, 1863. Before being forced to retreat, the 54th lost 272 of the 650 men engaged in the attack.

in every theater of operations during the Civil War. Through it all, they had to endure discrimination from white officers and enlisted men. Until late in the war, black soldiers were even paid less than white troops. "I will never fight by the side of a Niger [*sic*]," protested a white soldier, "& that is the feeling of the army." In reply to such attitudes, the well-known black leader Frederick Douglass said simply, "Give them a chance. I don't say that they will fight better than other men. All I say is, Give them a chance!"

THE SUCCESS OF BLACK TROOPS

Their chance came at places such as Fort Wagner in Charleston Harbor, where the all-black 54th Massachusetts Infantry Regiment covered itself with

Recruited from among free men and former slaves, many of the black troops saw action on battlefields across the South. The majority of black units performed garrison and labor duties.

54TH MASSACHUSETTS

One of the first black regiments recruited in the North, the 54th Massachusetts Infantry Regiment, was mustered into Federal service in May 1863. Colonel Robert Gould Shaw, the 25-year-old son of wealthy Boston abolitionists, was the regiment's first commander. Among the rank and file were two sons of the black abolitionist Frederick Douglass.

Deployed to South Carolina upon completing training, the regiment first saw action on James Island, where it lost 46 men while repelling a Confederate attack. Two days later, the 54th Massachusetts made its famous assault on Battery Wagner in Charleston Harbor, where Shaw was killed and 272 other men became casualties. Afterward, the regiment saw action in Georgia and during the battle of Olustee, Florida. The regiment was mustered out of the service September 2, 1865.

glory; and near Petersburg, Virginia, where 38 regiments of United States Colored Troops withstood the test under fire during a 10-month siege. Twenty-three blacks won the Medal of Honor at Petersburg.

In all, nearly 200,000 black soldiers served the North during the war. "I have given the subject of arming the Negro my hearty support," proclaimed Lieutenant General Ulysses S. Grant. "This, with the emancipation of the Negro, is the heaviest blow yet given the Confederacy. . . . By arming the Negro we have added a powerful ally. They will make good soldiers, and taking them from the enemy weakens him in the same proportion they strengthen us."

SLAVES AND SOLDIERS

✦

*T*he officers met by candlelight the night of January 2, 1864, in the commanding general's tent, on the outskirts of Dalton, Georgia, and couldn't believe what they were hearing. Confederate General Joseph Johnston and all but one of his corps and division commanders in the Army of Tennessee listened in stunned silence to Major General Patrick R. Cleburne. With the South threatened by ruin and defeat, Cleburne proposed "that we immediately commence training a large reserve of the most courageous of our slaves, and further that we guarantee freedom . . . to every slave in the South who shall remain true to the Confederacy in this war."

The reaction inside the tent was as icy as the chilly winter night outside. One officer present expressed the common sentiment when he later wrote that it was a "monstrous proposition," revolting to Southern sentiment, Southern pride, and Southern honor. When Confederate President Jefferson Davis learned of Cleburne's proposal, he ordered the letter suppressed. The matter was closed—for the time being.

Several newspapers in the South had earlier suggested much the same idea as General Cleburne's, with similar feedback. "You cannot make soldiers of slaves," General Howell Cobb of Georgia warned. "The day you make a soldier of them is the beginning of the end of the revolution. And if slaves seem good soldiers, then our whole theory of slavery is wrong."

THE BLACK ROLE

Blacks did, however, play vital roles for the Confederate military.

Most Southerners were not eager to use slaves as soldiers.

Many blacks, both slaves and freemen, were employed as cooks, teamsters, musicians, medical attendants, and servants. Many thousands wielded picks and shovels to erect miles of earthen fortifications and trenches. And on occasion, armed blacks performed guard duty.

Rarer still were the instances of blacks who saw combat with Confederate troops. "There were four colored men in our battery," wrote John Parker, a slave in action at the first battle of Bull Run (First Manassas) in July 1861. "We opened fire about ten o'clock. . . . My work was to hand the balls and swab out the cannon." In 1863 a *New York Times* journalist reported, "The guns of the rebel battery were manned almost wholly by Negroes, a single white man, or perhaps two, directing operations."

Though debate was long and bitter, the Confederate Congress finally enacted legislation in March 1865 for 300,000 black soldiers to fill the ranks of the Confederate army. By then it was too late. The war ended a few weeks later.

Fort Pillow massacre

MASSACRE OF BLACK SOLDIERS

Fighting was especially ferocious when black soldiers encountered Confederate troops in combat. The massacre of black troops is alleged to have occurred on several occasions. Documented cases of such atrocities did occur at Fort Pillow, Tennessee (April 12, 1864); Saltville, Virginia (October 2, 1864); Poison Springs, Arkansas (April 18, 1864); and Petersburg, Virginia (July 30, 1864).

In each instance, captured, wounded, or unarmed black soldiers were murdered by vengeful Confederate troops. About the action at Fort Pillow, a Federal soldier wrote: "As soon as the rebels got to the top of the bank there commenced the most horrible slaughter that could possibly be conceived. Our boys when they saw they were overpowered threw down their arms and held up . . . their hands in token of surrender, but no sooner were they seen than they were shot down, & if one shot failed to kill them the bayonet or revolver did not."

General Lee requested that the slaves be armed for use as soldiers, but the Confederate Congress did not authorize black troops until shortly before the end of the war.

NORTHERN PRISONS

✵

*I*t occupied 30 acres along the Chemung River in lower New York State, a few miles from the Pennsylvania border and about a mile above the city of Elmira. In the early months of the Civil War, a U.S. Army barracks located there welcomed eager young recruits before they were marched off to combat. Midway through the third year of the war, the old barracks were expanded, scores of tents were pitched, and stout timber walls were built to enclose the once-lush acreage. Six weeks later, 9,600 Confederate prisoners of war were crammed into the stockade. By the end of the year, more than 1,200 of the prisoners would be dead. The living would nickname the place "Hellmira."

The deplorable living conditions that developed at Elmira differed little from those in any other prison during the Civil War, North

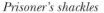

Prisoner's shackles

This view of the prison at Elmira shows wooden barracks that had been erected to replace scores of tents. Nevertheless, Southern prisoners continued to suffer the effects of the harsh northern weather conditions.

and South. Neither side, however, intended to abuse its prisoners when the war began. In fact, neither side had expected the war to last very long, so they hadn't prepared to detain and shelter prisoners for any length of time. Rather, until April 1863, each side frequently paroled and exchanged its captives. Soldiers who were actually held captive were temporarily housed in existing forts, local jails, or warehouses and vacant buildings.

INCREASING NUMBERS

The parole and exchange of prisoners all but ceased by the end of 1863. Exchange agents had begun to detect unfair practices as the war dragged on, and the number of prisoners became unmanageable. The introduction of black soldiers into the war also had an impact. The South refused to exchange blacks suspected of being runaway slaves and threatened to hang their white officers for inciting slaves to revolt.

A group of Confederate prisoners are surrounded by Union guards and observers. More than 200,000 men on both sides were captured during the course of the war. About 26,000 Confederates and 22,000 Federals died as prisoners.

Consequently, prisoner of war populations skyrocketed. Northern and Southern officials scrambled to find or make places to keep them—Fort Delaware, for example. "It is useless to attempt a description of the place," wrote a Confederate prisoner. "A respectable hog would have turned up his nose in disgust at it." Camp Chase in Columbus, Ohio, was equally bad, largely due to the camp commandant, Charles Allison. A government inspector found Allison "utterly ignorant of his duties and . . . surrounded by the same class of [officers]." The inspector added wryly: "But he is a lawyer and a son of the lieutenant governor."

Substandard housing, poor sanitation, lack of medical care, and meager quantities of bad food were the universal curse in prisoner of war camps. About Johnson's Island in Lake Erie, Confederate Captain H. W. Henry wrote: "The prisoners would rake the slop and garbage of the cook house and gather every scrap that showed any sign of nourishment." Of Camp Morton in Indianapolis, an inmate recalled that "all the rats which could be caught were eaten."

RETRIBUTION

After the war, blame for the collective evils of Civil War prisons, both North and South, fell on the shoulders of Henry Wirz, who had been commandant of the Confederate prison at Andersonville, Georgia. He was arrested and tried for "murder in violation of the laws and customs of war." Though his trial was a mockery of justice, Wirz was found guilty and hanged in Washington, D.C., in November 1865.

Confederate prisoners waiting to be transported north from Chattanooga in 1864. Prison populations overflowed on both sides once Union General Ulysses S. Grant suspended prisoner exchange in April 1864. "Every man we hold," Grant wrote, "when released on parole or otherwise, becomes an active soldier against us. . . . If a system of exchange liberates all prisoners taken, we will have to fight on until the whole South is exterminated."

Opposite. Opened in May 1864, the Elmira prison became notorious for the conditions its Confederate inmates were forced to endure. Wooden barracks erected to replace the tents as winter approached failed to ease a death rate of nearly 25 percent among prisoners.

SOUTHERN PRISONS

✴

*B*y all appearances, nothing was remarkable about the building that stood at the corner of Carey and 20th streets near downtown Richmond. A three-story brick structure, measuring 150 feet by 100 feet and divided into eight large rooms, it had been home to Libby & Son Ship Chandlers & Grocers before the Civil War.

But appearances can be deceiving. During the war, Libby & Son housed up to 1,200 captured Union officers at a time. They were densely packed into dank, drafty, bug-infested, tomblike rooms and placed under the control of Richard Turner, a Confederate prison official one inmate described as "a vulgar, coarse brute . . . the greatest scoundrel that ever went unhung." In February 1864, Libby Prison witnessed the greatest mass breakout of the war when more than 100 inmates escaped. Fifty-nine eventually made it back to Union lines.

Federal officers were imprisoned here at Libby Prison, located along the James River in Richmond. When Federal raids reached the outskirts of Richmond by mid-1864, prisoners were permanently transferred to prisons farther south.

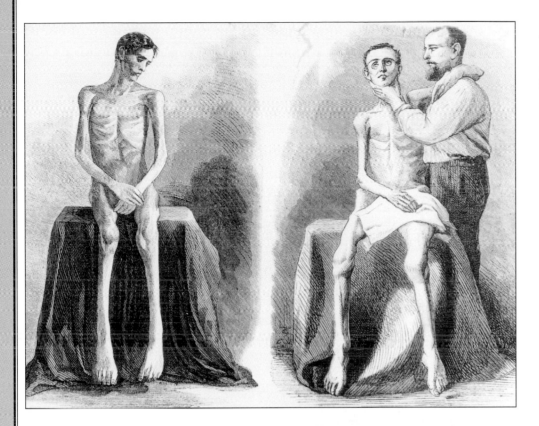

Prisoners being examined at United States General Hospital, Annapolis, Maryland. Malnutrition and disease were commonplace among prisoner of war camps in both the North and South.

Union soldiers outside a Confederate prison in Petersburg, Virginia, after the Confederates evacuated Petersburg in April 1865. The building was converted to a prison from a tobacco warehouse.

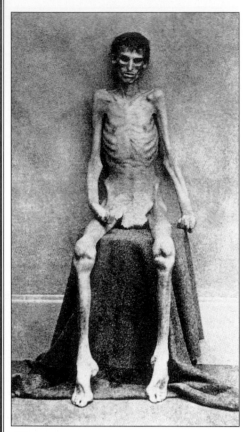

This photograph of a Union soldier after his release from Andersonville speaks eloquently about the terrible conditions at that notorious prison camp. "[I]t is hardly possible to conceive of greater accumulation of woes. . ." wrote a Union survivor, ". . . than fell to the prisoners at Andersonville."

A portion of the notorious prison camp at Andersonville. Located in southwestern Georgia, this 16-acre site received its first Northern prisoners in February 1864. Almost 13,000 men died there by war's end, due primarily to malnutrition and disease.

BELLE ISLE

As bad as conditions were in Libby Prison, the unspeakable misery of being held captive in the South was widespread. Not far from Libby was Belle Isle, in the James River, where thousands of enlisted Union men were confined. Their fate is told by poet Walt Whitman, who saw a boatload of former prisoners returned to Washington from there. "Can these be men," wrote Whitman, "these little, livid brown, ash streaked, monkey-looking dwarfs? Are they really not mummied, dwindled corpses? They lay there, most of them quite still, but with a horrible look in their eyes and skinny lips, often with not enough flesh to cover their teeth."

ANDERSONVILLE

Whitman could just as well have been describing the condition of prisoners from any of the stockades in the South. More than 200,000 Union soldiers became captives. Of these, more than 30,000 died. The prison at Andersonville in Sumter County, Georgia, was the most notorious of all, and by far held the greatest number of prisoners at a given time (33,000 in August 1864). Originally designed to hold 10,000, Andersonville became a death trap for 13,000 Union captives. "Rations very small and very poor," wrote a prisoner in his diary. "The meal that the bread is made out of is ground, seemingly, cob and

Convicted of inhuman crimes against pris oners at Andersonville, where he served as commandant, Heinrich (Henry) Wirz was executed on November 10, 1865. Having emigrated to America from Switzerland in 1849, Wirz was appointed to his Andersonville command in March 1864. Offered a last-minute reprieve if he implicated Jefferson Davis in the deaths of Northern prisoners, Wirz responded, "Jefferson Davis had no connection with me as to what was done at Andersonville."

all, and it scourges the men fearfully. Things getting worse. Hundreds of cases of dropsy. Men puff out of shape and are perfectly horrible to look at."

SALISBURY

Deadlier still was Salisbury Prison in North Carolina, where 34 percent of its 10,000 captives died. "The filthiness of the prison increased," wrote a prisoner, "vermin were literally swarming over us. . . . I have seen them countless numbers on the clothing of the dead. As soon as the body began to grow cold . . . they would crawl to the outside, and out on the end of the hair and beard until one would wonder the person had not been eaten alive by them."

Twenty-four years after the war, with memories still vivid, Libby Prison was dismantled and moved to Chicago for an exhibition. There, one young visitor listened to accounts from a veteran about the treatment endured by captives of the South. The youngster ranted and cursed the Confederacy. "That's all over now," replied the Union veteran. "If the truth were known, I guess we did pretty nearly as bad in some of our prisons."

THE COMMON SOLDIER

Enthusiasm for war spread throughout the North and South once Fort Sumter fell. Volunteers flocked to sign up for what everyone believed would be a short conflict. "Every person, almost, was eager for the war," wrote one Confederate volunteer, "and we were all afraid it would be over and we not be in the fight." Against the opinion of almost everyone, however, the war did not turn out to be a short-lived frolic. It took four years to end the conflict. In that period of time, many men served, and many died.

✦

"The Battle of Kennesaw Mountain," by Kurz & Allison

BILLY YANK

✦

With the onset of war, strange, new emotions swept through the homes of soon-to-be Union soldiers. "Sunday was a sorrowful one at our home," recalled a young 19-year-old preparing for war. "My mother went about with tears in her eyes, while I felt disappointment that I could not express and therefore nursed my sorrow in silence."

Concerned parents often weighed their sons down with baggage in order to ensure that all their needs would be met. "My knapsack was so heavy," one youth recalled of his trip from home, "that I could scarcely stagger under the load."

INITIAL ENTHUSIASM

Cities and towns throughout the North raised whole companies and regiments for the purpose of preserving the Union. There was much excitement and pageantry as families and friends saw them off to war. Recalled one young recruit: "At the wharf an immense crowd had gathered and we went on board our steamer with mingled feelings of joy and sorrow."

Bugle from Battery A, Chicago Light Artillery

Soldiers of Company B, 170th New York Infantry, read newspapers and letters from home, smoked, and played cards as they waited for orders to advance during the Wilderness campaign of 1864. This regiment of Irish Americans suffered heavy casualties three weeks after this photograph, during fighting along the North Anna River.

A private of Company F, 4th Michigan Infantry Regiment, strikes a martial pose for the photographer. Organized at Adrian, Michigan, in May 1861, the regiment participated in every major campaign of the Army of the Potomac until it was mustered out of service in June 1864. Many of its members continued to serve in other units.

Drum used in the 9th Regiment of Vermont

Federal soldiers encompassed the same spectrum of nationalities found in the Northern population. These artillerymen and cavalrymen in a variety of uniforms represent the diversity in the army.

These well-supplied Federal soldiers in a trench facing Petersburg, Virginia, presented a stark contrast to sparsely equipped Confederate soldiers who were less than 100 yards away.

Two young Federal telegraph operators pose at a headquarters camp near Petersburg, Virginia, in August 1864. By 1864 the Federal armies had laid more than 6,500 miles of telegraph wire to create vital communication links between the various commands. The overall casualty rate of telegraph operators during the war was nearly 10 percent.

There was very little difference between the Northern and Southern recruits. Most were between the ages of 18 and 29, Protestant, and unmarried. Just as with their Confederate counterparts, the issue of slavery was not the primary motivation for Union men to enlist. Devotion to preserving the Union and the enthusiasm and excitement of going to war were the primary reasons most young men flocked to the recruiting stations.

About half of the volunteers had been farmers, with the other half representing more than 300 different occupations. Their range of experience was much greater than that of individuals called to the Southern cause. The diverse skills of the typical Union recruit provided an invaluable pool of resources to the army, from bridge building to repairing wagons and railroads.

Although immigrants served in the Confederate armies, the Union army attracted a larger percentage of foreign-born enlistees. About 10 percent of the enlistees were German, 8 percent Irish, and 6 percent English and Canadian.

HARDSHIPS

Once away from home, recruits found that life was not going to be easy in the army. The common problem of transporting fresh food to the front was shared by both sides. The flour cracker called hardtack was a dietary staple but was not always in the best of shape when it reached the front. "It was no uncommon occurrence," one Union veteran recorded, "for a man to find the

"The Wounded Drummer Boy," by Eastman Johnson

CHILDREN AT WAR

Almost half of the more than 2 million Union soldiers were under the age of 19. Lax enlistment standards and indifferent examination techniques allowed easy access for underage recruits. More than 800,000 youths who enlisted were 16 or 17 years old. Approximately 100,000 were "no more than 15," according to a postwar study.

Boys 16 and under could enlist as musicians. Often during battle they would set their instruments aside to bear stretchers and aid the wounded. The war's most celebrated youngster, 12-year-old Johnny Clem, served with the 22nd Michigan Infantry and shot a Confederate officer at the battle of Chickamauga.

Hardtack and eating utensils

surface of his pot of coffee swimming with weevils, after breaking hardtack in it; but they were easily skimmed off and left no distinctive flavor." Hardtack was often called teeth-dullers, worm castles, and sheet-iron crackers.

THE TEST OF FIRE

As in all wars, most men questioned their ability to withstand the test of fire: "Will I fight or run?" Many times, however, soldiers did not have much time to ponder that question, as they were sent into battle soon after enlistment and without proper training. "Within three weeks from the day this regiment was mustered into service," wrote one soldier, "and before it had ever had what could properly be called a battalion drill, it was in the battle of Antietam."

The effects of battle quickly wore men down and embittered them. A soldier from New York wrote home:

Confederate bodies along McPherson's Ridge, casualties of the first day of fighting during the battle of Gettysburg, Pennsylvania, July 1–3, 1863.

On our way to the picket line, I saw fifteen unburied Confederate soldiers lying where they had fallen. It was not a pleasant sight. . . . I thought of the sorrow and grief there would be in fifteen homes somewhere; and for what had these young lives been sacrificed? . . . There should be some way to settle political differences without slaughtering human beings and wearing out the bodies and sapping the strength of those who may be fortunate enough to escape the death penalty.

By the middle of 1864, the soldiers were seriously questioning the purpose of their roles in the fight. One soldier wrote home:

The feeling here in the army is that we have been absolutely butchered, that our lives have been periled to no purpose, and wasted. Those in high command, such as corps commanders and higher officers, still . . . have time and again recklessly and wickedly placed us in slaughter-pens. I can tell you, Father, it is discouraging to see one's men and officers cut down and butchered time and again, and all for nothing.

Eventually the war ended for these young men who aged so much in four short years, but the bonds they formed throughout the hardships would be remembered the rest of their lives. "We have shared the incommunicable experience of war," wrote Oliver Wendell Holmes, Jr., an officer from Massachusetts. "We have felt, we still feel the passion of life to its top. . . . In our youths, our hearts were touched by fire."

THE HAVERSACK

"It is amusing to think of the follies of the early part of the war," a veteran wrote, "as illustrated by the outfits of the volunteers. They were so heavily clad, and so burdened with all manner of things, that a march was torture." A long march or two was all the convincing some soldiers needed to toss away such unnecessary equipment as extra boots or bulky overcoats.

The haversack, however, was one item many soldiers on both sides found essential. Measuring about a foot square, the canvas sack had a waterproof coating and was designed to hold all sorts of things. "After they had been in use for a few weeks," recalled a Union soldier, "[they were used] as receptacle for chunks of fat meat, damp sugar tied up in a rag, broken crackers and bread, with a lump of cheese or two." The white cotton linings "took on the color of a printing office towel."

JOHNNY REB

✦

"So impatient did I become for starting," a young Arkansas soldier wrote about his excitement to rush to war, "that I felt like ten thousand pins were pricking me in every part of the body, and started off a week in advance of my brothers." Many young Southern men flocked to recruiting centers in February and March of 1861, anxious to get to the war before it was over.

Each participant had his own motivation for going to war. While preservation of slavery was the primary provocation for some, most recruits in the early stages of the war were driven more by passion than politics. As the war progressed and the enemy invaded their homes, their motivation turned more to preservation and survival.

More than two-thirds of the recruits to the Confederate army were farmers. Although the minimum age was 18, many younger youths were passed through the rather lax recruiting process.

New recruits typically brought with them up to 100 pounds of baggage when they left home. Families and friends loaded them with several sets of clothes, every toiletry item imaginable, several pairs of underwear, gloves, and all measures of personal weapons. Once they made their first campaign march, however, they tended to discard everything but the bare essentials. In addition to the clothing on the soldier's back, the only items carried were typically a rifle, a knapsack, a cartridge box, a blanket, a rubber blanket, a canteen, and a haversack, which contained pipe and tobacco, soap, and food forage picked up during the march.

FOOD SHORTAGES

While plentiful at the start of war, food became more scarce for the common soldier as the war progressed. Although the standard diet was prescribed to be portions of meat, flour, sugar, and coffee, on few days were all four available. Normally the diet consisted of whatever food made its way to the front. Pure coffee was often hard to come by in the South. "How much I miss the

A pair of young Rebels pose in their uniforms with an antiquated flintlock.

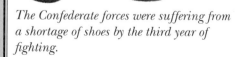

The Confederate forces were suffering from a shortage of shoes by the third year of fighting.

good coffee I used to get at home," one young Texan recorded. "I would cheerfully pay one dollar for as much like it as I could drink. . . . We got some ground coffee from the Yanks in the Seven Days fight."

The lack of coffee beans led to many improvised solutions. Soldiers often substituted chicory, peas, corn, peanuts, and a variation of other substances for their coffee ration. The *Confederate Receipt Book*, published for civilians in 1863, recommended the following: "Take sound ripe acorns, wash them while

Garbed in overcoats, these three Confederate privates of the 3rd Georgia Infantry appear ready for cold weather. Winter conditions generally limited active campaigning. Both Union and Confederate armies used the time to rest, regroup, and reequip themselves. The lucky soldier might also be granted a furlough to visit home during this season.

Though photography was barely 30 years old at the time of the Civil War, technical advances had made photos inexpensive and readily available for soldiers to record their participation in the war. These Confederate soldiers display a variety of uniforms. Ornate uniforms like that worn by the young Southern cadet in the upper left-hand picture disappeared soon after the war began. Shortages of all kinds plagued the Confederacy and affected what soldiers wore.

in the shell, dry them, and parch until they open, take the shell off, roast with a little bacon fat, and you will have a splendid cup of coffee."

One of the main food staples was hardtack, a tough, impenetrable flour-and-water biscuit. It was often discovered that boxes of hardtack had become the homes of maggots and weevils.

PAYMENT

At the start of the war, Confederate volunteers were paid $11 per month. Even though rampant inflation lowered the value of the dollar throughout the war, it wasn't until 1864 that the monthly payment was increased to $18 per month. Not only was this payment next to worthless due to inflation, but soldiers had to wait months before being paid. "Yesterday we were paid up—wages to Jany. 1, 1864 and commutation for clothing for the year ending Oct. 8, 1863," observed one Confederate. "As the 'old issue' of Confederate notes will soon be worthless, it seems the Treasury Department is very anxious to get rid of it—hence the large installment of wages we received."

INEXPERIENCED SOLDIERS

The average recruit was not a trained soldier. Confederates were known for their ferocity in battle and laxness at all other times. They were not a disciplined lot and rarely followed orders voluntarily. Officers had to earn their men's respect. When they did, their men would follow them to their deaths. A member of the 3rd Louisiana recalled:

Col. M'Intosh, though very affable and pleasant in his manner, had nevertheless something so commanding in his deportment that he carried men with him in spite of themselves, and, although I would just as soon have been somewhere else than to be the first man marching up to that battery, yet I felt that I would rather die three times other than display the slightest fear under the eye of that man.

Once in the army, it didn't take these young recruits long to realize that going to war was not an exciting adventure, but a monotonous, extremely dangerous existence. "If anyone had told me before the war that men could have borne for month after month . . . what we have, I would have thought it all talk," a young Alabama captain wrote to his father. "And I recollect when we first came into the service we grumbled at fare that we would think the greatest luxuries."

The reason men joined the army and accepted all the personal hardships was to fight, and many were anxious for that first opportunity. Once arrived, however, war had lost most of its glory. "None can realize the horrors of war, save those actually engaged," observed one young member of the 6th Georgia. "My God, My God, what a scourge is war."

This Confederate infantry private is well equipped for the photo, but as the war lengthened, the Confederate army suffered shortages.

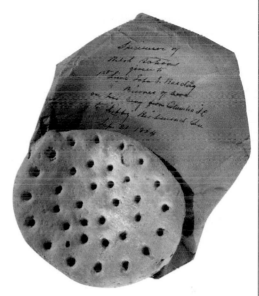

HARDTACK

If the adage is true, that "an army travels on its stomach," then the armies of the blue and the gray covered a good bit of the distance on hardtack. Otherwise called crackers, army bread, or hard bread, hardtack was a staple food of soldiers during the Civil War. A simple flour-and-water biscuit, hardtack measured approximately three inches by three inches and was a half inch thick. It was often eaten plain—or crumbled, boiled, or fried. "Hardtack was not so bad an article of food, even when traversed by insects," recalled one veteran. "Eaten in the dark, no one could tell the difference between it and hardtack that was untenanted."

NORTHERN UNIFORMS

✤

*I*t was the first battle of Bull Run (First Manassas). Even through a thick haze of gun smoke that clung to the side of the hill, Union Major Barry could see that the mass of soldiers coming his way were wearing blue uniforms. He quickly ordered the artillery commander not to shoot. "Those are your battery support," he told Captain Griffin. "They are Confederates!" Griffin shouted back. But Major Barry was certain that the troops approaching were the reinforcements he had been promised. The cannon were ordered not to fire.

The mistake was Barry's, however. The approaching troops belonged to the 33rd Virginia, a Confederate infantry regiment. They bore down on the Union line through the billowing smoke clad in blue. Charging within point-blank range, the Virginians fired a volley with devastating results, which echoed doom for the Union army.

A wide variety of uniforms characterized the early stages of the war. Union recruits were just as likely to wear gray as Confederates were likely to don the blue. Unprepared for a long conflict, the Union Quartermaster Department, which was responsible for clothing the armies, simply didn't have enough uniforms to go around. The United States Regular Army had standardized uniforms, but the vast majority of new recruits wore outfits provided by their individual state or militia organization.

By the second year of war, the Union had a "standardized blue uniform" that was eventually adopted by most volunteer units. What officers and enlisted men alike wore from the top of their heads to the tips of their toes was set forth in official army regulations. However, as time passed, a great deal of freedom was allowed in the daily application of the rules. Comfort was usually uppermost in the mind of the soldier.

"The more they serve," one veteran said of his campmates, "the less they look like soldiers and the more they resemble day laborers who have bought second-hand military clothes."

SOUTHERN UNIFORMS

✲

*a*rthur James Lyon Fremantle, a lieutenant colonel of the British army, got a good look at the Confederate troops. "[A] remarkably fine body of men," he wrote in his journal. "[They look] quite seasoned and ready for any work. Their clothing is serviceable, so also are their boots; but there is the usual utter absence of uniformity as to color and shape of their garments and hats: gray of all shades, and brown clothing, with felt hats predominate."

The cut and color of Confederate uniforms varied wildly, and this remained the case throughout the war. The Confederacy simply didn't have the resources and means to manufacture uniforms in abundance. Each state was relied upon to clothe its own regiments at first. "Texans, Alabamians, and Arkansians . . . certainly are a queer lot to look at," an observer wrote during the Gettysburg campaign in 1863. "They carry less than any other troops; many of them have only got an old piece of carpet or rug as baggage; many have discarded their shoes in the mud; all are ragged and dirty, but full of good humor and confidence in themselves."

"Cadet gray," a uniform color popular among the militia, was the origin of the familiar Confederate gray regulation uniform. The fancy, ornate attire prevalent among the militia units at the start of the war had long since disappeared by 1863. Much of what Southern troops wore was homespun, or outfits of simple design based upon whatever material was handy. Admitted a Texan leaving for the war: "We were a motley-looking set. In my company were about four shades of gray, but the trimming were all black braid. As far as pride went, we were all generals."

As needs demanded, Confederate soldiers stripped the dead of their clothes or concocted uniforms from civilian garb. Coats and pants, dyed with the juice from walnut hulls, gave a distinctive light-brown or butternut color to the homemade outfits. "No soldiers ever marched with less to encumber them," a Confederate veteran proudly recalled, "and none marched faster or held out longer."

UNION CAMP LIFE

✷

*T*he summer rain had stopped. The soldiers began to hang their coats and blankets out to dry. Three stories below the window of Walt Whitman's Washington apartment, the Union cavalry camp came to life. "[P]erhaps fifty or sixty tents," wrote Whitman, looking out onto a lot across the street. "Some of the men are cleaning their sabres . . . some brushing boots, some laying off, reading, writing—some cooking, some sleeping . . . a hundred little things going on."

An army camp was the soldier's home away from home. He spent more time in camp than he did on the march or in battle. And it was here that he learned the first lessons of soldiering. "Besides guard mountings and dress parades, five or six hours a day were consumed in company, regimental and brigade drills," wrote a New York private. "The men were worked hard, and . . . generally understood that . . . to be a soldier was no loafing business."

Photographs of family members comforted soldiers far from home.

A Federal kitchen during a winter encampment. Complaints about the quality of the food were common. "I'll bet when I get home I shall have an appetite to eat most anything," observed a volunteer from Vermont. "I have seen the time when I would have been glad to picked the crusts of bread that mother gives to the hogs."

EVERYDAY ACTIVITIES

When not on the drill grounds, the simple chores of everyday life occupied much of a soldier's time in camp. He cooked, barbered, mended his uniform—skills in many cases he was using for the first time in his life, and with varying degrees of success. One infantryman claimed he mended his trousers

A member of the 31st Pennsylvania Volunteers with his family at Camp Slocum outside Washington during the winter of 1861. It was common for families to join soldiers, particularly officers, during winter encampments.

More than 2,300 chaplains served in the Federal army throughout the war. Sixty-six died in service, and three were given the Medal of Honor. In this photo, Father Thomas Mooney is celebrating Catholic mass for members of the 69th New York Infantry. The regiment's commander, Colonel Michael Corcoran, stands to the left of the priest.

Union soldiers enjoy a bath during a lull in the fighting after the battles around Spotsylvania, Virginia. During active campaigns, soldiers had little opportunity for personal hygiene. "Some of the men were just as particular about changing their underclothing at least once a week as they would be at home;" recalled a veteran, "while others would do so only under the severest pressure."

To help supplement drab army rations, the government appointed civilian vendors, or sutlers, to sell a wide variety of goods in camp. Unscrupulous sutlers often jacked up prices and took unfair advantage of troops. Many of these profiteers became the target of pranks and vandalism from disgruntled soldiers.

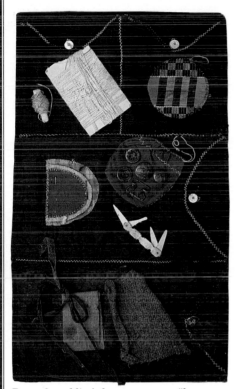

Part of a soldier's baggage was a "house-wife," a sewing kit containing needles, thread, buttons, and extra patches of fabric.

"as good as a heap of women would do." Barbering was another matter. "True, many men never used the razor in the service," wrote a Union cannoneer, "but allowed a shrubby, straggling growth of hair and beard to grow. . . . Many more carried their own kit of tools and showed themselves frequently shedding innocent blood." Greater care was taken with preparing food. "When the army was in settled camp," recalled a veteran, "company cooks generally prepared the rations. These cooks were men selected from the company, who had a taste or an ambition for the business."

PASTIMES

Camp life was not all drill and drudgery, however. The day's work would usually end by early evening. Until lights-out sounded at about 9:30 P.M., soldiers engaged in a variety of pastimes. The men played cards, read, wrote letters home, recounted their activities in diaries, and otherwise occupied themselves. Some among the more talented volunteers entertained their campmates with music. "In some tents vocal or instrumental music was a feature of the evening," remembered a Union veteran.

Noted a soldier about army camp life: "Men who . . . were accustomed to nothing more strenuous than the handling of a yard stick and dry goods . . . or light clerical work, lawyers, book keepers, school teachers, and . . . men of wealth now found themselves as privates in the ranks subject to orders of superior officers, doing the work of porters and laborers in all kinds of necessary drudgery."

COFFEE

"It was coffee at meals and between meals," remembered a soldier, "and men going on guard or coming off guard drank it at all hours of the night. The coffee ration was most heartily appreciated." Generally issued in the whole-bean form, coffee was often combined with a soldier's sugar ration. They were stored together in his haversack so coffee would be ready to brew at a moment's notice. A form of "instant" coffee also existed during the Civil War. Confederate soldiers, however, rarely had coffee in sufficient quantities and would frequently seek it in trade from Billy Yank whenever the opportunity arose.

CONFEDERATE CAMP LIFE

✳

*a*t the first sign of winter, most soldiers had the same concern on their minds. "Chilling rains, cutting sleet, drifting snow, muddy roads, all the miseries," recalled a Confederate artilleryman, "pressed him to ask and repeat the question, 'When will we go into winter quarters?'"

WINTER DWELLINGS

Wintertime was a special challenge to soldiers in camp. They had to contend not only with living under severe weather conditions but also with the monotony of living in the same confined space for months on end. Their first task was to build sturdy shelters. Winter quarters came in all sizes and shapes, usually limited only by the soldiers' imaginations and resourcefulness. Recalled a Confederate veteran:

> The old pines fall rapidly under the energetic strokes of the axes . . . the logs are cut into lengths, notched and fitted one upon another, and the structure begins to rise. . . . At last the topmost log is rolled into place. . . . Short logs of oak are to be split into huge shingles for the roof, and tough tedious work it is . . . the chimney . . . of notched sticks or small logs, rises rapidly till it reaches the apex of the roof and is crowned with a nail keg or barrel.

Thus small cities of crude huts spread across the landscape. As a finishing touch, soldiers often nicknamed their winter homes. Names like Swine Hotel,

Prayer books and hymnals carried by soldiers

A view of Confederate winter quarters near Centreville, Virginia, in March 1862. More men died from the diseases spread throughout camps like these than on the battlefield.

Artist Conrad Chapman gave an idyllic depiction of life in a Confederate camp near Corinth, Mississippi, in May 1862. In fact, more soldiers died from disease in seven weeks at this location than died during the battle of Shiloh, Tennessee, the month before.

Buzzard's Roost, and Devil's Inn appear in their memoirs. "Everything is complete, everything looks nice," wrote a soldier in a Tennessee regiment. "Our bed is composed of some chestnut lathing . . . covered with sage grass. We have got a big fire, took our seat before it and feel with great obligation to our heavenly father for giving us the comfortable dwelling that I now sit in."

PASTIMES

There were the usual camp routines and pastimes during winter as during any season: drills, mounting guard, and policing the campsite during the day; card playing, checkers, reading, writing, and socializing during off-duty hours. But winter also had its unique pastime: snowball fights. Individuals, small groups, and at times units the size of regiments and brigades participated. Gen-

Smoking accessories

FRIENDLY ENEMIES

During lulls between battles, it was not uncommon for soldiers in each army to greet and exchange goods with their enemies. After all, they did share a common language and culture as well as the experiences of soldiering. Tobacco, sugar, coffee, and newspapers were among the popular items to trade. When opposing lines were separated by a river or stream, a favorite practice was to float the goods back and forth aboard little handmade sailboats.

The soldiers also exchanged good-natured taunts and insults that they called "smart talk" or "jawing." Such practices were forbidden by regulations, but officers generally looked the other way. "We maid a bargain with the rebs not to shoot at one another heare [*sic*] an the scourmish line," wrote a Union private in 1864, "unless one side or the other went to advance, so it makes it mutch plesanter."

The carefree, relaxed attitude of these Confederate cannoneers of the famed Washington Artillery of New Orleans belies the heavy action they saw. Fighting under General Bragg in the Army of Tennessee, the company saw 42 of their own killed and 100 wounded during 40 battles and engagements.

erals themselves participated in one such battle near Dalton, Georgia, in March 1864. Snowball wars, observed a Virginia private, "were sometimes fought with such vigor as to disable the combatants."

Soldiers weren't necessarily happy to see the snow thaw. From his winter camp near Manassas, Virginia, a Confederate soldier wrote with humor that the whole "vicinity is literally a lake of mud. . . . Men and horses are often completely buried . . . and you see their heads protruding above the mire."

SICKNESS AND HOMESICKNESS

The camps could also be death traps. With large numbers of men living in tight quarters week after week, they became breeding grounds for sickness. Sickness of another kind was on the mind of a young Southern recruit as he stood guard over the army's winter camp on a snowy Christmas morning. "The novelty and fascination of my surroundings soon lost their charm," he wrote. "I must have had a slight attack of homesickness, for I began to think of home and my mother and father away out in Texas. . . . I honestly believe that genuine homesickness killed more soldiers in the army than died from measles."

By the looks of their uniforms, these two soldiers who peer stoically into the camera are veteran campaigners. Clothing often marked the man during the war. "In this army," quipped a Southerner during the Atlanta campaign, "one hole in the seat of the breeches indicates a Captain—two holes a lieutenant and the seat of the pants all out indicate[s] that the individual is a private."

Confederate soldiers of the 9th Mississippi Infantry perform some of their camp chores at Warrington Navy Yard in Pensacola, Florida.

THE NEW SCIENCES OF WAR

*T*he Civil War produced technological innovations that transformed the science of warfare. Many weapons that would be put to destructive use in 20th century warfare were first developed from 1860 to 1865. Torpedoes, land mines, machine guns, submarines, repeating rifles, and steam-powered iron ships were successfully developed. Other technologies put to military use for the first time included telegraphs, railroads, and even observation balloons.

✳

"Engagement between the Monitor and the Merrimac,"
by Xanthus R. Smith

NORTHERN IRONCLAD SHIPS

✳

*F*olks living along the Mississippi River in the fall of 1861 had never seen the likes of these vessels. Seven long, low, slope-sided iron monsters belching thick plumes of steam laboriously parted the murky brown waters of the Mississippi bound for Cairo, Illinois. To one newspaper reporter, "they looked like enormous turtles." To other wide-eyed spectators on shore, it must have looked as though these giant man-made creatures were more likely bound to sink.

POOK TURTLES

The USS St. Louis, *one of seven ironclads called Pook Turtles, was hit 59 times by Confederate artillery and disabled during the attack on Fort Donelson on February 14, 1862. Renamed* Baron de Kalb *in September 1862, the ironclad continued to battle Confederate forces until it was sunk by two torpedos near Yazoo City, Mississippi, on July 13, 1863.*

These were the creations of marine engineer and inventor James B. Eads and designer Samuel Pook, and each craft measured 175 feet long by 51.2 feet at midsection. A sturdy timber framework, shielded with iron plates 2.5 inches thick, enclosed a gun deck mounting 13 heavy cannon. Though the ships weighed more than 500 tons apiece, their flat bottoms drew only six feet of water. Nicknamed Pook Turtles after their designer and for their tough shell-like construction, these ironclads were ideally suited for river combat.

A converted New York ferryboat, the Commodore Perry saw service on the York, Pamunkey, and Nansemond rivers along the Virginia Peninsula. The ferryboats were especially suited for use on rivers because of their shallow draft and ability to move with ease in either direction. Designed to carry heavy loads, they were ideal for mounting cannon.

River combat is just what President Abraham Lincoln and military planners in Washington had in mind when they summoned Eads in the spring of 1861. A bold, strong-willed businessman who had established himself as an expert on river travel, Eads accepted a contract that few others would undertake. His challenge was to construct seven huge gunboats, fully armed and ready for their crews, in 65 days.

Within two weeks, conveying his directions via the telegraph, Eads had more than 4,000 workers scattered around the country employed on the project. They worked around the clock. Just 45 days later, the first United States ironclad was launched. Six more iron gunboats followed soon after, forming the backbone of the Western gunboat flotilla. An assortment of sailors manned the ships. Seamen from the Great Lakes, from ocean-going vessels, and from riverboats composed the 250-man crews.

THE MISSISSIPPI STRATEGY

Control of the Mississippi River and the network of smaller rivers that pierced the heart of the Confederacy was a key Union objective. Army and navy

The public found the innovative features of the Monitor *interesting*. Harper's Weekly, *one of the popular newspapers of the time, published illustrations of the ship's interior.*

forces handled the task together. Eads's ironclads and other armed vessels were Flag Officer Andrew H. Foote's most powerful weapons. Working their way up the Cumberland and Tennessee rivers in February 1862, the iron flotilla helped blast Confederate forts Henry and Donelson into surrendering. These victories secured Kentucky and central Tennessee for the Union.

Next, with an army force under Major General John Pope, Foote targeted the Confederate strong point at Island No. 10 in the Mississippi River. A monthlong duel followed, but the Southern garrison was finally battered into surrendering.

THE MONITOR AND THE MERRIMACK

Meanwhile, about 800 miles to the east, another innovative Union ironclad made its debut. The *Monitor*, with a single armored turret mounted on a flat, iron-plated deck, faced the Confederate ironclad *Virginia* (also known as the *Merrimack*) in the first battle between armored warships. At stake were the wooden sail and steam craft of the Federal blockading squadron. "Gun after gun was fired by the *Monitor*," wrote a witness, "which was returned with whole broadsides from the rebels, with no more effect, apparently, than so many pebblestones thrown by a child . . . clearly establishing the fact that

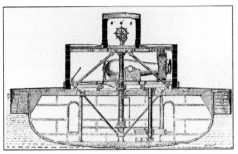

This sectional view of the USS Monitor shows the mechanism for the revolving turret, which housed two 11-inch smoothbore guns. This ship had a wooden frame covered by a thick armored hull. More than nine months after its fight with the CSS Virginia, the Monitor sank in a storm off Cape Hatteras, killing four officers and 12 men.

In July 1862 the officers of the USS Monitor posed in front of its well-known turret.

Lieutenant William Flye of the USS Monitor, wearing a straw hat, inspects the ironclad's turret. Effects of cannon fire from the CSS Virginia are clearly visible on the Monitor's iron plates.

The effects of Confederate cannon fire are visible on the deck of the ironclad gunboat USS Galena. *The* Galena's *sloped, armored sides constructed of interlocking iron bars proved unsuccessful when hit by plunging cannon fire.*

wooden vessels cannot contend successfully with the ironclad ones."

The *Merrimack* was so battered it never threatened the blockade fleet again. After hammering each other for about four hours, the iron ships parted and returned to base. The dramatic battle was a strategic victory for the *Monitor.* More important, the engagement proved the value of ironclad warships in general and the effectiveness of inventor John Ericsson's *Monitor* design in particular. As the war progressed, dozens of *Monitor*-like ironclads, some with two turrets and one with three, joined the blockade fleet in action against Southern coastal forts.

OTHER IRONCLADS

On the rivers, in the meantime, the Union added more armored gunboats to its flotilla and contin-

Union sailors and marines aboard the gunboat USS Mendota *pose for the photographer. Commissioned in May 1864, the* Mendota *was stationed in the James River, Virginia, where it engaged Confederate shore batteries.*

ued to wreak havoc on Confederate river defenses. At Memphis in June 1862, they battled Southern land batteries and a makeshift fleet of gunboats. "The roar of the cannon and shell shook the houses on shore on either side for many miles," recalled a naval officer. "The screaming, plunging shell crashed into the boats, blowing some of them and their crews into fragments . . . the Confederate fleet was destroyed." On the Mississippi River, only Vicksburg, Mississippi, and Port Hudson, Louisiana, remained in Confederate hands. "Vicksburg is the key," Lincoln said. "The war can never be brought to a close until the key is in our pockets."

While General Ulysses S. Grant battled Confederate forces on land, Admiral David D. Porter relied on his ironclads to pound Vicksburg from the river. Each force met stiff resistance. Grant also relied on Porter's gunboats to transport troops and supplies safely past enemy batteries. "It was as if hell itself were let loose," a Union soldier recalled. "The gunboats . . . keep up a continual fire," wrote Admiral Porter. Vicksburg eventually surrendered on July 4, 1863. Four days later, Port Hudson fell, and the Mississippi River, in the words of President Lincoln, "again goes unvexed to the sea."

Along the Southern coast, Union ironclads spearheaded the final assaults against the few harbors that remained in Confederate hands. The Northern ironclads overpowered Mobile Bay, Alabama, and Fort Fisher protecting Wilmington, North Carolina.

Launched on February 14, 1862, the USS Galena was one of the first Union ironclad ships. Because it was protected by only three inches of iron plating, many doubted it would be able to withstand heavy enemy fire. In its first action, at Drewry's Bluff, Virginia, in May 1862, it suffered heavy damage. After the action, its armor plates were removed and it was placed on blockade duty for the rest of the war.

SOUTHERN IRONCLAD SHIPS

✴

*W*ith their ship stuck in a sandbar in Hampton Roads, Virginia, the crew of the *Minnesota* watched helplessly as the Confederate ironclad *Merrimack* (or *Virginia,* as it was officially known in the South) shot the other Union warships to splinters. It first hit the *Cumberland,* a 24-gun sloop and one of the most powerful vessels in the Union fleet. The *Cumberland*'s shot bounced off the Southern ironclad "like an India rubber ball," a Union soldier recalled. With cannon blazing, the *Merrimack* rammed the helpless Union ship, "and in fifteen minutes," reported Captain G. J. Van Brunt of the *Minnesota,* "I saw [the *Cumberland*] going down by the head."

Next, the *Merrimack* "engaged the *Congress,* throwing shot and shell into her with terrific effect," Van Brunt wrote, "while the shot from the *Congress* glanced from her iron-plated sloping sides, without doing any apparent injury." Only darkness and a low tide saved the *Minnesota* from becoming the *Merrimack*'s next victim—for the time being, anyway. "We enjoyed ourselves," a seaman on the *Minnesota* remembered, "for none cared to look forward to the morrow, as there was but one termination possible as far as we knew then."

THE MONITOR

A light fog was lifting at dawn on March 9, 1862, when the *Merrimack* got under way and headed toward the *Minnesota* to finish her off. Suddenly, the

The Confederate ironclad Atlanta *plied the river near Savannah, Georgia. In June 1863 it steamed downriver to attack Union blockade vessels. During the attempt, the* Atlanta *ran aground and was forced to surrender. The* Atlanta *is shown here serving in the U.S. Navy in the James River, Virginia.*

Union ironclad *Monitor* appeared from behind the *Minnesota*, where she had anchored overnight. "No words can express the surprise with which we beheld this strange craft," a Confederate observed. A companion likened it to "a tin can on a shingle."

The two iron ships banged shot after shot off one another. "I opened upon her with all my broadside guns," wrote Captain Van Brunt, "which would have blown out of the water any timber-built ship in the world." With its armor badly damaged and its steering impaired, the leaking *Merrimack* was unable to damage the *Monitor*. "I can do her about as much damage," a gunner on the *Merrimack* told an officer, "by snapping my thumbs at her every two minutes and a half." But about four hours passed before the two iron monsters departed the watery battlefield. They had changed the future of naval combat forever.

This artist's depiction, "The Battle of the Ironclads," shows the guns of the Confederate Merrimack, *to the right, and the Federal* Monitor *exchanging point-blank cannon fire. The one-day engagement occurred on March 9, 1862, in Hampton Roads, Virginia.*

TORPEDOES

Not to be confused with the modern self-propelled variety, the 19th century torpedo was a self-contained mass of gunpowder designed to be detonated against an enemy vessel. The Confederacy especially relied on such devices to defend its harbor and river facilities. Twenty-two Union ships, including four ironclads, were destroyed by Confederate torpedoes. Union torpedoes were responsible for destroying six Confederate vessels. Scores of other ships on both sides were damaged by these "infernal machines." Their use also prompted one of the most memorable quotes of the war. "Damn the torpedoes! Flank speed!" exclaimed Union Admiral David Farragut as he steamed into Mobile Bay on August 5, 1864.

"The knowledge that a simple touch will lay your ship helpless, sinking without even the satisfaction of firing one shot in return," wrote a Union naval officer, "will sober the most intrepid disposition."

From the beginning of the war, Confederate navy authorities had staked their futures on ironclad warships. "I regard the possession of an iron-armored ship as a matter of the first necessity," wrote Confederate Navy Secretary Stephen Mallory on May 8, 1861. Mallory had few options, however. The Confederacy began the war with virtually no navy and lacking the resources and industry to create one. What few ships they had were captured or abandoned U.S. vessels. Arrayed against them was a force that eventually would become the most powerful navy in the world.

BLOCKADE RUNNERS

Caught in the grip of the Union blockade, the South relied on daring and innovation to combat the armed might of the North. On the high seas, the Confederacy used sleek, fast, powerful ships like the *Shenandoah* and the *Alabama* to attack merchant vessels and disrupt Northern commerce. In its harbors and on its rivers, the South defended itself with strong, well-armed

Commanded by Raphael Semmes, the CSS Alabama *became the scourge of Union commerce. Between 1862 and 1864, the Confederate sea raider captured or destroyed more than 60 vessels. The ship came to an end off the coast of Cherbourg, France, when it was sunk under the gunfire of the USS* Kearsarge *on June 19, 1864.*

fortifications and ingenious devices such as the torpedo and submarine. "The torpedo is destined to be the least expensive, but most terrible engine of war yet invented," warned a Union navy captain. "No vessel can be constructed as to resist its power."

"RAM FEVER"

Where the South excelled, within its limited means, was in the development and use of ironclad warships. By concentrating what resources it had, the Confederacy built many ironclads. Most of them followed the pattern of the *Merri-*

Officers on the deck of the USS Kearsarge, the ship that sank the CSS Alabama.

mack. By "fighting with iron against wood," Secretary Mallory aimed to make up for the Confederate navy's "inequality in numbers."

From that fateful day in March 1862 when the *Merrimack* attacked the Union blockade fleet at Hampton Roads, Confederate ironclads gained a formidable reputation. "A terrible disease is prevailing in the fleet here," a Union officer wrote home. "Commanding officers seem to be most severely attacked with it. . . . It is termed 'ram fever' and is supposed to be brought on by occasional sights at a rebel ironclad . . . an infernal machine . . . filled with . . . every other sort of diabolical contrivance for blowing up, running down, sinking, smashing and otherwise destroying us Yankees."

Despite some success, Confederate ironclads managed only to delay, not prevent, the inevitable. In fact, many of the vessels proved to be their own worst enemies. Makeshift construction techniques and inefficient engines—products of an agricultural economy—accomplished what Union guns failed to do. One by one, the Southern ironclads were run down and captured, abandoned, or destroyed.

THE HENRY RIFLE

✳

Colonel Lafayette Baker could see them coming across the bridge at Cox's Mills, Virginia, in the summer of 1863, before he heard their "wild yells." "A heavy force of mounted rebels," he recalled, "was charging up the hill." He could also see they outnumbered his blue-clad troopers two to one. But Baker knew the odds were on his side.

"On, on they came," wrote the Union colonel. "Cooly our men waited. Not a shot was fired till they were within easy range." Then at a given signal, the Union rifles blazed, punching rapid-fire volleys of .44-caliber slugs into the Confederate ranks. Within minutes, the lopsided fight was over. The enemy fled in confusion.

Armed with the 15-shot Henry repeating rifle, the Union troopers had made quick work of the enemy. Though the rifle saw very limited action, it was one of the most advanced weapons of its time. It had been developed by Benjamin Henry and patented in October 1860. The innovative lever-action weapon fired a metal-cased cartridge from a magazine located under the barrel. It was manufactured only in the North, and Confederates who faced the weapon came to call it "that damned Yankee rifle that can be loaded on Sunday and fired all week."

Men of the 7th Illinois Infantry with Henry repeating rifles, which they obtained at their own expense.

Short-sighted military authorities considered the weapon too wasteful of ammunition and purchased only 1,730 of the repeating rifles for selected units. However, many of the 10,000 Henry rifles used during the war were purchased by states and individual soldiers for about $35 to $40 each.

About the Henry rifle, one Union officer wrote: "Under ordinary circumstances, I believe it utterly impossible to make a successful charge on troops armed with them."

SOUTHERN WEAPONRY

✳

*W*e are testing our guns today," one Confederate artillery sergeant remarked in 1863 on the effectiveness of Southern-manufactured guns. "The target was placed at 1,000 yards; we fired seven shots, not one of which struck the target. As we have splendid gunners, Col. Polk had the rifle guns condemned." Prior to 1863, the primary source of artillery for Confederate armies was captured Union guns and British imports. As the supply of enemy guns dwindled, however, they had to turn to their own factories to produce the "long arm" of the infantry.

"There must be something very rotten in the Ordnance Department," wrote Confederate General D. H. Hill. "Our shells burst at the mouth of the gun or do not blast at all. The metal of which the new guns are made is of the most flimsy and brittle character, and the casting is very bad."

The ancient smoothbore weapons Confederate infantrymen started with were generally ineffective beyond 80 yards. By mid-1862, these worthless firearms were replaced by rifled weapons. Curved grooves were cut into the smooth barrel of these guns to provide a rapid spin to the bullet as it left the barrel. This spin increased the potential accuracy of the shot to more than 400 yards.

The two most popular types of rifles were the .577-caliber Enfield, manufactured in England, and the .58-caliber U.S.-produced Springfield. Whereas both rifles were used extensively on both sides, the imported Enfield became the most popular in the Confederate ranks. The English-manufactured Whitworth rifle was also popular among Southern sharpshooters. Mounted with a telescopic sight, this gun had an effective range of 1,500 to 1,800 yards. At a range of about a mile, the bullet deviated by less than 12 feet.

The Springfield rifle was the most widely used firearm during the war. Its rifled bore, interchangeable parts, and conical ammunition set it apart from guns used in earlier conflicts.

NORTHERN WEAPONS TECHNOLOGIES

✵

*A*lthough telegraph systems were in common use by 1861, the Civil War was the first armed conflict in which this technology was widely used. Insulated wire, either strung across poles or along the ground, provided both armies with the ability for speedy communications. Since the enemy could very easily tap into wire and intercept messages, codes were used by both sides. Federal communications experts were more successful at breaking codes than their Confederate counterparts.

OBSERVATION BALLOONS

The use of observation balloons by Federal troops also began early in the war. Aeronaut Thaddeus Lowe was contracted to supply seven balloons to the army by June 1862. The largest was the *Intrepid,* which, when filled, was 38 feet wide by 45 feet high. It took about three hours to inflate and required a team

A Federal telegraph operator is portrayed working through the night. While the operator receives a dispatch from the War Department in Washington, the mounted orderly waits to convey the message to generals in the field.

of 30 to 50 men. The preferred observation altitude was 300 feet, from which the aeronaut had a view of more than 15 miles. "Even if the observer never saw anything," a Confederate officer observed, "his balloons would have been worth all they cost, trying to keep our movements out of sight." Although effective, particularly when high ground was not available, balloons proved to be very unwieldy for an army traveling on campaign and were used sparingly after the Virginia Peninsula campaign of 1862.

The balloon Intrepid, *pictured here being inflated, was one of seven military observation balloons approved by the U.S. government in August 1861. Aeronaut Thaddeus Lowe commanded the fledgling balloon corps, which made more than 3,000 flights until May 1863, when Lowe resigned due to lack of support.*

WEAPONS

A number of types of weapons were developed just prior to or during the war, such as the Burnside carbine and the Dahlgren gun. Many were impractical inventions never authorized by the War Department, such as the double-barreled cannon and the 35-barreled "pale horse." One of the most innovative, practical killing machines was the Gatling gun. Hand cranked, it had six barrels that, when working, could fire up to 600 rounds per minute. Although the Gatling gun was never purchased by the War Department, Major General Benjamin Butler bought 12 of them at $1,000 each for limited use during the siege of Petersburg, Virginia.

RICHARD GATLING

Though he was a Southerner by birth, business opportunities took Richard Gatling north as a young man. Possessing considerable mechanical skills, he patented and manufactured several farm implements. Gatling turned his abilities toward military ordnance when the Civil War began. By the second year of the conflict, he had invented a steam-powered naval ram and a rapid-fire gun. The first Gatling gun was manufactured in Indianapolis. His first crude model fired 250 rounds per minute.

Gatling kept improving his weapon as the war progressed. Nevertheless, the army did not officially adopt the weapon until 1866. Gatling eventually improved the gun to fire 1,200 shots a minute. Until his death at age 85, Gatling continued to innovate weapons and farm implements.

This cover from the June 14, 1879, issue of Scientific American *shows Federal soldiers practicing firing the "New Model Gatling Gun." The only notable service these guns saw during the war was along the Federal lines at Petersburg, Virginia, in 1864.*

A smoothbore musket manufactured at the National Armory in Harper's Ferry, Virginia, in 1835. Rifled weapons replaced most smoothbore guns by the second year of the war.

The Spencer repeating carbine was popular among Federal cavalrymen.

Tough, ambitious Union Rear Admiral John A. Dahlgren (1809–1870) designed cannon that saw extensive use during the war. Chief among these was the Dahlgren gun, a heavy-caliber weapon that became common armament in the Union and Confederate navies.

The Colt revolver was the most popular handgun used by Federals during the war. This is the army .44-caliber model. A six-shot percussion revolver, it weighed more than two pounds and was usually carried in a holster.

The navy model of the Colt revolver differed from the army version in that it was .36-caliber. Although the models were designated for army or navy issue, they were often interchanged between the branches.

The "Dictator" was a 13-inch mortar that weighed more than 17,000 pounds and could hurl a 220-pound ball more than two miles. This iron monster was transported via railroad to Union siege lines around Petersburg, Virginia, to bombard the Confederate defenses.

Boys, some in their preteens, were not an uncommon sight aboard naval vessels. The adventurous sailors were called powder monkeys. They helped serve the ship's cannon, staff the galley, and otherwise performed a host of routine duties. This lad poses beside a cannon on the deck of the USS New Hampshire.

Abraham Lincoln's youngest son, Tad, played with this toy cannon.

MINES AND TORPEDOES

Throughout the war, Confederates experimented with all types of land and underwater mines. Considering them unworthy of a "chivalrous nation," Northern commanders were reluctant to use this technology. They did employ them on occasion, however. The most effective use of a spar torpedo, or explosives attached to a pole at the front of a boat, was the Union attack on the Confederate ironclad *Albemarle* near Plymouth, North Carolina, on October 27, 1864. With 14 volunteers, Lieutenant William Cushing set off in a small steamer mounting a torpedo. Under heavy fire, Cushing released the torpedo. As it floated up against the Confederate ship, he pulled a lanyard that set off an explosion that sunk the enemy vessel. In the tumultuous waters resulting from the explosion, Cushing and his crew were forced to abandon their small steamer. Of the 15 who set off on the mission, two drowned and 11 were captured. Only Cushing and another avoided capture.

Visual signaling, using flags in daylight or flames at night, was a crucial method of communicating during the Civil War. The construction of lofty platforms such as the Union tower pictured here at Bermuda Hundred, Virginia, made signals visible over greater distances.

Accompanying the Union armies to conduct surveys and explorations and to reconnoiter uncharted sites and areas for defenses was the Corps of Topographical Engineers. As the result of a reorganization in 1863, the topographical engineers were combined with the Corps of Engineers. The Confederate Army also included engineering specialists.

SOUTHERN WEAPONS TECHNOLOGIES

✦

*O*utmanned and lacking in critical resources, Confederate military leaders turned to technological innovations as one way to gain the much-needed edge over the enemy. They began to experiment with observation balloons before the Federals did, but they found the balloons to be impractical for regular deployment in the field.

WILLIAMS RAPID-FIRE GUN

Few prototype weapons were invented by Southerners. One of the most successful, however, was the Williams rapid-fire gun. A breechloaded artillery piece, it had a four-foot-long barrel and was mounted on a two-wheel carriage. This weapon differed from other artillery pieces in that it was hand-cranked and capable of firing up to 20 rounds per minute with a maximum range of 2,000 yards. Ideal for cavalry, it was used by Confederate forces in both the eastern and western theaters. "We had heard artillery before," one Union officer observed, "but we had never heard anything that made such a horrible noise as the shot from these breechloaders."

NAVAL TECHNOLOGIES

Since the Federal navy was slowly strangling the Confederacy with operations along the Atlantic and Gulf coasts and up the Mississippi River, naval

This painting of the Confederate submarine H. L. Hunley *was made by Conrad Wise Chapman. It recorded the first sinking of an enemy vessel by a submarine. When its victim, the USS* Housatonic, *sank, the* Hunley *with its crew went down with it.*

An ironclad, 50-foot long, cigar-shaped torpedo boat, the CSS David *guarded the waters off Charleston, South Carolina. Several craft of similar design were constructed to defend the inland and coastal waters of the Confederacy. The semisubmersible vessels were such a threat to Union ships that Rear Admiral John A. Dahlgren offered a cash reward for their capture or destruction.*

Torpedo boats like the one pictured here were built by the Confederate navy in a desperate attempt to breach the Federal blockade. The prototype, the 50-foot-long David, *lent its name to the type—they were all called* Davids.

innovations were given a great deal of attention by the Confederate War Department. Torpedo boats, submarines, rams, and torpedoes were all experimental projects during the war. Torpedo boats were named "Davids" by Confederates and were about 50 feet long, cigar-shaped, and semisubmersible with crews of four sailors. They each carried up to 100 pounds of explosives. Although they were frequently deployed and designed to sink Federal blockaders, there are no recorded incidents of any Union ship being sunk by these vessels.

Both sides were involved in a race to develop a practicable submarine, but only one, the Confederates' *H. L. Hunley,* recorded a sinking of an enemy ship. This submersible vessel was manually operated by an eight-man crew. It was armed with a torpedo holding up to 90 pounds of gunpowder. A propeller shaft extended through its interior. Three crews were lost testing the submarine; one group included its inventor, Horace L. Hunley. Once the *Hunley*'s operation was stabilized, it was put into service at Charleston Harbor, South Carolina. On February 17, 1864, it set off on the mission to sink the Union sloop *Housatonic.* It quietly skimmed slightly below the harbor's surface. Although the submarine was discovered, the submarine crew managed to explode the torpedo, sinking the *Housatonic.* Unable to escape, the *Hunley* and its crew went down with their victim.

Confederates did not limit their use of torpedoes to spars on ships. In an effort to protect their coastal and river defenses, they deployed them in underwater minefields. They experimented with many different types of torpedoes. Singly deployed or in groups connected across a channel with ropes, torpedoes did not stop the Union advance, but they did cause a great

Commissioned in November 1861, the sloop of war USS Housatonic *was stationed along the South Carolina coast. On February 17, 1864, it was sunk by a torpedo carried by the CSS* H. L. Hunley. *The water was so shallow that the* Housatonic's *rigging remained above the water, providing refuge for most of its crew.*

deal of concern and caution on the part of Federal commanders. Four Union ironclads and numerous other ships were sunk by these devices.

LAND MINES

The use of torpedoes by Confederates was not limited to the water. They also experimented with them as part of their land defenses. Two types were developed, one set off by a trip wire and another detonated by more than seven pounds of pressure on a sensitive fuse. The most effective use of the mines was in the Union attack on Fort McAllister near Savannah, Georgia, on December 13, 1864. Most of the 134 Federal casualties were from planted mines. One Federal officer wrote that from that point forward, these devices worked "as much by their moral effect as by actual destruction of life."

Hand grenades were used by both armies. This sketch shows the reaction of Union troops as a Confederate shell lands within their lines during the siege of Petersburg, Virginia. Knowing that it will explode in seconds, the horrified soldiers attempt to dodge for safety.

NORTHERN TRENCH WARFARE

✳

*L*ee's army will be your objective point," Ulysses Grant's orders to Major General George Meade read in the spring of 1864. "Wherever Lee goes, there will you go also."

From May 4 to June 12, 1864, the Federal Army of the Potomac fought several major battles with Robert E. Lee's forces, which brought them to within nine miles of Richmond. But the cost in human life was high. In little more than a month, the Union army had suffered 54,292 casualties, about 45 percent of the force that began the campaign. In the minds of many, Grant had changed from the savior of the nation to a butcher.

Even President Abraham Lincoln's wife became a critic of the new lieutenant general. "Grant is a butcher and not fit to be at the head of an army," Mary Lincoln wrote. "He loses two men to the enemy's one. He has no management, no regard for life. . . . I could fight an army as well myself." The support of the President, however, never faltered. "I begin to see it," Lincoln wrote to Grant after the Wilderness campaign. "You will succeed."

Located about 23 miles south of Richmond, Petersburg was a supply and transportation center for the Confederacy. In June 1864 Petersburg became the focus of a 10-month siege for control of the Confederate capital. Petersburg fell to General Ulysses Grant's Union forces on April 2, 1865. Richmond fell the next day.

Realizing that a direct attack on Richmond would result only in more casualties with little effect, Grant decided to swing his army south, cross the James River, and strike Petersburg, Virginia, a major rail center linking Richmond to the rest of the Confederacy. A stubborn defense by a small band of Confederate troops bogged down the Federal advance long enough to allow Lee to bring his army to Petersburg.

The siege of Petersburg began on June 18 and lasted over ten

Sharpened timber stakes angled toward the enemy, called a fraise, jut from the earthen walls of Union Fort Sedgwick outside Petersburg.

One Union veteran likened the terrain around Petersburg to "an immense prairie dog village." Here, the Federal line stretches as far as the eye can see.

Federal soldiers relax outside a bombproof shelter. Reinforced with heavy timbers, sandbags, and several feet of earth, these shelters were erected to protect soldiers, munitions, and supplies from mortar shells and other cannon fire.

months. After six weeks of almost steady fighting, the opposing armies began to burrow into the ground, constructing a series of trenches that in places were less than 100 yards apart. One Federal viewed these ditches as "an immense prairie dog village." Plagued by insects and rats, the ditches' uninhabitable living conditions made them a death trap for many. "No one could say at any hour that he would be living the next," a veteran later wrote. "Men were killed in their camps, at their meals, and . . . in their sleep."

Once the two armies were well entrenched, it became obvious that a frontal assault on either side would be suicidal. Lieutenant Colonel Henry Pleasants, commander of the 48th Pennsylvania, proposed an alternative to assault. He recommended digging a tunnel below the Confederate line and blowing a hole in it. His idea was dismissed as "claptrap and nonsense" by Union engineers and initially opposed by both Meade and Grant. However, Pleasants convinced his corps commander, Major General Ambrose E. Burnside, of the plan's feasibility, and Burnside in turn secured Grant's approval.

Four tons of powder were placed at the end of a 586-foot-long shaft. The explosion, at 4:45 A.M. on July 30, 1864, tore a 170-foot-long crater in the enemy position. When the hapless Union troops assaulted the position, they charged into the crater rather than around it. Eight hours later, Confederate troops managed to seal the hole in their line, inflicting almost 4,000 casualties on the poorly led Union troops while sustaining the loss of 1,500 men. "[It was] the saddest affair I have ever witnessed in the war," Grant later wrote.

The siege settled into a series of skirmishes and battles that slowly extended the Federal line to the west, stretching the undermanned Confederates to a breaking point. On April 2, 1865, a Federal attack along the Petersburg line managed to drive the Southerners from their defenses. The siege was over. The war in the East would end only seven days later.

TACTICS

Soldiers fighting shoulder to shoulder in long lines or dense masses was typical of Civil War combat. Based on Napoleonic tactics, the idea was to concentrate the greatest amount of firepower against an enemy formation. These battle techniques had been developed when short-range, smoothbore weapons were in use. Such tactics proved less effective and more deadly with the advent of rifled weapons during the Civil War.

Many Union and Confederate officers, however, had been schooled in Napoleonic methods and were slow to adapt their battle maneuvers to the new-style armament. It wasn't until later in the war that soldiers began to dig in for protection, making hastily constructed breastworks a common feature on many battlegrounds.

Napoleon Bonaparte

SOUTHERN TRENCH WARFARE

✦

In 1864, following fierce battles at the Wilderness, Spotsylvania Court House, and Cold Harbor, Confederate General Robert E. Lee found his army with its back to Richmond. His army had sustained 32,000 casualties, a reduction of about 46 percent, in little more than a month. He was short on replacements and found it increasingly difficult to supply those who had survived.

While he pondered Ulysses Grant's next move, his adversary had stolen a march on him and was poised to take Petersburg, an important rail center south of Richmond. A stubborn Confederate defense allowed Lee the time to move a body of his troops to Petersburg, repelling any further Union assaults. His army dug in and began constructing a series of trenches, beginning a process that would last for almost ten months.

The trench system was similar on both sides of the line. Low-lying forts were connected by a series of trenches, often two or more rows deep. Rifle pits and picket posts extended in front of the positions. Officers and men lived in bombproof structures within the forts.

To strengthen a defensive position and impede an enemy advance, soldiers, given time, might construct chevaux-de-frise as pictured. A log 6 to 9 feet long was studded with sharpened stakes and placed in front of the line. Attacking troops caught in the teeth of these deadly obstacles made easy targets for defenders.

As General Grant pushed his forces ever westward in an attempt to cut off Petersburg from the rest of the South, Confederate soldiers constructed earthworks wherever they went. By the end of the siege, the landscape was scarred for miles around the city.

As the siege of Petersburg dragged on, officers and enlisted men alike burrowed into the ground for protection from enemy bombardment and snipers. Soldiers in both armies constructed a variety of ingenious shelters, making use of whatever material was at hand. This is the interior of a Confederate fortification.

Because of its importance to the defense of Richmond, capital of the Confederacy, Petersburg itself was surrounded by fortifications. Named after its builder, Confederate Captain Charles H. Dimmock, the "Dimmock Line" consisted of a chain of more than 50 earth and timber forts linked by trenches and armed with a variety of cannon.

In the predawn hours of July 30, 1864, a portion of the Confederate trench system was ripped apart by a huge explosion. Of the survivors of the explosion, one officer observed: "Some scampered out of the lines; some, paralyzed with fear, vaguely scratched at the counterscarp as if trying to escape. Smoke and dust filled the air."

By the time the Federals started to attack, after the explosion, Confederate officers had been able to put together a patchwork defense. Luckily for the defenders, instead of charging around the crater, the Federals charged into it. "When they reached our lines," one defender observed, "instead of treating the opening as a mere passageway . . . they halted, peeped and gaped into the pit, and then, with the stupidity of sheep, followed their bell-wethers into the crater itself, where, huddled together, all semblance of organization shattered." Southern troops merely rushed to the edge of the crater and shot into the confused mass of attackers. It took eight hours, but the Confederates were able to once again join their line, killing or wounding about 4,000 enemy troops.

As Grant slowly extended his line to the west, Lee was forced to do the same with his already overtaxed force. The Confederate commander never desired the situation he found himself in at Petersburg. "This army cannot stand a siege," he had written before his army became bogged down south of Richmond. "We must end this business on the battlefield, not in a fortified place." Grant had sent a force under Major General Philip Sheridan to destroy Virginia's breadbasket in the Shenandoah Valley. "If the war is to last another year," Grant stated, "we want the Shenandoah Valley to remain a barren waste."

Hunger, sickness, and disease depleted Lee's force. Bad news from home and the other fronts also lowered morale to such a level that the number of desertions increased monthly. By the spring of 1865, Lee's army had thinned dangerously. "My own corps," Confederate General John Gordon remembered, "was stretched until the men stood like a row of vedettes, fifteen feet apart. . . . It was not a line; it was the mere skeleton of a line."

On April 1, Sheridan had shattered Lee's right flank, prompting Grant to order an attack along the whole front the next day. The Confederate position was overrun, causing Lee to retreat. Within hours Richmond fell, and the end of the war in the East was only seven days away.

After four years of war and several unsuccessful Union campaigns to take the Confederate capital, Richmond fell the night of April 2–3, 1865. As soldiers and civilians fled the city, a fire erupted about 3:00 A.M. Flames and explosions destroyed much of the city between the Capitol Building and the James River. In this painting, refugees flee on a bridge over the James River.

MEDICAL CARE

*M*edical advances we take for granted today were unheard of during the Civil War. Germ theory had not yet evolved. Thermometers and hypodermic syringes were new inventions and were never used on a wide scale. Unfortunately, the recruits flocking to both armies entered a war in which advanced technology made killing more efficient than in past wars. This combination resulted in thousands of needless deaths during the four bloody years of conflict.

✦

"The Death of General Sedgwick," by Julian Scott

MEDICAL CARE IN THE UNION ARMY

✶

In 1861 the U.S. Medical Department consisted of an aged surgeon general, 30 surgeons, and 83 assistant surgeons. This small force was woefully inadequate for the task ahead, and it was soon increased. For volunteer regiments, the War Department mandated that each unit should have one surgeon and one assistant surgeon, each to be appointed by state authorities.

THE NEED FOR SURGEONS

As the war expanded and needs increased, more surgeons were appointed. The establishment of permanent hospitals required manpower, and the Medical Department hired "contract surgeons" in an attempt to fill the numerous vacancies. The department authorized the creation of a corps of medical cadets as well as some medical inspectors and purveyors. Each volunteer unit was authorized to enlist a second assistant surgeon. By the end of the war, the Medical Department contained 189 medical officers, while the volunteer branch counted 547 surgeons and assistant surgeons, 2,109 regimental surgeons, and 5,532 assistant surgeons. Contract surgeons numbered 5,617 men.

Two wounded Federal officers. On the right is Major Lewis R. Stegman, who led the 102nd New York in the Atlanta campaign until shot in the thigh and forced to remain out of action for months. On the left is Lieutenant Donner of an Ohio regiment, also wounded and using a cane for support.

Photographer Hass S. Peale captured this image of a tent hospital at the Union base on Hilton Head Island, South Carolina. Surgeons posed for the camera's lens, an agonizingly slow process that must have been even slower for the poor man lying on the operating table.

Unfortunately, the pressing need for medical expertise meant that any person claiming medical knowledge could obtain an appointment. A veteran of the 63rd Pennsylvania later wrote:

> While there were some noble, humane and self-sacrificing physicians in the army . . . unfortunately these formed a minority to the unskilled quacks whose ignorance and brutality made them objects of detestation to the soldier. . . . Brutal as well as ignorant and careless of the poor soldiers placed in their care, they helped to fill many graves where our army marched. After awhile, when a large number of these would-be doctors had been kicked out of the army, the service improved.

Regimental surgeons often set up their temporary field hospitals as close to the battle area as possible to expedite medical care. In this scene from the famous Gettysburg Cyclorama painted by French artist Paul Philippoteaux, a surgeon works on his patients under cover of a farm outbuilding.

An 1864 image taken at Fort Monroe, Virginia, showing Union surgeons about to amputate the leg of a wounded soldier. One surgeon holds a saw while another, to his left, steadies the leg with a forked retractor. Any blood that results will fall into the basin placed below the leg. Because of the long exposure times needed for photography at the time, a photograph like this would have to be posed.

Emory Upton, a brevet major general at war's end, wrote in his memoirs: "The ablest as well as the most ignorant practitioners in the land were eligible for appointment. Such as came into the army without receiving a previous license or diploma were permitted to experiment with the lives and health of their patients until, found incompetent; or, detected in malpractice, they were at last brought before a board and dismissed from service."

In the 1860s medical school generally consisted of a two-year course of instruction. The second year was but a repeat of the first. The student then apprenticed with a doctor and afterward set up his own practice.

THE SOLDIER'S MEDICAL EXAMINATION

When each soldier enlisted, regulations specified that he was to undergo a medical examination to make sure he was fit for service. However, the haste to raise troops in 1861—as well as the pressure upon company captains to make sure their companies each had the required number of bodies—frequently meant that the required exam was cursory at best. If a man who had plowed on a farm or worked in a factory lifting heavy boxes enlisted, he was usually passed without any close scrutiny; after all, his civilian occupation was arduous enough that army life would be no problem. But thousands of men who never should have been passed managed to enter military service. Of the million men who enlisted in 1861 and 1862, some 200,000 were discharged for disability—in other words, they were physically unfit for sustained service in the field.

SANITATION AND DISEASE

Once the regiments were assembled in camp, the men became targets of common illnesses that quickly manifested themselves. Camp sanitation was universally bad—not on purpose, but through ignorance of the importance of cleanliness. Each camp had a latrine dug, but many soldiers would not submit

to being seen in the open, so they relieved themselves wherever they wished. Between this odor, food garbage, and slaughtered animal remains, camps smelled pretty bad.

The smell and rotting garbage brought flies—and mosquitoes in the spring and summer months—by the thousands. Diseases quickly followed. During the war, 199,720 Union soldiers died of disease. More than 27,000 died of malaria, while thousands more died of typhoid fever, smallpox, tuberculosis (then called consumption), dysentery, and diarrhea.

Diarrhea, called the Virginia quickstep, the runs, and other such names, was caused by a combination of bad food, improper diet, and improper sanitation. Physicians, unable to accurately distinguish between diarrhea and dysentery, differentiated the two illnesses by the presence or absence of blood in the stools. At any rate, doctors of the time treated diarrhea as a disease, not a symptom. To make matters worse, most doctors treated loose bowels with purgatives—castor oil, salts, opium, whiskey. Such doses only aggravated diar-

When General George B. McClellan decided to change his supply base from the York to the James River as the Seven Days' Battles opened in front of Richmond, he abandoned the large hospital at Savage's Station. The overcrowded hospital, filled with sick and wounded Yankees, ran out of space, and men were forced to remain outdoors, as shown in this view.

THE VETERAN RESERVE CORPS

In order to alleviate a shortage of manpower, the U.S. War Department in 1863 began to organize units of men deemed unfit for combat—generally wounded and convalescing soldiers. First called the Invalid Corps, the men wore sky-blue uniforms and were organized into two battalions, with numbered companies in each battalion.

The corps' name was changed in March 1864 to the Veteran Reserve Corps, and the troops issued regulation uniforms to enhance enlistments. These companies of soldiers performed garrison and escort duty in the rear areas, thus freeing other units to join the main armies. Units skirmished with John Mosby's Partisan Rangers in northern Virginia and manned fortifications during Jubal Early's July 1864 attack on Washington.

rhea and killed thousands of men. In the Federal army alone, 57,265 men died from diarrhea or dysentery.

MORE SERIOUS DISEASES

The sudden introduction of men into army service also brought forth other killing diseases. Many soldiers, having grown up in rural areas, had never been exposed to childhood diseases, and measles by far was the deadliest killer. "Though we enlisted to fight, bleed and die," wrote John M. Gould of the 1st Maine, "nothing happened to us so serious as the measles." Country boys, not used to crowded living conditions, felt the brunt of measles and other communicable diseases. Surgeons were of no help because no one understood the disease. One surgeon went so far as to blame the wheat straw used in the men's mattresses as the cause.

Smallpox was equally dreaded. When a couple of cases broke out in Captain J. Merrill Linn's Company H, 51st Pennsylvania, while the regiment was stationed on Roanoke Island, the company was banished to a small earthwork fort until medical personnel were sure that the disease would not spread. After one soldier of the 11th Michigan died in a hospital from the disease, the regiment soon heard about it. It "come very near causing a general mutiny," wrote one of the men, observing several of his comrades clamoring to leave camp to avoid contamination.

Civil War–era medical personnel had to deal with these diseases as best as their limited amount of knowledge would allow. In the 107th Pennsylvania, the surgeon treated smallpox and measles by subjecting the entire regiment to a diet of mush and molasses. Favorite medicines for other camp illnesses included turpentine, calomel, castor oil, blue mass (a mercury and chalk combination), whiskey, and quinine. Surgeons seemed to think that dispensing medicine would make the men happy simply because they were getting something, even if that "something" had no relation to the illness at hand.

THE WOUNDED

Once the soldiers entered combat, however, the medical staff was able at least to do something to help. For every soldier killed outright in battle,

These Yankees were shot during the successful Union attack on Marye's Heights in May 1863. They have already been to the hospital and are awaiting evacuation to the rear. The man on the left has had his right arm amputated, and the soldier lying in the stretcher has lost his lower right leg.

This wounded Union soldier's Zouave uniform is clearly evident, including the short jacket, baggy trousers, fez headgear, and white gaiters (spats) worn over the shoes. The man's right arm is in a sling, and he appears to be weak or dazed from his ordeal, although the photo was probably staged.

another four or five were wounded. Infantry weapons accounted for more than 95 percent of all wounds; artillery projectiles caused the rest. Rarely were men who had been stabbed with bayonets brought into field hospitals.

Pistols and muskets—both rifled and smoothbore—fired projectiles ranging in size from .36 caliber to mammoth round balls of .75 caliber. These slow-moving lead bullets literally knocked their victims over with force. More than one country boy thought being wounded felt like being kicked by a mule.

The lucky ones suffered flesh wounds when the bullets tore through clothing, entered their bodies, and missed vital arteries and bones. Others were not so lucky. When a soft lead projectile hit a bone, it usually flattened on impact, widening its hole and splintering the bone.

FIELD HOSPITALS

When a regiment went into battle, its medical staff followed along and set up field hospitals as near the front line as safely possible. Under the direction of the assistant surgeons, stretcher bearers—generally the bandsmen and other

Several nurses among their patients pose for the camera inside Washington Square Hospital. A sign at the far end of the ward read, "The true characteristic of a perfect warrior should be fear of God, love of country, respect for the laws, preference of honor to lawlessness, and to life itself."

noncombat personnel—combed the fields in search of wounded men. Most were located quickly and taken back to the regimental hospitals for treatment. Hospitals were commandeered buildings or simply tents pitched wherever needed. As the war progressed, the Union armies tended to group hospitals by division and corps, saving the most talented physicians to act as surgeons while less well-trained doctors performed other tasks.

Union Zouave soldiers staged a series of photographs taken in Virginia in 1864. The series, of which this scene is a part, depicted ambulance drill; an officer directs stretcher bearers on the proper way to place wounded men in an ambulance wagon.

Following their ordeal in the forward hospitals, surviving patients were sent to evacuation hospitals located outside the immediate combat zone. From there, sick and wounded men were sent by boat, train, or wagon to general hospitals located throughout the North, usually in such cities as Washington, Philadelphia, and Chattanooga. During the war, the Union established 204

This rare photo shows Nurse Anne Bell posed with two of her patients, probably in Nashville late in the war. Two crutches and medicine bottles can be seen behind her.

general hospitals with a capacity of 136,894 beds; these hospitals admitted more than a million cases.

TREATMENT FOR THE WOUNDED

Surgery for the wounded was crude and ineffective. Soldiers gathered from the battlefield and taken to field hospitals were divided into two groups—those who would probably survive and those who wouldn't. In the latter case, wounds of the abdomen and chest were fatal three-quarters of the time, whereas head wounds, especially if the bullet penetrated the bone, resulted in an 85-percent death rate. These men were put aside and tended to only when time permitted. That a fraction of them survived—without medical care—is a marvel of the human spirit of resistance.

Photographer Peter S. Weaver captured this posed scene at Camp Letterman, Gettysburg's largest hospital, in October 1863. A surgeon prepares to operate on a patient's foot while others look on. The man with the white beard and hands on hips is the Reverend Gordon Winslow, at the time acting as Sanitary Inspector of the Army of the Potomac.

Flesh wounds were examined and generally treated with cold-water compresses and opiates to ease the pain. Most of these men survived, but the risk of infection was always present, and gangrene could attack even the most minor wound.

For the men wounded in the arm or leg, the hospitals breathed terror. The flood of wounded and the limited time and expertise did not allow the surgeons to practice quality medical care. Not only was bone setting very risky and time-consuming, but it was made impractical by the large amount of splintering damage caused by lead bullets.

Instead, surgeons resorted to wholesale amputations to save the men's lives. Wounded men were placed upon crude operating platforms and given an anesthetic—chloroform, opium, or ether. The surgeon cut through the flesh and muscle with a knife and hacked through the arm or leg with a saw. One New Jersey soldier who watched two such operations was horrified: "Neither of them seemed to be under the influence of chloroform, but were held down by some four men, while nothing but a groan escaped them, as the operation proceeded."

UNSANITARY PRACTICES

The cause of infection was unknown in those days. Surgical procedures were done without proper sanitation. Bloody bandages were reused. Surgeons wiped their bloody hands on the same dirty towels. Instruments went unwashed. Often, doctors did not search wounds thoroughly and missed bits of uniform and dirt carried into the wound by the lead bullets. The victim was then bandaged up and carted off to wait for transportation to a general hospital.

General hospitals, located far from battle zones, were not without risks. Overcrowding led to spread of diseases that killed off weakened survivors of combat. Improper sanitation also contributed to hospital deaths. Loneliness and homesickness hurt the soldiers' convalescence. Milton McJunkin of the 85th Pennsylvania was sent to a hospital with a bad case of consumption. Lack of mail from his home saddened the ill McJunkin, and he never recovered. A relative finally came to take him home on furlough, but the soldier died en route.

MEDICAL DISCOVERIES

In spite of such savagery, there were a few medical advances. By accident, a Union surgeon in charge of a hospital observed that wounded men placed in outdoor tents convalesced faster than those in enclosed wards. At the time, it was widely believed that "miasmas" from swamps and ponds fouled the air and endangered sick and wounded men. But by the simple act of opening windows, patients grew healthier. Middleton Goldsmith, a Union surgeon in charge of hospitals in Kentucky and Ohio, discovered that bromine was an effective cure for gangrene.

This image, one of a series made for the Quartermaster Department in 1862, shows a model in the dress uniform of a hospital steward. Unlike surgeons and assistant surgeons, hospital stewards did not operate on wounded men but performed the useful tasks of compounding and administering medicines and looking after patients.

CONFEDERATE MEDICAL CARE

✳

When the Confederacy was formed in 1861, its government instituted a medical department similar to that of the United States. David C. De Leon was the first surgeon general, but in July 1861 he was succeeded by Samuel P. Moore, who held the office until the end of the war. Like his Northern counterpart, Moore was sometimes tactless and high-handed, but his administration of Southern military medicine was generally successful. In 1863 Moore organized the Association of Army and Navy Surgeons and sponsored the publication of *A Manual of Military Surgery*. Moore also established hospitals of the pavilion type, with each building a separate ward that could be abandoned if conditions permitted. These hospitals were better ventilated and more spacious than standard designs.

RISK OF DISEASE

Southern medical knowledge was equal to the North's. Soldiers were equally ignorant of sanitation; subsisted on improper diets; lived in squalid, crowded camps; and died by the thousands. Owing to a lack of proper records, Southern losses have never been officially established. The best educated guess indicates that at least 164,000 Rebels died of disease, and this number is probably far too low.

The Southern soldier faced a greater risk of disease than did his better-fed and better-clothed opponent. The lack of proper uniforms in the Southern armies is legendary; most Civil War books include the familiar tales of barefoot marching, bloody feet, and lack of proper winter clothing.

The hot Southern climate also produced its share of problems. Mosquitoes were so big that one Southern infantryman stationed near Vicksburg wrote

A Civil War surgeon's kit included all sorts of saws and knives designed for amputating damaged limbs; a skilled surgeon could remove an arm or leg in 15 minutes. Such speed could save a soldier's life if infection did not set in.

home that they were "almost able to shoulder a musket." Writing from Mobile in 1862, a Texan wrote that his only battles thus far were with the hordes of fleas on his person. Soldiers both North and South fought repeatedly with "graybacks," as the hundreds of lice that infested every uniform were known.

At the battle of Cedar Mountain in August 1862, the Confederate field hospital shown here treated the wounded. The Confederate medical corps had not yet developed the shortage in medical supplies it suffered later in the war.

SHORTAGES

Southerners were just as prone to measles, typhoid fever, diarrhea, dysentery, and smallpox as the boys in blue. The sudden widespread appearance of such illnesses shocked even the most experienced doctors. Many were unable to cope with these onslaughts. The Confederacy managed to muster only 2,600 surgeons, or one for every 324 men.

A major problem that the Confederacy never solved was the shortage of medicine and supplies. The initial shortage was compounded when, on July 13, 1861, the Lincoln administration passed into law the Trading with the Enemy Act. This law placed an embargo against the South. It included all medicines and medical supplies—even medical texts and instruments. As a result, there were constant shortages of everything, and suffering was rampant throughout the South.

SUBSTITUTES

To alleviate the lack of drugs, Moore and his staff compiled a list of some 400 plants that were be-

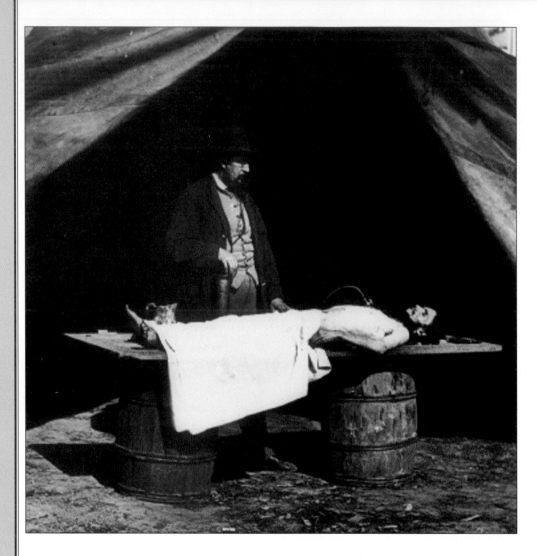

While embalming methods were well known in the 1860s, most soldiers slain in battle were buried in trenches on the battlefields or in more proper cemeteries with marked headboards for identification. The decomposition that soon set in made it imperative that bodies be buried immediately or embalmed for the long trip home to a local cemetery.

lieved to have various healing properties. Moore then established a botanical garden to grow the plants for experimentation. Opium was procured by growing poppies; other plants, such as sassafras, watercress, wild mustard, wild garlic, and artichokes were already available in many places.

By trial and error, Moore and his associates painstakingly drew up acceptable substitutes for unavailable drugs. For example, when queried about what to do when there was no quinine available for combating malaria, Moore recommended a substitute made from "dried dogbark 30 parts, dried poplar bark 30 parts, dried willow bark 30 parts; whisky, 45 degrees strength; two pounds of the mixed bark to one gallon of whisky. Macerate [steep almost to a solution] fourteen days. Dose . . . one ounce three times a day." It is unknown whether or not this concoction worked, but the patients probably didn't care!

Moore also established chemical laboratories throughout the South to produce castor oil, turpentine, chloroform, and adhesive plaster. Even so, output could never keep up with demand. However, since Southerners were already partial to home remedies, lack of proper medicine may not have been felt as badly as a modern observer would believe.

Owing to chronic shortages, a system for evacuating casualties as was devised in the North never materialized in the Confederacy. The South's limited transportation facilities contributed to untold agony for wounded soldiers. After the victory at Chickamauga, Georgia, in September 1863, the single rail-

Ambulances, despite their names, were little more than simple wooden wagons pulled by two horses or mules. The wagons were springless, and wounded soldiers suffered untold agonies as they bounced along rutted dirt roads toward rear area hospitals.

On May 4, 1863, photographer Andrew J. Russell captured this image of dead soldiers of the 18th Mississippi who had attempted to defend Marye's Heights at Fredericksburg from attacking Union troops of the Sixth Army Corps.

way to Atlanta was clogged with carloads of wounded, many of whom waited up to five days to be evacuated. When General Robert E. Lee retreated from Gettysburg, the wagon train of wounded men was 17 miles long—and was an easy prey for roving Union cavalry units.

HOSPITALS

Like Washington, Richmond became a city of hospitals, with 34 active at one point. Winder Hospital, with a 4,300-bed capacity, was the largest, while Chimborazo, located just east of the city, was perhaps the most famous. Hospitals were terrible places. Most were overcrowded and dirty. With a lack of supplies and medicines, patients were taken care of by the staff as best they could.

DISCOVERIES

Southern doctors made some accidental medical discoveries during the war. At Chattanooga, surgeons were out of chloroform and were thus unable to use this liquid drug to kill maggots that infested many wounds, especially of amputees. They were amazed when maggot-infested wounds healed more quickly, because the maggots acted as scavengers and ate diseased tissue. This "cure" had been known in medieval times but had been forgotten by 1861. To replace their use of gauze, which was in short supply, Confederate doctors started using cotton for bandages. Wounds healed better and resisted infection, but at the time doctors didn't understand that excluding air from the wound kept germs out.

Timothy O'Sullivan photographed this group of dead Union and Confederate soldiers somewhere on the Gettysburg battlefield. Unfortunately, the hazy background precluded modern identification of the specific site. Note that the dead soldiers are missing their shoes—it was common for Confederate soldiers to take shoes from those who would never need them again.

One of the most famous Civil War photographs by Alexander Gardner shows a dead Confederate sharpshooter behind a rock barricade in Devil's Den at Gettysburg. Sleuthing by photo expert Bill Frassanito revealed that the body originally lay some 75 yards away from the wall and was dragged into position for this classic shot.

THE U.S. SANITARY COMMISSION

✶

*T*hroughout the North, local groups raised money and obtained donations of clothing, food, and other items for the soldiers. Pennsylvania had its own state agency, while the Michigan Soldiers' Relief Association aided its own soldiers. The single largest Union relief agency was the U.S. Sanitary Commission, formed in June 1861 to impose order on a chaos of benevolence. The agency's board of directors chose Frederick Law Olmsted, the landscape architect who had laid out New York's Central Park, to direct the commission.

Initially opposed by President Abraham Lincoln and his cabinet, the Sanitary Commission eventually converted doubters into believers. Their sanitation reports embarrassed the army. To help hard-pressed surgeons, the commission's medical experts compiled booklets on a wide range of topics— scurvy, dysentery, and amputation, to name a few. As a result of commission pressure, the army replaced the aged surgeon general and grudgingly accepted commission suggestions on reform of the medical department.

From offices across the North, women volunteers funneled donations to commission warehouses for distribution to soldiers. Throughout the war, the Sanitary Commission distributed more than $25 million in aid. Commission wagon trains followed the armies and arrived on battlefields as soon as possible, bringing medical supplies and food to wounded soldiers and their sur-

Officers and nurses of the Sanitary Commission gathered at Fredericksburg, Virginia, in 1864.

Wounded soldiers as well as civilians in front of the commission's headquarters.

Whenever a Sanitary Commission wagon train appeared at a military camp, its arrival drew crowds of expectant soldiers.

geons. Volunteers staffed hospital boats, railroad cars, and wagons to transport wounded when the army was unable to provide adequate transportation.

The commission also established "soldiers' homes" as lodging for troops in transit. One of the best known was the Cooper Shop Volunteer Refreshment Saloon in Philadelphia. Until it closed in July 1865, the Cooper Shop facility dispensed more than 800,000 meals to passing regiments. It also provided medical service, washrooms, paper and stamps, and a laundry room.

Beginning in the fall of 1863, the Sanitary Commission sponsored a series of fairs to raise money for its activities. The first was held in Chicago and included exhibition halls filled with captured battle flags, farm machinery, and art. Such fairs alone raised more than $4 million for the commission.

All in all, the relief drive led by the commission aroused patriotism, kept up soldier morale, and in general helped unify the Northern populace behind the war effort.

CHRISTIAN COMMISSION

Established in November 1861, the U.S. Christian Commission worked closely with the U.S. Sanitary Commission in supplementing medical and food provisions supplied to soldiers by the Federal government. Sustained solely by private funding, the commission held benefits throughout the North to raise funds. The mission was to provide physical, moral, and spiritual relief to soldiers. In addition to supplying free writing materials for letters home, commission members also established Bible-reading rooms in the more permanent camps.

Members often volunteered for nursing and other medical positions in hospitals. Following the battle of Gettysburg, more than 30,000 wounded from both sides were left behind in the Pennsylvania village, left to be cared for almost exclusively by the Christian Commission and other privately sponsored relief associations. Perhaps the most famous member of this organization was poet Walt Whitman.

CHIMBORAZO HOSPITAL

Samuel Preston Moore (1812–1889) organized an association of physicians to exchange knowledge, designed the pavilion-shaped hospital, and published a surgical manual.

Medical kit

lanned by Surgeon General Samuel P. Moore, Chimborazo Hospital was the first general hospital constructed in Richmond that utilized the pavilion system. Chimborazo was constructed on a high plateau just east of the city. The James River lay immediately to the south, and a creek bordered the site on the west. These water bodies, when combined with the hill's eastern slope, gave the site excellent drainage and a good supply of water. Sweating slaves constructed about 120 buildings in the 40-acre complex. Most were ward buildings, whitewashed wooden structures 75 feet long with room for 30 to 40 cots. Altogether, the hospital could handle 3,000 patients at a time. The Seven Days battles led to overcrowding, with more than 3,500 admitted.

The hospital opened in October 1861, with Dr. James B. McCaw in charge. Using a hospital fund provided by the army to ensure that each patient received a balanced diet to speed recovery, McCaw proved an able administrator.

Chimborazo was a typical army hospital. The hot climate meant that the smell of sick men and gangrene permeated the pine boards. Hordes of flies tormented staff and patients alike. So overworked was the medical staff that visitors sometimes claimed that wounded men went four or five days without care.

This view of Richmond's Chimborazo Hospital illustrates the fine geographical location of the facility—on a hill, which provided better drainage for the site.

To alleviate these problems, the Confederate Congress in September 1862 passed a law that authorized the hiring of matrons to assist the medical staff. Laudable as this legislation was, though, it did not help. Full-time nursing was not regarded as an acceptable occupation for women, and most men refused to work with members of the opposite sex. Chimborazo, however, by some stroke of luck, managed to hire a number of women for most wards. Patients later recalled that the mere presence of women in the wards raised morale and helped in recovery.

Chimborazo faced the usual shortages throughout the war—food, silverware, dishes, soap, bedding, clothing, bandages, and more. McCaw battled with the Quartermaster and Commissary Departments over jurisdiction in order to acquire badly needed supplies.

The hospital remained open until Richmond fell and the Federal army occupied the grounds. Shortly thereafter, the facility was closed. More than 77,000 patients had been admitted to Chimborazo; more than 20 percent of them died, with 16,000 buried in nearby Oakwood Cemetery.

NORTHERN CASUALTIES

✦

Succinctly put, the Civil War was the bloodiest conflict in American history. Until Vietnam, more Americans had died in the Civil War than in all other American conflicts combined. Because of fragmentary records, we will never know precisely how many men served in the Civil War or how many were killed, wounded, captured, or missing.

Officially, the Union army recorded 2,778,304 enlistments, although many soldiers enlisted more than once in different regiments. Of this total, 178,975 were black soldiers, 3,530 were American Indians, and 105,963 served in the navy and marines.

Of the more than two million Northerners who served in the war, casualties exacted the following cost:

Total deaths	359,528	Other causes	20,728
Killed in battle	67,088	Wounded	275,175
Mortally wounded	43,012	Navy:	
Died of disease	199,720	Killed and mortally wounded	1,804
Died as prisoners of war	24,866	Died of disease and accidents	3,000
Killed by accident	4,114	Wounded	2,226

Union battle deaths included one army commander (Major General James B. McPherson, killed at Atlanta, July 22, 1864), three corps commanders, 14 division commanders, and 32 brigadier generals in command of brigades. Also, 35 generals died of disease, including Edwin V. Sumner, David B. Birney, John Buford, and Charles F. Smith.

Statisticians adding up the fighting in the war came up with 1,882 incidents in which at least one regiment was engaged. In 112 of these battles, one of the two sides had at least 500 men killed and wounded.

A group of Union dead at Gettysburg. In addition to the absence of shoes (doubtless taken by needy Southern troops), their pockets have been rifled. The bodies show the effects of bloating and rigor mortis. The entire battle area was permeated by the smells associated with unburied bodies of both men and animals.

SOUTHERN CASUALTIES

✦

*B*ecause large numbers of Confederate records were destroyed when Richmond fell in 1865, the exact number of Southern casualties has never been ascertained. Even figures for losses in specific battles change over the years as historians find new muster rolls or casualty lists and revise earlier research.

The best summary details 94,000 Southern soldiers killed in battle or mortally wounded plus 164,000 deaths from disease, for a total death count of 258,000. An incomplete wounded summary included 194,026. Those who died in Northern prisons have been estimated to be between 26,000 and 31,000.

Southern enlistments have been estimated at a low of 600,000 to a high of 1.4 million, with a widely accepted estimate being 1 million. The gray armies included more than 1,000 regiments, battalions, independent companies, and artillery batteries. On the whole, few new units were raised after 1862; the Davis administration preferred sending recruits and conscripts to units already in the field. This procedure enhanced the effectiveness of the units and prevented the chaos of completely new units—a scenario that occurred several times in the North. One Pennsylvania regiment was so mixed up and demoralized upon being fired upon that, in order to calm the men down, its colonel lined his men up and had them go through the manual of arms while under fire!

Of the South's general officers, one army commander, Albert Sidney Johnston, was killed (at Shiloh). Four corps commanders, seven division leaders, and 62 brigadiers in charge of brigades were also slain.

Dead Confederate defenders at Petersburg, Virginia, on April 3, 1865.

Slain Georgians of Brigadier General Paul J. Semmes' Brigade, killed in the field just west of the Rose Woods at Gettysburg. Photographer Alexander Gardner's photographic wagon appears on the horizon to the left of the trees.

THE MEDIA

New inventions such as the telegraph and photography profoundly affected the distribution of news about the Civil War. It was the first war to be covered in depth by newspapers and the first to be extensively recorded in photographs. Big-city newspapers, both illustrated and common versions, dominated the media. They captured the essence of the Civil War for the waiting families at home.

✦

"Newspapers in Camp," by Edwin Forbes

NEWSPAPERS OF THE NORTH

✳

*C*ivil War–period newspapers differed vastly from today's large papers. They had no banner headlines; these did not come into being until William Randolph Hearst's papers instituted them in the 1890s. The entire paper usually consisted of four, eight, or twelve pages, with five to seven columns of closely packed news and advertisements. Papers copied widely from each other to disseminate timely news stories. Comics were unheard of, and most papers were published once a week. Larger city papers appeared daily except Sunday, the day on which no papers were printed.

THE ILLUSTRATED WEEKLIES

At the forefront of modern papers were the few illustrated weekly newspapers that had appeared just prior to the outbreak of war. *Frank Leslie's Illustrated Newspaper* had started in 1855, *Harper's Weekly* in 1857, and the New York *Illustrated News* in 1859. All three papers were printed in New York City and were fiercely competitive. As the war progressed, each issue became chock full of scenes ranging from the swirl of battle to the grisly aftermath, from camp life to troops on the march.

The August 8, 1863, edition of Frank Leslie's Illustrated Newspaper *featured a sketch showing the surrender of Vicksburg, Mississippi, to General Grant.*

William Waud drew this 1864 sketch of returned prisoners of war exchanging their rags for new clothing. The artist wrote: "The figures on the right are coming in with the new clothing, in the Centre pitching the old rags overboard, & going out on the left to get their rations."

During the war years, these three newspapers hired approximately 30 "special artists" to accompany the Union armies and sketch scenes that could be reproduced in the papers. These men produced more than 2,500 sketches that appeared in the papers throughout the war. The best-known artists were Winslow Homer, Alfred Waud, William Waud, Arthur Lumley, Theodore R. Davis, William T. Crane, James E. Taylor, Frank H. Schell, Edwin Forbes, and Henri Lovie.

When the war started and these men, as well as countless journalists, reached the front lines and followed the troops, the government did not know what to do. As it happened, the government never adopted an official policy

This 1883 woodcut portrays the editorial room of Frank Leslie's Illustrated Newspaper. *Such scenes were common in the 1860s as well. The haphazard pile of wastepaper on the floor is the only indication of the hectic pace common to editorial rooms.*

toward media coverage of the war. Instead it allowed each field commander to deal with the press as he saw fit. Most commanders simply ignored the press or tried to make the best of the coverage, while others weren't amused. William T. Sherman, a great commander by 1865, had numerous problems with adverse press coverage of his administration in Kentucky in 1861, suffered a nervous breakdown, and had to be relieved. George Meade, angry over unfounded press rumors about his generalship, took matters into his own hands and banished the offending reporter.

THE DANGER TO SPECIAL ARTISTS

The special artists lived lives of danger and privation. Since the men were not government servants or soldiers, they did not receive army rations or supplies. Sympathetic generals or other officers helped artists if they wished; oth-

ALFRED WAUD

The preeminent special artist of the war was English-born Alfred Waud (1828–1891). He had 344 of his sketches published by *Harper's Weekly* and the New York *Illustrated News*. He was "blue-eyed, fair-bearded, strapping and stalwart, full of loud cheery laughs and comic songs, armed to the teeth, jack-booted, gauntleted, slouch-hatted, yet clad in the shooting-jacket of a civilian," according to a fellow member of the press. The list of engagements at which he was present included Bull Run (First Manassas), Burnside's North Carolina expedition, Peninsula Campaign, Antietam, Fredericksburg, Chancellorsville, Gettysburg, Wilderness, Cold Harbor, Shenandoah Valley Campaign, Petersburg, and Appomattox.

Arthur Lumley captured a reconnaissance balloon on the James River in pencil and sepia wash for Frank Leslie's Illustrated Newspaper.

erwise, the artists were permitted to purchase food from officers' messes and buy leftover quartermaster supplies. Some were captured by Southern troops and imprisoned or detained for a short period of time before being released. On occasion, generals asked these correspondents for help; General Meade pressed Alfred Waud into service to draw for him the scene Waud witnessed from the top of a signal station.

The luckier ones survived unhurt and avoided the deadly diseases common to army camps. *Leslie's* artist John Hillen was captured at Chickamauga but managed to escape. During Sherman's Atlanta campaign, he was wounded while sketching under fire. Henri Lovie became a running target for Union pickets who mistakenly thought he was an enemy scout. Lovie recalled later that he had "no objections to running reasonable risks from the enemy, but to be killed by mistake would be damnably unpleasant!"

HOW THE ARTIST WORKED

The usual tools of the artist were simply pencil and paper, whether the paper be white, gray-green, buff, tan, or brown. Each artist carried a sketchbook of varying sizes, depending on personal taste. They usually rode horses to get from place to place quickly, keeping to high ground to be able to survey a battlefield rapidly and choose the best vantage point from which to sketch.

Working as quickly as possible, the artist sketched the scene before him and filled in as many details as he was able. A survey of surviving original sketches shows that most were unfinished; if the artist had the time to detail only one window of a house or cannon of a battery, he knew that artists at the paper would be able to fill in the remaining details. In quieter times—in camp, in winter quarters, or during a siege—the artist had more time to complete each sketch before sending it off by mail, courier, or special express to his newspaper.

"My Studio," by Edwin Forbes, shows a snug little tent with space for an easel and three-legged stool. An artist enjoyed the luxury of a tent in winter quarters or when the army was not marching, but during battle he took shelter wherever he could find it.

Above at left is the sketch "Pennsylvania Soldiers Voting," by William Waud; at right is the published engraving from Harper's Weekly, *October 29, 1864. The engravers removed the folding stool in the center foreground and added detail to the uniforms and the foliage.*

PUBLISHING THE SKETCH

Once the sketch arrived, artists at the paper engraved the scene in reverse onto a block of boxwood with a whitened, polished surface. Each block was made up of a number of sub-blocks, depending on the desired size of the sketch to be printed. If time permitted, one artist engraved the entire block. More often than not, though, the block was subdivided and different engravers assigned to complete the copying as rapidly as possible. One might specialize

The New York Herald *was the only Northern newspaper to organize its correspondents who covered military operations. While other reporters eked out an existence dependent upon the goodwill of officers, the* Herald *provided tents, supplies, and forage for its employees. Timothy O'Sullivan captured this image of the* Herald's *staff at Bealton, Virginia, in August 1863.*

in backgrounds, one in buildings, one in soldiers. Together, they would recopy the battlefield artist's work. This cumbersome process could not hope to capture the original sketch's immediacy and style. Usually the special artist's sketches became stylized and monotonous.

Normally the original sketch appeared in the illustrated newspaper for which it was intended in about two weeks. If geography and transportation were a problem, a sketch might not appear for two or three months, or sometimes never at all.

Newspaper vendors were very popular with soldiers of both armies. Here a supplier of New York, Philadelphia, and Baltimore papers plies his trade in November 1863.

ARMY REACTION

Soldiers eagerly awaited newspapers and were critical observers of the war scenes. Literate men in blue wrote home and advised civilians about which artists were the best as well as which were inaccurate. Major Edgar A. Kimball of the 9th New York praised Frank Schell's rendering of the bayonet charge of his regiment at the battle of Roanoke Island; other Union soldiers, though, thought Schell's vantage point did not allow him to see the true state of affairs about this engagement.

At times the newspapers also relied on photographs to help convey the sense of the war to their readers. Images of generals and of battles, campaigns, or incidents for which none of their special artists were present were sometimes based on photographs and graphic rendition of them by engravers. Occasionally, fearing that competitors might "scoop" a story, the papers would include scenes entirely made up by city-based artists. These woodcuts were easy to spot because the papers, not wishing to intentionally mislead their readers, failed to include any bylines under such illustrations.

SOUTHERN NEWSPAPERS

✳

Unlike the North, the newly formed Confederacy did not have any illustrated papers of its own in 1861. To remedy this shortage, the *Southern Illustrated News* started publication in Richmond in 1863. Although it survived until 1865, this single paper failed to have much of an impact on its limited number of readers. Its few illustrations and political cartoons could not match the splendor of the New York publications.

Throughout the war, Southern readers got their information from and looked at pictures in the Northern illustrated weeklies. Robert E. Lee and other generals commented more than once that they eagerly looked for Yankee newspapers, illustrated papers included, to read about their opponents and the latest military information.

FRANK VIZETELLY

England became the major source of illustrations portraying the Southern viewpoint. The *Illustrated London News* was that nation's chief illustrated paper. Shortly after hostilities commenced, the London paper sent a special artist named Frank Vizetelly to cover the war for English readers.

Vizetelly arrived in Washington just in time to follow the Union advance in July 1861. He witnessed the debacle at Bull Run (First Manassas) and wrote a scathing text for his illustration: "Retreat is a weak term to use when speaking of this disgraceful rout, for which there was no excuse. The terror-stricken soldiers threw away their arms and accoutrements, herding along like a panic-stricken flock of sheep."

After covering the Union naval expeditions on the Mississippi River early in 1862, Vizetelly returned to Washington, where his candid reporting of Union problems prevented him from following the Army of the Potomac to the Peninsula.

Frank Vizetelly was the premier correspondent of the Illustrated London News covering the American Civil War for English readers. Vizetelly's scathing tales of mismanagement early in the war did not endear him to Northern authorities.

Frank Vizetelly's sketch of Southern cavalry leader Jeb Stuart appeared in the Illustrated London News *of October 4, 1862. Vizetelly's surviving sketches are one of the best contemporary records of the Southern war effort.*

This sketch of the Confederate ship Lillian *running the blockade into Wilmington, North Carolina, on June 4, 1864, is by Vizetelly.*

Consequently Vizetelly went South and spent the remainder of the war reporting on Confederate military operations. He traveled across the South, reporting from Fredericksburg, Charleston, Vicksburg, and Richmond. At Chickamauga, Lieutenant General James Longstreet made Vizetelly an honorary captain for his aid in carrying dispatches during the battle, which ended in a Confederate victory.

It is unknown how many sketches Vizetelly actually made. The *Illustrated London News* published 133 of them; others, sent via blockade runner to England, were undoubtedly captured or destroyed by Union naval action. Vizetelly himself returned to London for a visit in January 1864, then returned to Wilmington, North Carolina, via blockade runner. He covered the Shenandoah Valley campaign and by December was present at Fort Fisher when a Union amphibious operation attacked and captured the fort in January 1865.

Retreating Confederate soldiers burned bales of cotton to keep the crop from falling into Union hands as the Federals occupied Memphis in June 1862. Vizetelly drew this sketch and instructed the printer to finish the scene—note the directions on the building.

If Union authorities had been able to read his account of the battle, they would have chuckled over how much Vizetelly had changed his tune since 1861:

> I was present in the fort during the entire engagement, three days in all, and never could I have credited such formidable means of attack were possessed by the Federals. Never has the world seen aught so fearful as the terrible concentration of fire brought to bear on the luckless sand work by the largest fleet armed with the most powerful ordinance [*sic*] yet employed for the reduction of a fortress.

Following the collapse of the Confederacy, Vizetelly returned to England, then went to Europe to cover other wars. In 1883 he was in Egypt and accompanied the army of Hicks Pasha when it marched to subdue the Mahdist uprising in the Sudan. He perished when Sudanese tribesmen annihilated the British army.

On the evening of July 18, 1863, a Federal storming column attacked Fort Wagner, defending Charleston harbor. Colonel Robert G. Shaw and his 54th Massachusetts regiment led the attack. Southern defenders repelled the attackers and inflicted more than 1,500 casualties. Frank Vizetelly penned this view of the morning after, as Southern troops inspected the grisly scene.

NEWSPAPER SUPPRESSION

✳

resident Lincoln, although an advocate of free speech, at times acqui-
esced in suppression of newspapers when a particular paper either will-
fully misrepresented government policy or became rabidly antigovernment.
The president also had power to arrest editors after he received the power to
suspend the writ of habeas corpus.

On May 18, 1864, two journalists circulated a presidential
proclamation that called for a national day of fasting and
orders for a draft of 400,000 men. This proclamation, giving
the sense that the Union was facing defeat, was actually a spu-
rious story attempting to raise the price of gold on bad news
of the war. Most papers suspected that the document was
amiss, and only two New York papers, the *World* and *Journal of
Commerce*, printed the story. Secretary of War Stanton shut
both papers down immediately. The local general thoroughly
investigated the matter and uncovered the gold plot. Three

*Newspaper editors anywhere in the country
were targets of mob action if their papers
printed material that was contrary to local
opinion. This illustration from* Harper's
Weekly *depicts a Northern editor being
tarred and feathered for printing pro-South-
ern sentiments. Several times during the
war, newspaper offices were ransacked and
editors thrown out of town.*

days later, the War Department allowed the papers to resume publication.

In June 1863 General Ambrose E. Burnside, in command of the Department of the Ohio, shut down the Chicago *Times* for "the repeated expression of
disloyal and incendiary sentiments." This paper called emancipation "a criminal
wrong" and had become very anti-Lincoln, antiblack, and antiwar. Lincoln,
deeply respectful of civil rights although understanding Burnside's order,
revoked the general's policy and allowed the paper to continue publishing.

At times Union soldiers took the law into their own hands and shut down
disloyal papers. In 1861 Samuel Medary launched a paper called the *Crisis*. Based
in Columbus, Ohio, this Democratic sheet printed antiarmy stories that deni-
grated Ohio soldiers. On the night of March 5, 1863, troopers from the 2nd
Ohio Cavalry, then bivouacked at nearby Camp Chase, attacked the *Crisis* office
and destroyed most of the contents. Local police were "persuaded" to remain
aloof while the soldiers completed their work and then went back to camp.

THE WANDERING NEWSPAPER

✳

*U*nlike their counterparts throughout the North, Southern newspapers were constantly under threat of Union occupation as Federal troops invaded the South and seized large chunks of territory. This is one of the reasons that many newspaper titles once published during the Civil War are no longer available for inspection.

Memphis fell to Union troops June 6, 1862. Here the Union flag is being hoisted over the post office at Memphis.

One such paper was the Memphis *Appeal,* a paper that had started publication in 1840 and by 1861 was the largest daily newspaper in Tennessee. Although it advocated compromise in 1861, the paper's editorial slant became staunchly pro-Confederate when Tennessee left the Union.

The *Appeal*'s press and other equipment left Memphis by rail just before the city was occupied by Union troops in June 1862. The editors set up shop in Grenada, Mississippi, only to flee again in November when soldiers from Ulysses S. Grant's army moved into the town. Until May 1863, the *Appeal* published in Jackson, the state capital, then moved to Atlanta when Grant's men seized Jackson. In Atlanta circulation topped 14,000 for its two daily editions. But the paper had to move again when Sherman's army captured Atlanta in September 1864. Then the paper moved 167 miles to the west to set up in Montgomery, Alabama. It remained there until April 1865, when Yankee troopers from James H. Wilson's Cavalry Corps seized the city.

The paper's staff again eluded capture by moving to Columbus, Georgia, where their luck ran out. Many staffers were taken prisoner and some of the equipment wrecked, and editor Benjamin F. Dill was brought before General Wilson. "Have we caught the old fox at last?" exclaimed the general. "Well I'll be damned." After some laughter and backslapping, the general and editor drank whiskey together. The press survived and was returned to Memphis, where the paper resumed publication in November. Today the Memphis *Commercial Appeal* continues the tradition of its earlier name.

NORTHERN PHOTOGRAPHERS

✳

Mathew B. Brady had this photograph taken of himself the day after the battle at Bull Run. Brady's genius for the new art of photography made his name synonymous with Civil War photography even though he himself, after 1862, did not take many images.

On June 20, 1864, Brady was photographed in captured Confederate Battery 8 in the Petersburg defenses. The earthwork fort was now occupied by the 12th New York Battery. Brady, wearing his customary straw hat, stands in the center of this image, observing the effects of the artillery's firing.

The science of photography began in France in the 1830s, when Louis Daguerre invented the daguerreotype process. Although photography studios appeared in America in the 1840s, it took almost 20 years for the country to become aware of the possibilities that photographs offered. By 1860, however, more than 3,000 photographers were listed throughout the United States.

MATHEW BRADY

Mathew Brady (1823–96) was an eminent American photographer whose studios in New York and Washington captured the images of the most famous people of the prewar period. When war erupted in 1861, Brady later wrote that "I felt I had to go. A spirit in my feet said 'go' and I went." Brady's towering fame was thereafter associated with his images of the Civil War—generals, privates, contraband slaves, forts, supply depots, and dead bodies.

No photographer was ever able to photograph a battle in action. The photographic process of the time, which required the use of a wet collodion glass plate, was simply too slow. Any motion in a scene being captured on glass was reproduced as a blur. When people stood or sat for views, many photographers used a wire headstand on their subjects to ensure stillness; sharp-eyed viewers

have no trouble picking out the wooden bases of these stands as they poke out from behind their subjects.

Brady himself, owing to failing eyesight, did not do much field work, if he did any at all. He was assisted by a staff of photographers that included Alexander Gardner and Timothy O'Sullivan, although they left Brady in the middle of the war. These men captured images on the major battlefields of the war in the east.

In the west, George N. Barnard made his fame by photographing the wild mountain country of Tennessee and Georgia that had never been seen by those in the eastern United States. His views of Lookout Mountain and associ-

Shown here is Mathew Brady with one of his horse-drawn processing wagons. Once an image was taken, the photographer could develop the film by working under the dark cover at rear of the wagon.

Photographer George N. Barnard's portable darkroom and related equipment attracted the attention of a group of General William T. Sherman's veterans near Atlanta. Barnard was commissioned to photograph the captured city and its defenses, and he did a superb job.

George N. Barnard took this photograph of the East Tennessee & Virginia Railroad bridge over the Holston River at Strawberry Plains, Tennessee, probably in the autumn of 1864. One of Barnard's assistants appears behind a second camera on the right side of this image.

ated battlefields became widely known. He followed Sherman's advance on Atlanta in 1864 and was contracted by the government to photograph the captured Southern forts around the city.

PHOTOGRAPHER FOR THE ARMY

Captain Andrew J. Russell was the army's sole official photographer. Russell had enlisted in the 141st New York Volunteer Infantry, then was reassigned to General Herman Haupt's U.S. Military Railroad Construction Corps. The captain was a photographer by trade and was charged with photographing the efforts of Haupt's railroad crews in rebuilding bridges and track to bring supplies to the troops operating in Virginia. As a result, Russell took photos of installations, bridges, railways, supply ships, and other associated matériel.

TYPES OF PERIOD PHOTOGRAPHS

In addition to the views of generals and battlefield scenes, the war resulted in the widespread use of the *carte de visite* (visiting card), a 2.5×4-inch cardboard stock featuring a mounted portrait on one side

Alexander Gardner captured this view of Richmond's "Burnt District" on April 6, 1865. Retreating Southern troops set fire to everything that might be of value; as a result, perhaps 1,200 buildings went up in flames—the arsenal, tobacco warehouses, railroad bridges, commissary depot, and other buildings. The conflagration smoldered for over two months.

and the photographer's mark on the reverse. Soldiers of both sides rushed to available studios to be photographed in order to send copies to loved ones at home. Tens of thousands of these have survived and portray the officers and common soldiers who fought in the Civil War.

Another common period photograph was the ambrotype, a variety of the collodion process that produced a photographic negative that could be rendered into a positive image by backing it with black material.

Finally, the tintype, commonly termed the melainotype or ferrotype at the time, was a photograph made on a blackened iron sheet. The tintype did not need glass for the exposure, which made the image appear in reverse; thus, in looking at a tintype, all letters and numbers appear in reverse image. The cheap cost associated with the tintype made it very appealing for the common soldiers, thousands of whom used this process to record their images.

Timothy O'Sullivan photographed the headquarters of Major General Irvin McDowell, commanding the Third Army Corps, in July 1862.

CONFEDERATE PHOTOGRAPHERS

✦

*P*hotographers of the Confederacy were very few. Surviving evidence suggests that several photographers made the rounds of historic sites and military camps when hostilities began in 1861, then seemingly disappeared for the rest of the war.

J. D. EDWARDS

Such an example is J. D. Edwards, a shadowy figure who remains obscure. A New England native, he was working in New Orleans in 1860 as an ambrotype portrait taker. He had been contracted by the U.S. Army to take photographs of the Custom House and Marine Hospital as they were built. When Louisiana troops left for Pensacola, Florida, Edwards apparently followed along, hoping to capture images of the new war. He took several views of the Southern camps and forts around the city, as well as some long-range shots of Union-held Fort Pickens. Once the war moved on, however, Edwards moved to Atlanta but apparently did not photograph any more scenes; what he did afterward is a mystery.

In February 1861, two months before the war started, Charleston photographer George S. Cook took his camera to Fort Sumter and persuaded the officers of the garrison to pose for him. Shown here is Kentucky-born Major Robert Anderson, commander of the fort.

Richmond photographer Charles Rees took several wartime photographs of the city. His images were found in 1865 and appropriated for use by Northern publishers. In this view, Rees captured the infamous Libby Prison and its commandant, Thomas P. Turner, standing at center of the group in the foreground.

GEORGE S. COOK

Another leading photographer was George S. Cook of Charleston, South Carolina. Connecticut-born Cook finally settled in Charleston and from there went north to manage Brady's gallery while Brady toured Europe. By the time Fort Sumter was fired upon, Cook was back in Charleston, having already taken images of Major Robert Anderson and his staff. After the fort's surrender, Cook photographed the bastion's interior and was later kept busy taking images of officers and men as well as installations for the area commander, Pierre G. T. Beauregard.

By 1863 Cook had established a prosperous business supplying photographic materials to other Southern photographers. Some of this material he obtained via the blockade runners, some from Northern sources surreptitiously. In September 1863 Cook was present in Fort Sumter, taking images of the battered fort. He placed his camera on the parapet and managed a sensational image of Federal monitors firing at the fort—and his camera! Following the war, Cook moved his studio to Richmond, where it continued to operate into the 1950s.

OTHER PHOTOGRAPHERS

Other Confederate photographers are less well known. A. J. Riddle of Georgia captured images of Yankee prisoners at Andersonville. A few other identified images have survived, in addition to the surviving images of Confederate soldiers, but, on the whole, Union photographers by far outnumbered their Southern counterparts.

HOW A TYPICAL PHOTOGRAPH WAS TAKEN

First the cameraman needed a glass plate, usually 8 by 10 inches for larger views, or 4 by 10 inches for stereo views. These were carried in dustproof boxes. When ready to photograph, the artist coated a plate with collodion made of a solution of nitrocellulose in equal parts of sulphuric ether and 95-proof alcohol. The surface of the plate was then sensitized by adding bromide and iodine of potassium or ammonia. After letting this mixture evaporate to the right consistency, the plate was immersed from three to five minutes in a bath holder solution of silver nitrate. This had to be done in total darkness, or an amber light at best. The plate then went into a holder for insertion into the camera, already aimed and focused. The photographer then uncapped the lens to permit an exposure of from five to thirty seconds, depending on available light. Following the capping, the photographer then had only a few minutes to develop the plate in a solution of sulfate of iron and acetic acid. Then he washed the plate with a cyanide of potassium solution to remove any surplus silver. Finally he washed it yet again, dried it, and varnished it.

ARTISTS OF THE NORTH

✳

*I*n addition to the special artists who sketched the war for the illustrated weeklies, a number of other artists captured the essence of the Civil War in their paintings and sketches. Some of these men actually served in the armies, whereas others learned from veterans and executed superb renditions of Civil War camp and battle scenes.

WINSLOW HOMER

On the Union side, two names stand out above all others. Winslow Homer (1836–1910) was already working for *Harper's Weekly* when the war began and served as a special artist for over a year. Thereafter, he made numerous excursions to the front lines. Altogether, 26 of his illustrations appeared in *Harper's*. He is best known, however, for his oil paintings that he executed from his sketches, such as "Prisoners from the Front" (1865). After the war Homer became famous for his natural scenery paintings.

In a sketch by Winslow Homer, a young woman takes a letter for a hospitalized Union soldier.

Entitled "The Army of the Potomac—A Sharp-shooter on Picket Duty," this engraving was one of Winslow Homer's finest wartime efforts.

GILBERT GAUL

Gilbert Gaul (1855–1919) was too young to serve in the war, but after his studies at the National Academy of Design in New York, he devoted himself exclusively to painting Civil War scenes and illustrating books then being published about the war. Although Northern born, Gaul developed a sympathetic eye to Southern scenes. Several of these, such as "Waiting for Dawn" and "With Fate Against Them," are among his finest efforts. He was one of the illustrators who worked for The Century Company on its "Battles and Leaders" series, and he also produced sketches for Boston newspaperman Charles Coffin's set of books.

In Winslow Homer's "Prisoners from the Front," a Union general examines a group of captured Southern prisoners escorted by a Union guard. The prisoners range from a young boy to an old man, indicative of the range of ages serving in the Confederate armies.

Gilbert Gaul's "Waiting for Dawn" depicts Southern cavalrymen camped out on a battlefield. The shivering men are huddled around campfires, surrounded by dead bodies of their foe. In the distance can be seen the camps of Union soldiers.

OTHER ARTISTS

Other veterans included drummer boy Julian Scott, who served in the Vermont Brigade of the Sixth Army Corps, and who later painted a host of accurate battle scenes. Charles W. Reed was a bugler for the famed 9th Massachusetts Battery and drew numerous sketches of army life in his letters home. After the war, he put his newfound talent to use and became an illustrator for many books written by comrades in arms.

LOUIS KURZ

Everyone has seen at least one Louis Kurz Civil War scene—the melodramatic, stylized battle scenes still being reprinted by some companies. A lithographer from Chicago, Kurz produced a Lincoln lithograph shortly after Lincoln's assassination. He is best known for the three dozen or so prints that he and his partner, Alexander Allison, introduced to a new generation of Americans in the 1880s and 1890s. Although error-ridden and stylized, Kurz prints were cheap, readily available, and eagerly purchased by people across America who had read about the war in books.

French artist Paul D. Philippoteaux was best known for his cyclorama paintings, including the famous cyclorama at Gettysburg. Philippoteaux also painted several other Civil War scenes, including this view of General Grant at the battle of Fort Donelson.

One of Kurz & Allison's prints shows Major General Philip Sheridan, at center, leading his army to victory over Jubal Early's Southern troops at the battle of Cedar Creek, Virginia, October 19, 1864. This print is inaccurate and stylized, but scores of such battle art translated the actual war into illustrations for the public.

SOUTHERN ARTISTS

✳

ALLEN C. REDWOOD

*I*n addition to Northern artists, the Civil War also spawned Southern artists who later used their abilities to record their experiences during the war. Allen C. Redwood (1844–1922) became one of America's greatest post-war artists, illustrating countless books and magazine articles. Redwood served in the 1st Maryland Cavalry and 55th Virginia Infantry, was thrice wounded, and captured twice. He settled in Baltimore after the war and entered a career as a writer and artist. He worked on the "Battles and Leaders" series for the Century Company, and he contributed his fine sketches to numerous Civil War books written by Northern and Southern veterans alike.

CONRAD WISE CHAPMAN

The son of distinguished artist John Gadsby Chapman, Conrad Wise Chapman (1842–1910) also served in the Confederate army, with the 3rd Kentucky.

Conrad Wise Chapman depicted one of the Confederate navy's "David" torpedo boats at a dock in Charleston harbor. A crew of men work on the dock and boat.

Chapman was wounded at Shiloh, then transferred to the 46th Virginia and saw action in that state and at Charleston. While stationed in the city, Chapman was detailed to make a pictorial record of the city and its defenses. He completed his sketches later, turning them into paintings that preserve a view of life in besieged Charleston.

WILLIAM L. SHEPPARD

William L. Sheppard (1833–1912) was a member of the famed Richmond Howitzers during the war. The budding artist's career took off after the war, when his illustrations of Southern life appeared in such magazines and newspapers as *The Century Magazine, Harper's Weekly,* and *St. Nicholas.* He illustrated books written by fellow batteryman John Esten Cooke and contributed to numerous other volumes. The talented artist also sculpted the monument to the Howitzers that stands in Richmond.

Another of Chapman's paintings shows a Confederate artillery battery that defended Charleston from Union attacks. The viewer's attention is immediately drawn to the Southern flag, tattered but still flying in the pale morning light.

THE HOME FRONT

*W*ar made a significant impact on Northern and Southern home fronts. Citizens on both sides faced sacrifices in support of the war effort, but for the people of the South, sacrifice became a tragic way of life. Very few had imagined the war would last beyond a year. By 1864 three years of personal loss, taxes, and conscription began to take their toll. The fire that initially burned passionately throughout the citizenry of both sides began to extinguish, and Presidents Abraham Lincoln and Jefferson Davis struggled to find ways to reignite it.

✦

"The 9:45 Accommodation," by Edward Lamson Henry

FOOD SHORTAGES IN THE SOUTH

✳

*T*he war was young. The clash of arms had favored the gray armies. The infant Confederacy hailed victories at Manassas (Bull Run) and Ball's Bluff, Virginia; Wilson's Creek and Lexington, Missouri; and numerous venues in between. And yet by autumn 1861, a specter of things to come was already beginning to descend upon the South.

BASIC FOODSTUFFS

"Flour was already unknown in that part of the Confederacy," a woman wrote of Mississippi, "coffee, and sugar were about as scarce . . . a pound of tea twenty-five dollars, and it rose to fifty dollars in two days . . . a pair of coarse shoes cost forty dollars. . . . We had scarcely any clothes." Meanwhile, a soldier's pay was only $11 a month—when he was paid at all.

By the winter of 1863, food and other supplies in the South were so scarce that Federal troops had to support Southern civilians in occupied areas. This sketch by Edwin Forbes shows a Southern family traveling to the Union commissary for rations in February 1864.

From Richmond came word of a shortage of salt, one of the major means for preserving meat. "The South requires, at lowest estimate, six million bushels of salt a year," reported the Richmond *Dispatch*. But after Union troops captured a salt works in western Virginia, "we know of no other sources of supply on which we can depend for more than a million-and-a-half at the most," the paper stated. The price skyrocketed as a result of the shortage, from $2 a bag before the war to $60 by the fall of 1862. Beef and pork slowly disappeared from dinner tables.

Food of all kinds became scarce on the home front, as the enormous demands of the armies had priority. "Is this war to be carried on and the Government upheld," wrote a Mississippian, "at the expense of the starvation of the women and children?" As word of the plight of families reached the armies, desertions increased. "We are . . . willing to defend our country," a soldier wrote, "but our families [come] first."

Inside Federal commissaries in occupied Southern territories, Union troops distributed provisions to civilians. Lack of supplies drove families to these commissaries in order to survive.

A group of Southern women, their faces veiled, ride to the United States commissaries for provisions. This became a very common sight in Federally occupied territories.

GROWTH AND DISTRIBUTION

The young nation, though rich in agriculture, could barely feed itself. Confederate victories on the battlefield early in the war and the prospects for a quick end to the conflict had made Southern planters reluctant to switch from growing cotton and tobacco, which fed their purses, to producing corn, grains, and other crops so vital to feeding people and livestock. Ironically, much of the food that eventually was produced often rotted in the fields or on railroad sidings because of the South's poor transportation and distribution system.

"The railroads were cut so constantly," wrote a hospital administrator, "that what had been carefully collected in the country in the form of poultry and vegetables . . . would be unfit for use by the time the connection could be restored." The South lacked the industry to maintain or repair its railroads, and most horses and good wagons had already been taken by the army.

By the middle of 1862, most Southern ports had been blockaded, shutting the South off from the vast markets of Europe. Farm workers were off fighting, leaving crops either unharvested or rotting unsold. Inflation was beginning to run unchecked. The little manufacturing that existed in the South was almost exclusively being turned to producing implements of war. Conscription laws did not exempt males with dependent families, leaving loved ones unprotected against the ravages of a society turned hostile due to deprivation and greed.

DISPLACEMENT AND INFLATION

Many families were displaced from their homes, fleeing from invading armies. The vast expanse of the rural South isolated those not touched directly

by invasion. Word of loved ones killed or wounded at the front only added more grief to lives already burdened with intense misery. "Every breeze chants the requiem of dying heroes," wrote a mother stricken by the death of her son.

As the war advanced, the Southern economy steadily deteriorated. Confederate money, printed in excess of $1 billion, failed to keep pace with spiraling inflation. The dismal Confederate economy gave rise to a saying that was common throughout the South: "You take your money to the market in a basket and bring home what you buy in your pocketbook."

"The gaunt form of wretched famine," one Southerner wrote from Richmond in March 1863, "approaches with rapid strides." With no relief in sight, bread riots such as the one that occurred in Richmond in April 1863 broke out in other cities of the South. "Our battle against want and starvation," wrote a Confederate supply officer, "is greater than against our enemies."

As the Union blockade tightened and the agricultural productivity of the Southern states drastically reduced, rampant inflation gripped the South. Civilians living in Federally occupied regions were rationed food. In this sketch by Alfred Waud, Alabamians go to a ration office prior to procuring supplies.

THE EXPANSION OF THE NORTHERN ECONOMY

✶

*I*t was harvest time in the fall of 1862. Tens of thousands of men across the North who otherwise might be bringing in the crops and preparing their farms for winter were instead away at war. Thus a traveler in rural Iowa at the time wrote, "I met more women driving teams on the road and saw more at work in the fields than men."

The following year, even more men were taken away from their farms by the military. Yet another observer would write of "a stout matron whose sons are in the army, with her team cutting hay. . . . She cut seven acres with ease in a day, riding leisurely on her cutter." It was evidence, the witness noted, of "the great revolution which machinery is making in agriculture." It was also evidence of how the Civil War had expanded the role of women in the Northern economy. The wheat harvest for those years illustrated the success the transformation had on agriculture. Whereas before the war 20 million bushels were exported to other countries, 60 million were now being shipped.

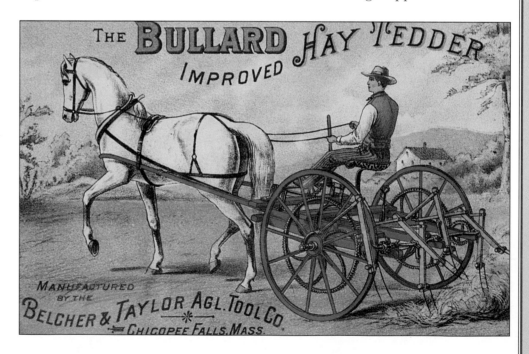

Before the war, labor for farming was available and cheap, and new machines progressed slowly. As manpower was diverted to the fighting, all kinds of improved farm machinery—mowers, reapers, cultivators, and threshers—became widespread.

INDUSTRIAL BOOM

The impact of mechanization and changes in the workforce were not restricted to agriculture. Northern industry enjoyed a war boom of major proportions. Labor-saving machinery and mass-production techniques helped Northern factories supply the endless needs of the military at the very same time that the military was taking many able-bodied laborers from the factories. Women, children in some cases, and a continuous influx of European immigrants helped to fill in the gaps in the workforce. "The nation is teeming with ingenuity," wrote a foreign observer traveling across the North, "and ever producing something new; everybody invents or improves something."

This prewar engraving shows a bountiful wheat harvest. During the Civil War, the demand for foodstuffs of all kinds grew remarkably despite the loss of the Southern market.

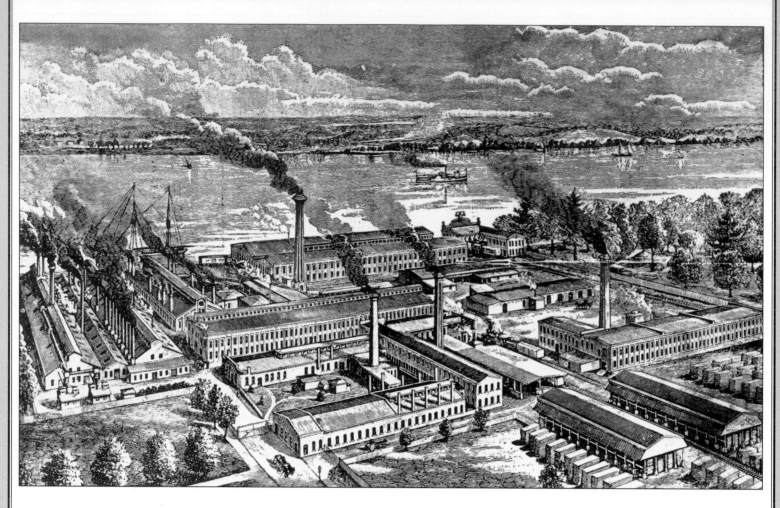

The Philadelphia factory of Henry Disston & Sons claimed to be the world's largest producers of saws.

ECONOMIC CRISIS

When the war began, the sudden and dramatic loss of Southern commerce and investments was a calamity to Northern businesses and banks. The Union was plunged into a financial crisis at the start of hostilities. As months passed with no end to the contest in sight, its ability to pay for the war appeared even bleaker. "What shall I do?" President Abraham Lincoln lamented to Quartermaster General Montgomery Meigs in January 1862. "The people are impatient; Chase has no money and tells me he can raise no more. . . . The bottom is out of the tub."

With economic doom on the horizon, Congress took emergency measures to stabilize the economy by passing legal-tender acts authorizing the printing of $450 million in currency as well as passing the first income taxes in the United States. Although these measures did not stop wartime inflation, they kept it at a manageable level.

ECONOMIC ACHIEVEMENT

The true savior of the Northern economy was the escalation of manufacturing and agricultural production. In contrast to their Southern counterparts, Northern manufacturers were able to meet both wartime and civil needs. In Philadelphia alone, more than 200 new factories opened during the course of the war. Binding the North together was a plentiful network of railroads of the

best quality. Working in unison, they permitted the free flow of men and equipment over great distances in the shortest times possible. And even in the grip of war, the North possessed the energy and materials to push its rails toward the Pacific Ocean to help bring the vast lands and resources of the West into production.

Boasting of the Union's economic achievements, a prominent businessman wrote in 1864 of "railroads pressed beyond their capacity with the freights of our people . . . more acres of fertile land under culture . . . and more prolific crops than ever before . . . whitening the Northern lakes with sails of its commerce . . . and then realize, if you can, that all this has occurred and is occurring in the midst of a war."

Homesteaders in Custer County, Nebraska

HOMESTEAD ACT OF 1862

Passed on May 20, 1862, the Homestead Act provided for the free distribution of public lands for settlement. The law required a settler to live on a quarter section of land (160 acres) for five years, make improvements, and pay an incidental legal fee of $10. The settler secured title to the land once these terms were fulfilled.

Since the act was put into effect on January 1, 1863, more than 1.2 million acres had been claimed by June 1864. Despite some abuse by speculators, the plan enhanced the population and development of the West. It also increased popular support for President Abraham Lincoln and the Republican party. Before the Civil War, Southern congressmen had blocked such legislation to prevent the spread of anti-slavery sentiment to the West.

THE CONFEDERATE DRAFT

✳

*F*rom one end of the Confederacy to the other," complained Confederate Superintendent of Conscription John S. Preston, "every constituted authority, every officer, every man and woman is engaged in opposing the enrolling officer in the execution of his duties."

THE FIRST AMERICAN CONSCRIPTION ACT

Even though they realized that the enactment of a draft would cause unrest throughout the young Confederacy, by the second year of war Confederate President Jefferson Davis and the Congress in Richmond felt they had no other choice. The Federals were raising large armies in Washington and to the west.

This 1861 woodcut shows a little band playing to draw men into the Confederate army.

Many of the Confederate volunteers who initially enlisted for a year at the start of the war expressed a reluctance to reenlist. Some form of conscription or draft would be necessary to maintain the Southern armies. On April 16, 1862, therefore, Congress passed the first conscription act in American history. It called for every white male between the ages of 18 and 35 to serve for three years.

It took Davis and his government only a few days to realize that some exemptions had to be established if the war machine at home was to continue to run. On April 21, Congress exempted government officials, ferrymen, pilots, employees in iron mines and foundries, telegraph operators, ministers, printers, educators, hospital employees, and druggists. By September 1862 the age of those eligible for the draft was raised to 45.

EFFECT OF THE DRAFT

Discontent toward the draft spread throughout the South. Conscription was fundamentally alien to

the notion of personal rights. This alienation was further fueled by the fact that the people most affected by the draft were poor whites whose families could least afford their absence. Better-off men could avoid being drafted. The "Twenty-Negro Law" permitted exemptions to owners or overseers of 20 or more blacks. Furthermore, those draftees from the upper class who were not eligible for one of the many exemptions had the ability to hire substitutes to serve for them.

Opposition to conscription grew until, in an attempt to heal some of the wounds caused by the draft, Congress ended the use of substitutes in December 1863. Two months later, in a drastic effort to fill the gaps caused by almost three years of war, Congress widened the age limits for conscription from 17 to 50 years. The quality of the soldier in the ranks declined in the later stages of the war, leading one journalist to observe: "The Yankees cannot do us any more harm than our own soldiers have done." Eventually, even blacks were impressed into the military for noncombat functions.

Confederate recruiters marching through the streets of Woodstock, Virginia, attracting young men to the military. Scenes like this were common during the early years of the war. As the fighting dragged on and the number of eligible men diminished throughout the South, however, the furor to join the army greatly diminished.

THE DRAFT IN THE NORTH

*P*arodying a popular poem, a satirist wrote:

> We're coming, Father Abraham, three hundred thousand more,
> We leave our homes and firesides with bleeding hearts and sore,
> Since poverty has been our crime, we bow to the decree,
> We are the poor who have no wealth to purchase liberty.

ENLISTMENTS

In 1861 and 1862, liberty for males between the ages of 20 and 45 was the freedom to choose personally whether or not to serve in the military. That freedom of choice was compromised by the Enrollment Act of March 3, 1863. For the first two years of war, President Abraham Lincoln and Congress avoided enacting a draft, but several factors finally forced their hand, causing them to act before their armies fell apart.

By the spring of 1862, Lincoln realized that the war would not be over soon and that some permanent system had to be developed to keep his armies fully manned. In July 1862 he signed the Militia Draft Act, giving states the authority to conduct drafts to fill their military quotas. This attempt at state-administered conscription, however, was rife with corruption and could not be depended on to supply the necessary manpower.

The enlistments of those April 1861 volunteers who had signed up for two years approached expiration. Heavy losses in the fall and winter of 1862, a marked increase in desertions, and the expiration of volunteers' enlistments concerned Lincoln and Congress. Bounties paid for volunteer enlistments were no longer enticing, and recruiting throughout the North drastically slumped.

THE DRAFT

By the spring of 1863, the Federal government felt there was no choice but to institute a national draft. The Enrollment Act of 1863 called for the registration of all 20- to 45-year-old males and

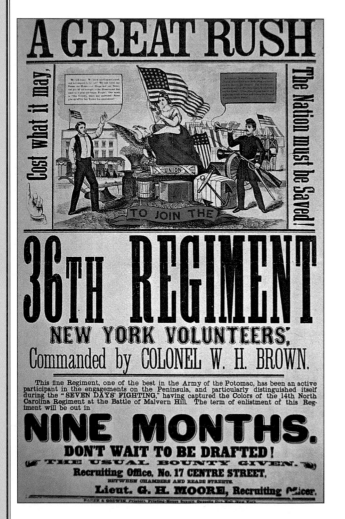

Volunteers to the army received a bounty, whereas conscriptees did not. Many men chose to enlist rather than wait to be drafted.

a house-by-house census of all neighborhoods to determine quotas to fill the call for 300,000 men. Bachelors would be called into the service first, followed by married men between the ages of 20 and 25.

Two provisions caused many to feel that this was actually a measure to fill the military ranks from the lower classes. If called, one could avoid serving in the army either by providing a substitute or by paying a $300 commutation fee. While politicians tried to sell these loopholes in service as a means to ensure stability in the private sector, most citizens—particularly from the middle and lower classes—saw it as a means for protecting the wealthy from the war. For embittered masses of people, the conflict had become a "rich man's war and a poor man's fight."

Because of the unpopularity of the draft, bounties were offered to new recruits who volunteered and soldiers who reenlisted. This sketch by George Law for Harper's Weekly *shows recruiting in New York City in 1864.*

The names of men eligible for the draft were often placed in lottery wheels to ensure an honest and fair system. Drafted men were given many loopholes to allow them to avoid military service, the most popular being the hiring of substitutes to serve in their place. A medical exemption was another common method for avoiding service.

Around 164,000 men, including paid substitutes, entered the Union army as a result of the 1863 draft, a small number compared to the more than 2 million who actually served. This newspaper sketch shows a group of draft recruits taking the oath of allegiance.

EFFECT OF THE DRAFT

Civilian riots broke out throughout the North after the enactment of the draft. Hostility was focused particularly on blacks, who had become not only the scapegoats of the war but also a potential threat to take away the jobs of lower-class workers.

The 1863 draft act proved to be a horrendous failure. In New York City, about 13 percent of the males who were called failed to report for induction. More than 55 percent of those who did report were given exemptions. The draft resulted in the induction of 35,882 men with all but 9,880 being substitutes. Subsequent drafts in 1864 were no more successful.

Conscription, however, was not a total failure. A major benefit of the laws was the increase in volunteer enlistments. Faced with the choice of being forced into service with no monetary benefit or the ability to receive a bounty upon volunteering, most chose the latter option. A spirit of national honor and duty also supplied men to the ranks. More males enlisted during the first nine months of 1863 than were drafted. This trend continued throughout the remainder of the war, with more than a million men volunteering during the final two years.

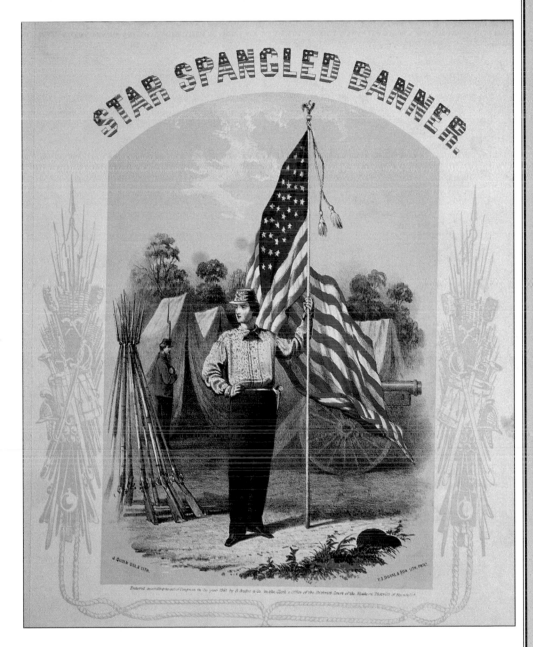

Patriotic songs such as "The Star-Spangled Banner"—which was written during the War of 1812 but was not the national anthem until 1931—stirred men to enlistment.

Richmond Food Riot

Several hundred women in Richmond marched to Capitol Square on April 2, 1863, demanding concessions from the governor. Failing to have their needs met, they surged into the shopping districts, smashing windows and stealing clothes and food.

On April 2, 1863, a mob of angry women, children, and old men marched through the streets of Richmond behind a "40-year-old Amazon with the eye of the devil" and a six-shooter in her hand. Minerva Meredith led a growing throng through city streets to Capitol Square, where they presented a list of grievances to Virginia Governor John Letcher and Richmond Mayor Joseph Mayo. Simply stated, the people were hungry. They wanted bread, and as well, they wanted an end to the inflated prices of food that had plunged many Southern families to the brink of starvation.

The governor listened sympathetically but failed to appease the crowd. The mayor read the riot act, directing attention to a battalion of soldiers standing nearby with their muskets and bayonets poised for action. Enraged, the crowd spilled into side streets chanting, "Bread! Bread!" They ransacked shops and warehouses.

Legend has it that soon Confederate President Jefferson Davis appeared in the midst of the looters, clambered atop an abandoned wagon, and pleaded with the rioters to cease. "You say you are hungry and have no money," Davis shouted, reaching into his trouser pockets. "Here is all I have." He flung money into the crowd. Davis next removed a pocket watch from his vest. "We do not desire to injure anyone," he cried, "but this lawlessness must stop. I will give you five minutes to disperse. Otherwise, you will be fired upon." The battalion of riflemen leveled their weapons and the mob slowly dispersed.

NEW YORK CITY DRAFT RIOT

✧

*I*n a matter of hours, an angry mob had "swollen to a frightful size," according to one witness. "[A] vast crowd of those who lived by preying upon others, thieves, pimps, professional ruffians, the scum of the city, jail birds, or those who were running with swift feet to enter the prison doors, began to gather on the corners, and in streets and alleys where they lived." Many armed themselves with clubs, crowbars, and paving stones. In time, the devilish masses spilled from the dark reaches of New York City and swarmed to the 9th District draft office with blood in their eyes.

It was Monday, July 13, 1863, and the angry New Yorkers were reacting to the beginning of a nationwide military draft brought on by a shortage of volunteers. By the middle of 1862, the gruesome stories from the battlefields, the long lists of soldiers killed in action, and the scores of overcrowded military hospitals had soured the public enthusiasm for the war.

Mobs of protesters roamed the streets of New York for three days, fighting pitched battles with police. Provost guards brought in to subdue the rioting New Yorkers had to use artillery force.

Over the next few days, the rioters brought a reign of terror to the city. Government offices, political officials and military personnel, and black residents of any age became the targets of the mob's wrath. It took several regiments of troops with artillery to force an end to savage street battles. In the end, more than 70 people were killed, hundreds more were injured, and property damage exceeded $1.5 million. Similar uprisings on a smaller scale erupted in Boston and other Northern cities. The "nation is at this time," wrote the editor of a Washington, D.C., newspaper, "in a state of revolution."

THE NORTH GREW TIRED

✳

*E*conomic success did not lessen the personal costs of war. Immigrants and members of the lower classes of Northern society carried the bulk of the burden. Attracted either by volunteer bounties, which could amount to as much as $1,500, or by the soldier's wage of $11 to $16 per month, many husbands and sons of poor families went off to war. These were also the families affected by the first Federal draft, leading to the feeling that this was a "poor man's fight."

The growing lists of casualties most affected families who could least afford the absence of males. Relief agencies sprang up across the North to provide needed services not only to soldiers but also to families who could no longer support themselves due to the death or maiming of the head of the household.

THE ELECTION OF 1864

By the start of 1864, the citizens of the North had grown tired of war. After the fall of Fort Sumter in 1861, a patriotic spirit swept through the North, with most civilians pitching in to make a contribution to the war effort. As casualty

Union dead at Devil's Den, outside of Gettysburg, Pennsylvania, on July 2, 1863. In less than half an hour of heavy fighting at Gettysburg, one Union regiment lost more than half its men. News of such heavy losses dispirited the North.

Union General Samuel Peter Heintzelman with his family. Personal sacrifices by the families of military men began to weigh down on Northern citizens.

The 1864 Democratic Presidential ticket, shown on this Currier & Ives poster, consisted of George B. McClellan and George H. Pendleton. More favorable news from the battlefront in 1864 enabled President Abraham Lincoln to be reelected with 55 percent of the popular vote.

lists mounted and personal sacrifices on the home front grew larger, however, an antiwar movement began to affect political policy. The Democratic Party, with an antiwar platform, chose George B. McClellan, the first commander of the Federal Army of the Potomac, as its presidential candidate.

With the military successes of 1864, however, particularly the capture of Atlanta and the destruction of the Shenandoah Valley—the breadbasket of the Confederacy—an end to conflict was in sight. These successes led to a resurgence of support for the war effort and led to President Abraham Lincoln's victory over McClellan in November. Although it may have temporarily waned, citizens' resolve for reuniting the Union never faltered, meeting with ultimate success in the spring of 1865.

FACING THE END

✳

This dramatic representation of the hard-ships faced by the South shows a family who once possessed great wealth reduced to abject poverty. In this sketch the blacks, who before emancipation were owned by this grieving woman, remained with her to care for her family.

By January 1865 the fate of the Confederacy had been sealed. With one Federal army marching almost unmolested through Georgia and the Carolinas and the other slowly strangling General Robert E. Lee's Army of Northern Virginia at Petersburg, Virginia, the passionate fire that had ignited with the fall of Fort Sumter in April 1861 was all but extinguished.

The hardships on the front were only made worse by desperate letters from home. "We haven't got noth-ing in the house to eat but a little bit of meal," one woman wrote to her spouse. "Try to get off and come home and fix us all up some and then you can go back. If you put off coming, t'wont be no use to come, for we'll all . . . be out there in the garden in the graveyard with your ma and mine." Such letters were received daily by men who were finding it difficult to remain com-mitted to the country they helped form less than four years earlier. What began as a "great experiment" was ending in a dismal failure.

Once it became apparent that the sacrifices made for the Confed-eracy were in vain, citizens and sol-diers found it difficult or impossible to continue under the burden of war. "Before God, Edward," one

woman wrote to her husband, "unless you come home we must die! Last night I was aroused by little Eddie's crying. . . . He said 'Oh, mamma, I'm so hungry!' And Lucy, Edward, your darling Lucy, she never complains, but she is growing thinner and thinner every day." By the spring of 1865, life on the Southern home front was breaking down, making it harder for soldiers to continue the fight for a dying country.

Women left at home learned to make do with little.

WOMEN IN THE WAR

The Civil War was not simply a man's war, for women played a significant role in the conflict as well. It has been estimated that 300,000 women aided the war effort by working in factories, as nurses, in soldiers' aid societies, as spies, and, in disguise, as soldiers. Some of these women became legendary, though most never achieved lasting fame. A few were scoundrels, while several gave their lives. Their stories make great reading.

✶

"The Field Hospital," by Eastman Johnson

UNION SPIES

✵

*B*oth the North and the South actively employed spies to gather military intelligence about the opposing side. In addition to the normal use of male spies, both sides used women as unofficial and self-appointed spies, with mixed results.

MRS. E. H. BAKER

Allan Pinkerton, who had headed a detective agency prior to the war, worked with the U.S. government and used females as spies. One of his agents, Mrs. E. H. Baker, had lived in Richmond before moving to Chicago. She went south in 1862 and returned to her Virginia home to spy on Southern naval activities; rumors of experimental submarines had unnerved the Union navy, and officers wanted information.

Allan Pinkerton was the founder of a detective agency who organized a wartime espionage network that became the Federal Secret Service. He hired both men and women to spy for the Union government. He is shown on horseback in camp in the Army of the Potomac during Lincoln's visit to the camps in October 1862.

Baker wormed her way into the confidence of Southern officers and actually was given a tour that included the inspection of one of these craft. She managed to return to Washington with notes on her visit that alerted the navy to these ships.

ELIZABETH VAN LEW

Elizabeth Van Lew, a member of the Virginia aristocracy, had been educated in the North and came to hate slavery. When the war started, she decided to keep the Lincoln administration informed of events in the Confederate capital. Using her slaves as couriers, she managed to keep Union authorities informed throughout the entire war and was never suspected of disloyalty to the Confederacy.

Writing in invisible ink with a cipher that she developed, Van Lew was a master of deception. She managed to get one of her female servants hired as a nanny at the Confederacy's presidential mansion, thus obtaining much valuable information. She aided escaped prisoners whenever possible, and she even offered her house as quarters for the new commander of Libby Prison when he arrived in the city. Ruined by the war, however, Van Lew was spurned by postwar society. She was appointed postmaster of Richmond by President Ulysses S. Grant but died in poverty.

PAULINE CUSHMAN

One of the more flamboyant spies was Pauline Cushman, reputed to have been the subject of the later silent movie series *The Perils of Pauline*. Cushman was born in New Orleans but was raised in Michigan. She was an aspiring actress whose soldier husband died of dysentery in 1862. Recruited into espionage service for the Union, Cushman—during a play in Louisville in early 1863—drank a toast to the Confederacy and was subsequently fired from the

Above: *A member of Richmond society, Elizabeth Van Lew nevertheless sympathized with the North. Throughout the war, she and her servants sent valuable information concerning Confederate military activities to Washington.* Left: *This cipher key was found in Van Lew's effects when she died, long after the war. The letters of the alphabet and the numbers 0 through 9 appear in the 6-by-6 grid, which has coordinate numbers at the side and bottom. Using this grid, the letter g, for example, would be represented by its coordinates, 56.*

Pauline Cushman in a photograph taken after this Union spy was caught by the Confederates, sentenced to hang, and rescued by advancing Union troops. Her career as an agent over, she returned to acting briefly and then lectured widely on her exploits.

cast. Her supposed Southern sympathies now established, she moved south to Nashville but was expelled for her Southern leanings.

Cushman was acting on army orders to learn what she could about General Braxton Bragg's plans. Suspicion fell upon her and she was arrested, with drawings and plans found on her person. A court-martial examined her case and sentenced her to be hanged. But before this sentence could be carried out, Union troops advanced and occupied Shelbyville, Tennessee, where Cushman was confined to a sickbed. She went on to tour the North, lecturing on her exploits and garnering accolades wherever she went. Her career went ever downward, however, and she died in 1893 from an opium overdose.

SARAH EMMA EDMONDS

One woman's disguise as a male soldier was so convincing that her comrades never discovered her identity until a reunion years after the war. Sarah Emma Edmonds was a Canadian who ran away from home to avoid marrying an older neighbor forced on her by her father. Under the alias of Frank Thompson, Sarah disguised herself and fled to the United States. She sold Bibles and in 1861—together with a male friend—joined the 2nd Michigan infantry.

Acting as a male nurse, Edmonds took care of sick Union soldiers. During the Peninsula campaign of 1862, she volunteered to spy on Confederate positions at Yorktown, Virginia. She disguised herself as a male contraband slave by painting herself with silver nitrate. The "slave" easily slipped through the enemy picket lines and helped other slaves dig entrenchments while gathering information about the number of enemy troops and the strength of their positions.

After returning to Union lines, Edmonds was sent back again and again to spy. Her disguises included that of a female Irish peddler, a female contraband, a dry goods clerk, and a young boy. Each time she was successful and reported her intelligence to Union officials. By the time the 2nd Michigan joined the Ninth Army Corps and went to Kentucky in 1863, Edmonds had contracted malaria from the Virginia swamps. To avoid medical treatment that would have revealed her true sex, Edmonds deserted in April.

While recovering at home, Sarah discarded her Frank Thompson alias and wrote a book about her military experience. She gave the proceeds from its sales to soldiers' aid societies. She married in 1867 and gave birth to three children. In 1884, she attended a reunion of the 2nd Michigan and shocked old comrades, who never suspected Frank Thompson was Sarah Edmonds! She later received a pension for her services, and when she died in 1898, she was buried in the Grand Army of the Republic (GAR) cemetery in Houston.

During her term of service, Sarah Emma Edmonds acted as a spy, using both male and female impersonations. Her comrades never suspected she was a woman and found out only at a reunion in the 1880s.

"Playing Possum," a scene from Nurse and Spy in the Union Army, *about the exploits of Sarah Edmonds.*

CONFEDERATE SPIES

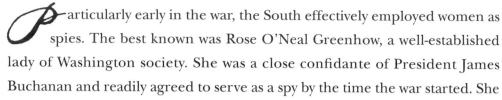

ROSE O'NEAL GREENHOW

Rose O'Neal Greenhow and her daughter in a Brady photograph taken after the famous spy was captured. The deeds of daring by early Southern spies, including Greenhow, were greatly exaggerated and grew into legends far beyond whatever espionage was successfully accomplished.

*P*articularly early in the war, the South effectively employed women as spies. The best known was Rose O'Neal Greenhow, a well-established lady of Washington society. She was a close confidante of President James Buchanan and readily agreed to serve as a spy by the time the war started. She helped to provide advance information about the Union army's plans to attack the Southern army located behind Bull Run. Forewarned, Confederate officers were ready and defeated the Yankees at the battle of Bull Run (First Manassas).

Greenhow's activities led to her arrest a month later, and she was eventually confined in Old Capitol Prison. After her exchange in June 1862, President Jefferson Davis sent her to Europe to campaign for support for the Confederacy. Greenhow decided to return to America in 1864. The blockade runner *Condor,* carrying Greenhow, ran aground off the North Carolina coast, closely pursued by a Union warship. Greenhow was carrying gold for the war effort and had sewn it into her dress. The lifeboat transporting her to shore overturned in heavy seas, and the weight of the gold drowned the famous spy. Her body was found the next morning, placed in state in the Capitol, and buried in Richmond.

BELLE BOYD

Virginia native Belle Boyd took up spying for Stonewall Jackson. She was captured but soon was released after General John A. Dix gave the young woman a stern lecture and allowed her to return home. Taken again in July 1862, she was sent to Old Capitol Prison in Washington, where she remained for one month until exchanged. After a third imprisonment, she went south and sailed to London, where she married. Belle returned to America as an actress whose career spanned only four years (1866–1869). She married three times and died of a heart attack while preparing to give a recital of her adventures to a Wisconsin GAR post.

Other Southern spies included Sarah Slater, who acted as a courier for Confederate agents in Canada and disappeared after the war, abandoning her North Carolina husband. Belle Edmondson lived in Memphis during the war and provided information as well as pharmaceutical supplies to the Confederacy. The Moon sisters—Lottie and Ginnie—lived in Tennessee and throughout the war successfully carried out several missions to aid Southern troops.

Belle Boyd spied for the Confederacy in northern Virginia early in the war, but she was captured three times.

MARY TODD LINCOLN

✳

No lady of the White House has ever been so maltreated by the public press," wrote the editor of the *Chicago Daily Tribune* in August 1861. During the Civil War the first lady was constantly attacked by the press, and her own personality foibles made such attacks easy.

Kentucky-born Mary Todd (1818–1882) had married Abraham Lincoln in 1842. Mary was strong-willed and tempestuous with a sharp tongue. She was undisciplined, a spendthrift with lavish tastes, and emotionally immature. But Lincoln loved her dearly and defended her time after time.

Mary fussed constantly over Lincoln's appointments, and her imperious manner made many enemies. Because four of her brothers and two brothers-in-law served in the Confederate army, she was constantly accused of spying for the enemy. In addition to her political troubles, the death of the Lincolns' 12-year-old son, Willie, in 1862 devastated her.

Her husband's assassination so grieved Mary that she took no part in the funeral ceremonies. She finally left the White House a month later and was never again stable. Her son Robert caused his mother to stand trial for insanity in 1875. She was released after a few months and went to Europe, returning to America in 1880. Mary Todd Lincoln died in isolation; the autopsy revealed a brain tumor that may have played a large part in her character.

VARINA HOWELL DAVIS

Described by the great statesman John C. Calhoun as an "intellectual equal," Varina Davis (1826–1905) was the right hand of her husband, Jefferson, throughout their marriage. She was witty, well informed, and bright. She was a devoted wife and mother and a ferocious defender of her husband's reputation.

An enemy called her Queen Varina, but as the war went on this nickname assumed a charm of its own. Varina worked to obtain leaves for soldiers on honeymoons, saved food so other women could have wedding receptions, and had clothes altered for those in need.

Varina was her husband's researcher and ghost writer on numerous occasions. President Davis suffered from neuralgia and had bad eyesight; his wife spent long hours assisting in the writing of his memoirs. After her husband died in 1889 of a bronchial ailment, Varina wrote her own memoirs, then gave the Davis estate to Mississippi to serve as a soldiers' home. She moved to New York City, where she supported herself by writing magazine articles.

Kady Brownell went with her husband, Robert, when he enlisted in the 1st Rhode Island infantry in 1861. She was present at the battle of Bull Run (First Manassas). Kady cared for the wounded of both sides and went home when Robert was discharged for his wounds.

WOMEN IN BLUE

*a*n unknown number of women served in the ranks of both armies throughout the war. Most were discovered quickly and banished from the camps. Sometimes women were unmasked by their mannerisms. A soldier in the 1st Kentucky Infantry was found out by the way "he" pulled on his stockings. Captain Emanuel D. Roath of the 107th Pennsylvania, while inspecting picket stations of the First Army Corps in April 1863, found that one of the sentries had just given birth—illustrating the laxness of medical examinations upon entrance into service.

A few nameless women were actually killed in battle. In 1934 a man digging a flower bed outside his Tennessee house found some bones and reported this to authorities. Subsequent investigation revealed parts of nine bodies, all clad in Union attire. The grave site, near the Shiloh battlefield, included the skeleton of a woman, who apparently had been killed by a rifle bullet found within the skeletal remains. Her identity remains a mystery.

"ALBERT CASHIER"

One woman served an entire three-year term without being found out. Jennie Hodgers enlisted under the moniker Albert Cashier on August 6, 1862, as a private in the 95th Illinois. This new regiment took part in General Ulysses Grant's Vicksburg campaign and fought at Brice's Crossroads, Nashville, and Mobile before being disbanded in 1865.

"Albert Cashier" survived the war and returned to farming. She participated in veterans' reunions and marched in Grand Army of the Republic (GAR) parades. In 1911, while working for a state senator, Cashier was involved in a freak automobile accident when "his" employer backed his car into Cashier. A doctor was called and the truth came out—Albert Cashier was a woman! Her erstwhile comrades, however, didn't care. They supported her and continued to reminiscence about her wartime experiences. After she died in 1915, the local GAR post erected a tombstone that read: "Albert D. J. Cashier, Co. G, 95 Ill. Inf."

"FRANK MAYNE"

When William Fitzpatrick enlisted in the 126th Pennsylvania, he was followed into service by his lover, Frances Day. Fitzpatrick died of disease a month later; on that same day, Sergeant Frank Mayne of Company F deserted. Later, Sergeant Mayne enlisted in a Western regiment and was mortally wounded in battle. On his deathbed, he told listeners that he was really Frances Day.

PERSISTENCE

Some women were persistent in their efforts to remain in service. Frances Hook joined the 90th Illinois. Upon being discovered and sent home, she reenlisted in the 8th Michigan—and later the 2nd East Tennessee Cavalry. Fanny Wilson started in the 24th New Jersey and was found out during the Vicksburg campaign. She was discharged from service but later enlisted in the 3rd Illinois Cavalry.

Some estimates claim that hundreds of women served in the Union army disguised as men. Frances Clalin is shown in the uniform of a cavalry trooper in the Missouri militia.

WOMEN IN GRAY

✳

a handful of stories exist about Southern women in uniform. When Union burial details swept the Gettysburg battlefield following General Robert E. Lee's retreat, those working in the area of Pickett's Charge reported that they buried a woman clad in gray.

Some tales of women in disguise have been disproved. In December 1864, it was reported, one of the Southern officers at the Johnson's Island prison camp startled Union authorities by giving birth. A local reporter, tongue in cheek, wrote that "this is the first instance of the father giving birth to a child that we have heard of." However, the paper employing this reporter always tried to find scurrilous stories about prisoners, and this baby tale appears to be one such concocted bit of falsehood.

Documented stories of Southern women in uniform are far rarer than those of Northern women, since a woman shouldering a musket was less imaginable in the tradition-minded South. Even the notion of women serving as nurses met so much opposition that the practice was not widely adopted.

WOMEN WHO SERVED

The few who have been recorded in history include Amy Clarke, who enlisted with her husband in the 11th Tennessee. Her husband was killed at Shiloh, and she was wounded, exposed, and banished behind Confederate lines wearing a dress. Lucy Thompson also went with her husband, serving in the 18th North Carolina. She was wounded twice and her husband killed; she survived her wounds and took her husband's body home for burial. Another Carolinian, Sarah Blaylock, enlisted as Sam Blaylock in the 26th North Carolina. When her husband received a medical discharge, "Sam" revealed her true identity and was sent home as well.

MADAME VELAZQUEZ

The most confusing and questionable Southern heroine was undoubtedly Madame Loreta Janeta Velazquez. Her 1876 memoir, *The Woman in Battle*, stirred debate that continues to this day. Was she a heroine or a fraud?

Loreta Janeta Velazquez in the guise of Lieutenant Harry Buford, C.S.A.

Velazquez claimed to have served the Confederacy as Lieutenant Harry Buford and fought at Bull Run (First Manassas), Fort Donelson, and Shiloh. In her book, she claimed to have helped raise a battalion of Arkansas troops, then served as a spy in Washington, where she met President Abraham Lincoln. At Shiloh, she was wounded by a shell and her identity discovered. She fled to New Orleans, her former home, and was there when the Union army took control of the city. Velazquez then served as a Southern spy, traveling throughout the North and South.

After the war, she married a third and fourth time, traveled extensively, and created a major controversy when her book appeared. General Jubal Early questioned her claims and thought she was a fraud. Modern-day historians have examined her work and concluded that her story *might* be based on fact. Many of the events she wrote about are verifiable, but her involvement in those events is not.

A scene from Velazquez's book, The Woman in Battle.

ANGELS OF THE BATTLEFIELD

DOROTHEA DIX

*T*he woman most responsible for arguing the case for female nurses was Dorothea Dix. This 59-year-old woman was already famous as an activist for the humane treatment of the insane. Seeing that the army was ill-prepared to handle medical problems, Dix visited the surgeon general with her proposal and was turned down. Undaunted, she called on every congressman she knew until on May 28, 1861, the War Department accepted her offer to select nurses for the Union army.

On June 10, Dix was commissioned superintendent of women nurses. To dissuade the "wrong" kinds of ladies from rushing to her cause, Dix issued an order that "no woman under 30 need apply to serve in government hospitals. All nurses are required to be plain-looking women. Their dresses must be brown or black, with no bows, no frills, no jewelry, and no hoop skirts."

Appeals to ladies' aid societies collected 5,000 shirts within a month of a government request for 500. Responses for other materials were so overwhelming that Dix had to appoint a woman to collect and store supplies until they could be sent to the proper distribution points.

Dix ran into personality problems with officers and used her authority to visit hospitals on inspection tours, a practice resented by male medical personnel. Nevertheless, she continued in her position as Union superintendent of nurses without pay throughout the war.

Reformer Dorothea Dix's practice of recruiting plain-looking women over 30 years of age led to much amusement in the hospitals and the press.

CLARA BARTON

Clara Barton, who later founded the American Red Cross, also participated in the war. She led a volunteer effort to assist wounded soldiers after the battle of Bull Run (First Manassas). The surgeon general later granted her a pass to travel with army ambulances "for the purpose of distributing comforts for the sick and wounded, and for nursing them." Barton served in this capacity in

In this highly dramatized painting, Clara Barton is shown tending a fallen Union soldier on the night after the bloody fighting at Antietam. Barton arrived with medical supplies and gained national prominence for her work on the battlefield.

This 1904 photo shows Clara Barton (1821–1912) as she appeared in later life. Barton, a Patent Office worker in 1861, actively sought aid for Union soldiers during the war, and in 1881 she founded the American Red Cross.

Virginia, Maryland, and South Carolina, attracting national attention for her efforts. In addition to caring for the sick and wounded, she visited returning prisoners of war to learn the fate of men missing in action so their families could be contacted.

MOTHER BICKERDYKE

"A woman rough, uncultivated, even ignorant, but a diamond in the rough," a contemporary described Mary Anne Bickerdyke. When the dreadful conditions of army hospitals in Cairo, Illinois, were known, "Mother" Bickerdyke was selected to head a relief commission to deliver supplies to the needy soldiers. A large, muscular widow, Mother Bickerdyke served in the western theater of war, participating in campaigns that generals William Sherman and Ulysses Grant commanded. The terror of colonels and generals alike, Mother was held in high regard by the soldiers she served. Numerous postwar accounts detailed her selfless sacrifices for the boys in blue.

Shown in later life, Mary Anne Ball Bickerdyke (1817–1901) supervised the building of about 300 field hospitals during the Civil War. She accompanied General Sherman on his march to the sea. After the war she served as a pension attorney for veterans.

CATHOLIC NUNS

Throughout the war, more than 600 Catholic nuns served as cooks, washerwomen, nurses, hospital administrators, apothecaries, and more. Sisters from 12 orders are known to have served with the Union armies. The Washington and Richmond governments arranged an agreement that allowed these sisters to travel south to help tend Confederate wounded and sick Union prisoners.

Nuns tended the wounded after many major battles. A group of sisters from Emmitsburg, Maryland, arrived at Gettysburg after the fighting had ceased. One group staffed the hospital ship *Red Rover* on the Mississippi River. Their efforts were not without loss; several nuns died of disease during their valiant services.

LOUISA MAY ALCOTT

Author Louisa May Alcott volunteered for hospital duty. After working a month, she came down with typhoid fever, was given repeated doses of calomel to cure the disease, and contracted mercury poisoning. Alcott lost teeth and hair as a result and was never again completely well.

Above left: *Louisa May Alcott published her first book,* Hospital Sketches, *in 1863 following several months of service in a "perfect pestilence box" in Washington. Her hospital work ended when she went home ill from her exposure to horrible conditions.* Above right: *Sister M. M. Joseph of the Sisters of Mercy, along with other members of her order, served in a military hospital in Beaufort, North Carolina.* Left: *This sentimental scene typifies mid-19th-century romanticism—the soothing hand of a woman, the grateful soldier, the loyal dog. But it was true that as soon as females appeared in hospitals, morale among the inmates improved. Female nurses helped feed the sick and wounded soldiers, listened with attentive ears, wrote letters to loved ones for those too weak to write, changed bandages, and generally helped with sanitation.*

CONFEDERATE WOMEN

✦

*U*nlike the North, the Confederacy never succeeded in enlisting widespread female aid as nurses and other hospital staff. Traditionally, Southern women did not work outside the home, and any attempts to do so—even during the dislocation caused by war—were opposed by somebody. Thousands of women probably served as nurses by war's end, but never in as large numbers as their Northern counterparts. There were exceptions, of course.

Felicia Grundy Porter, president of the Confederate Women's Relief Society, worked to establish hospitals for the Confederate wounded in Nashville, Tennessee.

SALLY TOMPKINS

Sally Tompkins was the only woman to hold a military commission. A Virginian by birth, Tompkins came from a wealthy family that moved to Richmond prior to the beginning of hostilities. When wounded men began arriving after the battle of Bull Run (First Manassas), Tompkins felt she had to help, so she approached a friend, Judge John Robertson, for help in establishing a hospital. Generous to a fault, the judge turned over his Richmond home for her use. She attracted other well-bred ladies, who brought their personal and monetary aid to the new Robertson Hospital. "The little lady with the milk-white hands," as she was known, carried on in spite of her frail appearance.

Later in 1861, when the government decided to take over all hospitals in the name of efficiency, Tompkins was allowed to continue her administration after President Jefferson Davis commissioned her a captain in the Confederate army. Robertson Hospital, between August 1861 and June 1865, received 1,333

Captain Sally Tompkins was given her commission for her hospital work.

admissions and numerous transfers with but 73 deaths—a remarkable record for the time.

PHOEBE YATES PEMBER

Phoebe Yates Pember obtained a nurse's appointment in 1862 and literally forced her way into Richmond's Chimborazo Hospital against male opposition. Several of those men opposing women working as nurses argued that the horrible sights so prevalent inside hospitals should not be seen by female eyes. Pember had an eloquent answer for her critics:

> In the midst of suffering and death, hoping with those almost beyond hope in this world; praying by the bedside of the lonely and heart-stricken; closing the eyes of boys hardly old enough to realize man's sorrows; much less suffer man's fierce hate, a woman must soar beyond the conventional modesty considered correct under different circumstances.

The patriotism of Southern women is illustrated in this 1862 woodcut. The women on the left are working to produce uniforms for soldiers; on the right, other women exhort their men to enlist in order to protect the South from Yankee invaders.

UNION WOMEN OF VALOR

✳

*I*n addition to working as spies, serving as soldiers, and ministering to sick and wounded men, Northern women served widely in other capacities. Thousands of women left their homes and worked in factories across the North to make up for the loss of manpower caused by the never-ending need for fresh troops.

FACTORY WORKERS

Factories of the day were perilous establishments, employing women and young boys to run sometimes dangerous machinery. The most hazardous jobs, without a doubt, were those associated with manufacturing ammunition for the army. Arsenals across the North employed women by the hundreds of thousands to make cartridges. Each cartridge, be it intended for a pistol or the more standard .58-caliber musket rifle of the period, had to be handmade. The slightest mistake, usually an unintended spark, could set off the unstable black gunpowder used in ammunition.

One such accident did occur on September 17, 1862, the same day as the bloody battle of Antietam. A few minutes after 2 P.M., three successive explosions rocked the Allegheny Arsenal in Pittsburgh. More than 80

With men away at war, women joined the workforce in increasing numbers. Working in arsenals and other government facilities, women performed the dangerous tasks of making ammunition for the army. The slightest spark could set off unstable black powder and cause a catastrophe.

employees were killed, most of them women as young as 14. Some were literally torn apart by the explosions; many bodies could never be identified. An investigation revealed that a supply wagon had ignited some loose powder that had been carelessly swept off the porch of one of the laboratories. Bits of unidentified bodies were gathered into 39 coffins and buried in the Allegheny Cemetery.

LEGENDS

Other women became legends, including a woman immortalized in John Greenleaf Whittier's poem "Barbara Frietchie." The poem's heroine, 95-year-old Barbara Frietchie, supposedly flaunted the U.S. flag in the faces of Southern troops marching through Frederick, Maryland, prior to the battle of Antietam. Stonewall Jackson was said to have been involved, but subsequent research—and the memoirs of others with Jackson—revealed that Jackson and Frietchie never met and that Southern troops did not pass her house. Still, owing to Whittier's epic but inaccurate lines, Barbara Frietchie was elevated into an instant symbol of American patriotism.

Dr. Mary Walker's Civil War involvement has been shrouded in mystery. A graduate of Syracuse Medical School, Dr. Walker was one of few women who became full-fledged physicians. When the war started, Walker tried to obtain a commission as a contract surgeon, but she failed until President Abraham Lincoln himself signed the order in January 1864.

The legend of Barbara Frietche arose from John Greenleaf Whittier's poem, which included the lines "'Shoot, if you must, this old gray head,/But spare your country's flag,' she said."

A view of members of the Soldiers Aid Society of Springfield, Illinois, in 1863. Women across the North banded together to make or collect supplies of bandages, clothing, writing paper and implements, and food for their loved ones in blue.

At Cooper Union Hall in New York, hundreds of women met to organize the Women's Central Association of Relief to aid sick and wounded Federal soldiers.

HARRIET TUBMAN

Dr. Mary E. Walker, who served as a contract surgeon, is wearing her Medal of Honor.

One of the foremost conductors of the Underground Railroad was former slave Harriet Tubman. In 1849 she left her Maryland home and went north to freedom. Over the years she returned south at least 15 times and brought back more than 300 slaves, including her own family, rescued from the "jaws of hell." Often called "Moses," Tubman recalled with pride that "my train never ran off the track and I never lost a passenger."

Tubman went south in May 1862 and spent at least two years helping runaway slaves and assisting Union commanders in gathering military intelligence. During her sojourn, Tubman worked hard to gain the confidence of suspicious local blacks. She gave up her army pay and rations and lived among the contrabands (slaves who escaped to the North), helping them procure clothing, food, and shelter. Tubman worked as a nurse to both contrabands and Union officers, eliciting praise from both.

In June 1863 Tubman went on a Union raid up the Combahee River to destroy railroad bridges and track and deny local supplies to enemy troops. During this foray, Tubman and her compatriots liberated 700 slaves.

Tubman returned north in 1864 and spent her remaining years at her home in Auburn, New York. She died in 1913. Her restored home is now a museum.

The new army doctor wound up serving in Colonel Dan McCook's brigade of the Army of the Cumberland. She was present during the opening stages of the Atlanta campaign and was taken prisoner by enemy troops as she ministered to civilians outside the advancing Union lines. After almost four months of captivity in Richmond, she was released and sent north. Walker was assigned to a women's prison in Louisville, then moved to a Tennessee orphan's asylum.

After leaving service in June 1865, Walker petitioned for appropriate recognition of her services. In November, President Andrew Johnson awarded her a Medal of Honor, which she wore proudly until 1919, when an army board struck 911 names of those the members felt did not deserve the nation's highest military award. In 1977 President Jimmy Carter signed into law a bill restoring Walker's award.

WORKING WOMEN

✸

FACTORY WORKERS

Like their counterparts in the North, Southern women went to work in factories to offset the loss of manpower to the army. One group of women, employed by cotton mills in Roswell, Georgia, faced the horrors of war when, on July 5, 1864, Yankee cavalry from General William T. Sherman's advancing army occupied the town. After a two-day delay waiting for instructions, the Union troops rounded up all employees and, after destroying the mills, transported more than 400 women to Marietta, Georgia. The factory women were unloaded and placed in the vacant buildings of the Georgia Military Institute.

The number of refugees swelled when the workers of the Sweetwater Factory, 16 miles southwest, were brought to Marietta. Then, the entire group was shipped north via train to Nashville, then on to Louisville. The refugees then disappear from recorded history. Sherman intended to send them to Ohio,

Noted Southern artist A. J. Volck penned this scene of Southern women at a home industry making clothing for the soldiers. Since the South had comparatively few manufacturing establishments, it had to rely on the generosity and patriotism of its women to help feed and clothe its armies.

Indiana, and wherever else they could earn a living, but until records are discovered, the Georgia factory women remain a mystery.

GOVERNMENT EMPLOYEES

The Confederate government made a practice of hiring women. After the passage of the Conscription Act of April 1862, Congress passed several resolutions affecting government hiring practices. One ordered that clerical positions in the Post Office and Treasury Department, "where so little exertion was required," be given only to women and disabled soldiers.

The Treasury Department, headed by Christopher G. Memminger, became the largest employer of women. The secretary noted that competition for each job was keen, with more than a hundred applicants for each position. It was his decision that led to the hiring of the most needy women for government service.

His women worked five six-hour days a week, being paid half the wages of male clerks. Most Treasury women worked as note signers, a job requiring speed and precision. Each woman signed or numbered 3,200 notes per day. Any mistakes, such as blotting or defacing, led to salary deductions. Their salaries failed to keep up with rampant inflation. In April 1864 Memminger transferred much of the department operations to cities farther south in order to relieve the food shortage in Richmond and to place the finishing operations near the printing presses to prevent fraud. Most treasury women resigned; only a hundred or so went to Columbia, South Carolina, to keep their jobs.

Christopher G. Memminger, the Secretary of the Treasury for the Confederacy, employed large numbers of women.

AMMUNITION EXPLOSION

The South's equivalent disaster to the Allegheny Arsenal explosion occurred in Richmond on Friday, March 13, 1863. Brown's Island, in the James River at the base of Seventh Street, had been turned into an ammunition-assembly factory employing young women. One of these employees, Mary Ryan, tried to unstick a friction primer and hit the device against a board. It exploded, and by the time authorities were able to sift through the wreckage of the building, at least 45 women and young boys had died. The women killed and mortally injured ranged in age from 10 to 33.

LEGACY OF THE WAR

*a*fter four years of bloody fratricide, the American Civil War was finally over. More than 600,000 men were buried in graves from California to Maine. The North's military, economic, and political might had finally crushed the South. But after the shooting stopped, unanswered questions remained. What was to be the fate of thousands upon thousands of freed slaves? Would the victors punish the vanquished? And where would the energies unleashed by the war take the reunited nation?

✦

"Surrender at Appomattox," by Tom Lovell

LINCOLN'S ASSASSINATION

✶

*I*n anticipation of President Abraham Lincoln's attendance, the performance at Ford's Theatre was sold out on the evening of April 14, 1865. Major Henry Rathbone and his fiancée, Clara Harris, accompanied the President and Mrs. Lincoln to the theater.

John Wilkes Booth, a staunch Confederate supporter, also entered the theater. A member of a nationally respected dramatic family, Booth was well known to the theater staff. Having appeared in the play several times, Booth knew when the audience would be most distracted by actions on stage.

As laughter filled the theater, it took Booth only 30 seconds to slip into the President's box, shoot Lincoln in the back of the head with a single-shot derringer, slash Rathbone in the arm, break his left leg leaping to the stage, and limp out of the theater exclaiming, *"Sic semper tyrannis!"*—"Thus be it ever to tyrants," Virginia's state motto.

Lincoln died the next morning. The lives of everyone else in the box that evening would be dramatically changed. Booth was captured and killed 11 days later. Mary Lincoln was declared insane in 1875 and spent several months in an asylum. Although Rathbone and Harris married two years later, his inability to save Lincoln helped drive Rathbone insane. He murdered his wife in 1894 and spent the rest of his life in an insane asylum.

President and Mrs. Lincoln sat in the box on the right when they viewed the play Our American Cousin *in Ford's Theatre, Washington. John Wilkes Booth stepped up behind the president, placed a derringer pistol less than six inches from the back of Lincoln's skull, and pulled the trigger.*

LEE'S SURRENDER AT APPOMATTOX

✳

By the morning of April 9, 1865, the Federal army of Ulysses S. Grant had been on the heels of the enemy for a week. Since the fall of Petersburg, Robert E. Lee's men had been on the run, hoping to beat Grant's army to waiting supplies at Appomattox Station, about 80 miles away. During his flight west, Lee lost a large portion of his command each day to fatigue or capture.

Palm Sunday, April 9, dawned with the Federals in possession of Appo-

Wilmer McLean's family left Manassas, Virginia, after the war began in 1861. He settled in this house in a small village named Appomattox Court House, away from all the fighting. And yet, on April 9, 1865, the war in Virginia came to an end in McLean's parlor room, where Lee and Grant met to make peace.

mattox Station, blocking the Confederate advance. "There is nothing left me," Lee practically whispered to himself, "but to go and see General Grant, and I had rather die a thousand deaths."

The two generals met in the home of Wilmer McLean, who had moved his family from Manassas Junction, the site of the first battle of Bull Run (First Manassas). Their meeting lasted only a few hours. "Whole lines of battle rushed up to their beloved old chief," a correspondent recorded as Lee slowly returned to his men for the last time, "and struggled with each other to wring him once more by the hand. Not an eye that looked on that scene was dry."

THE NORTH: PROSPERITY

✳

The coming of war brought prosperity to most sections of the Northern states. This area of the country had been suffering from a slight economic depression, which at first worsened after the Southern states left the Union and trade was disrupted.

The rush for army contracts gave rise to many new businesses. Uniform makers dotted the urban landscape. Others manufactured all sorts of leather goods—belts, knapsacks, percussion cap pouches, haversacks. In 1861 the government, as well as individual states, competed in European markets to purchase enough rifles to arm the volunteers. That year, the Springfield Arsenal in Massachusetts was able to provide only 1,200 weapons. Three years later, with wartime expansion in full bloom, the arsenal turned out 300,000 of its famous rifles.

Agriculture flourished even as tens of thousands of farmers left their fields and flocked to the Union colors. Even though Cyrus McCormick had invented his famous reaper before the war, its comparatively high cost had prevented most farmers from buying one. Farmhands continued to use hand scythes to cut wheat and corn. Still, the demand for food both for the army and for civilian workers in the cities stimulated American agriculture. President Abraham Lincoln appreciated its importance so much that he agreed with the creation of the Department of Agriculture as a cabinet-level agency.

This painting by N. C. Wyeth shows Cyrus McCormick watching the first public test of his new reaping machine in 1831. The high cost of such machines slowed their widespread use, but by 1865, as families moved west to claim new land, new technology allowed for quick westward expansion.

THE SOUTH: DESOLATION

The Civil War was fought in the South. Every state witnessed military or naval invasions and scores of skirmishes, actions, engagements, and battles. As a result, the region was simply wrecked. Economic and social dislocation was widespread. When Southern armies surrendered and were disbanded, there were no parades or welcome-home speeches. Regiments and batteries ceased to exist wherever they surrendered, and their men had to find their own way home. Returning veterans came home to find desolation. Many could not even find their families, who had fled or relocated ahead of advancing Federal armies. When General William T. Sherman destroyed Atlanta, its people had to move. Some returning veterans trying to locate their loved ones never found their prewar families.

Richmond's devastation in April 1865 is readily apparent in this Alexander Gardner photograph. Scenes such as this were all too common across the South. The war had been fought on Southern territory, and destruction of homes, factories, railroads, and farms was widespread.

Southern economic life was shattered beyond repair. The war freed the slaves and thus destroyed the South's economic underpinnings. The newly freed blacks had to compete with poor whites for land and labor, while former plantation owners found their way of life gone. Railroads were largely destroyed during the war. What rolling stock remained was generally in disrepair, its owners unable to buy parts until 1865. Telegraph lines had disappeared, and most river traffic had either been sunk or captured.

Most Southern cities had suffered severely. The core of Richmond burned in 1865, as did that of Charleston and Columbia, South Carolina. Atlanta had burned in 1864. Other cities were overcrowded with refugees from rural hinterlands who were desperately seeking food and shelter.

AN AMERICA TRANSFORMED

✳

The negative economic effects of the war on the North pale in comparison with the economic forces awakened during the conflict. In particular, the Republican-dominated Congress passed a number of laws that transformed America into a budding power to be reckoned with.

INCOME TAX

To help finance the war, Congress in 1861 enacted an income tax for the first time in American history. Revised in 1862, it taxed incomes between $600 and $10,000 per year at 3 percent and larger incomes at 5 percent. Many Americans would be touched by government bureaucracy for the first time. Prior to 1861 most citizens had contact only with the Post Office, the single government agency that mattered to the people.

GOVERNMENT BONDS

Another wartime idea was government-issued bonds that the average American could purchase. This wildly successful measure was introduced by Treasury Secretary Salmon P. Chase and foreshadowed similar measures adopted in the 20th century. Over $1.4 billion in revenue was generated during the war by the sale of these bonds.

CURRENCY

Two more financial measures survived and blossomed in postwar America. The Legal Tender Act of February 1862 authorized the government to

This 1895 cartoon illustrates the reaction of much of the public to increased income taxes in order for the government to balance its budget and dispense pension payments to Union veterans. The pension system was the largest single drain on the treasury during the decades following the Civil War.

begin printing paper money—the "greenbacks"—that would function in the same way as specie (coins). To be sure, there was some opposition to this bill; strict constructionists maintained that the Constitution allowed the government to "coin" money, not print it, but greenbacks soon became an economic staple. A year later, Lincoln signed into law the National Banking Act, which created an embryonic national banking system. This act eventually erased the prevalent system of state-issued banking notes and started the country on a more centralized system.

WESTWARD EXPANSION

The Homestead Act of May 1862 set the stage for western expansion after 1865. This measure allocated 160 acres to every family that settled on the land,

The Union Pacific railroad was built west from Council Bluffs, Iowa, and the Central Pacific was built east from Sacramento, California. On May 10, 1869, the two railroads met with great ceremony at Promontory Point, Utah, linking the West Coast with the Middle West and the East Coast.

made improvements, and remained for five years. According to one estimate, more than 200,000 people obtained free land during the westward movement.

A prewar goal was the construction of a transcontinental railroad. In the absence of Southern opposition, the Railroad Act became law in July 1862. In 1869 Promontory Point, Utah, witnessed the driving of the "golden spike" as the East and West coasts were linked by iron rails.

Of even more importance for the future was the passage of the Morrill Act. Long a dream of Vermont Representative Justin Morrill, this legislation set aside public land to be used for higher education in "agriculture and the mechanic arts." Since this public land lay in the Western states and territories, Eastern states choosing to participate could sell their land for capital to found universities. A few states took advantage of their newfound bonus right away and established schools in 1865. In the long run, schools like Penn State, Cornell, the University of Wisconsin, and Texas A&M were the result.

BUSINESS AND COMMERCE

All these laws helped transform America. The war itself created an atmosphere of business and commerce that showed how much money could be made by industrious individuals with drive and ambition. The tycoons who rose after the Civil War got their start during the conflict. John D. Rockefeller, Andrew Carnegie, J. P. Morgan, and Cornelius Vanderbilt, among others, rose to prominence on the crest of the forces unleashed by the war.

The Civil War did not cause the rise of industrial America. No great inventions came of the war effort. To

Andrew Carnegie (1835–1919) emigrated to America from Scotland in 1848 and by 1859 was a superintendent with the Pennsylvania Railroad. In 1872 he started the steel company that would create his great fortune. Believing that the duty of the rich was to distribute their excess wealth, he founded numerous philanthropic activities and funded public libraries throughout the English-speaking world.

In the 1850s "Commodore" Cornelius Vanderbilt (1794–1877) began investing in railroads, and in 1873 his New York Central railroad offered the first rail service from New York to Chicago.

be sure, suppliers developed better canning and packaging methods for the armed forces, steam warships took the place of sail-powered vessels, repeating rifles and cannon showed their killing power, and ironclad vessels began to replace wooden ships. But the Civil War did not produce inventions of the scale and importance of those produced by the two world wars.

Instead, the creation of larger-scale businesses, a decline in business ethics, and the evolution of social Darwinism all contributed to the postwar economic boom. In effect the Civil War was a watershed moment in American economic history because it destroyed Southern dominance in the federal government and allowed more progressive legislation to be passed, paving the way for the future of America.

The Civil War delayed the opening of the Massachusetts Institute of Technology in Boston from 1861 to 1865. A third of its income in its early years derived from the terms of the Morrill Land Grant Act. A leading institution for scientific education and research, MIT moved to Cambridge, Massachusetts, in 1916.

RECONSTRUCTION

✷

The short-term economic disaster to the South did not resolve itself as years went by. From 1860 to 1870 Southern agricultural and manufacturing capital declined by 46 percent. The South's share of the national wealth declined from 30 percent to just 12 percent.

THE CHANGE IN AGRICULTURAL LABOR

The major reason for all of this was the widespread economic dislocation across the South. The freeing of the slaves meant that the prewar labor system had to be revamped. The Southern answer was twofold. Sharecropping became the usual contract between landowner and laborer. In exchange for

In spite of increasing mechanization of American agriculture after the Civil War, many tasks still had to be done by hand. This scene, taken in the 1890s, shows black peanut pickers at work in Virginia. For many of the former slaves and their descendants, conditions were not much better than they were in 1861.

allowing freedmen to live on his land, the owner provided shelter and implements; the sharecropper then had to give the owner a percentage of the crops. The second was the crop lien system, which occurred if the freedman owned his land. If he was too poor to buy implements and seeds, he obtained them on credit, which was usually secured by a share of his crops.

This new labor system enabled whites to control the movements and economic well-being of the former slaves. To further restrict blacks, Southern state governments eventually passed a number of black codes that evolved into "separate but equal" laws upheld by the Supreme Court in 1896.

GOVERNMENT REORGANIZATION

Initially Southerners were largely unrepentant over their military defeat. President Andrew Johnson allowed the defeated states to elect their own governments without Congressional help. When Congress reconvened

In this 1882 editorial cartoon, the New South is seen to be adopting industry as the future and leaving behind "King Cotton," the most lucrative crop in the Old South before 1861. Slavery and its one-crop dominance became a thing of the past; diversity and industry aided the growth of the New South.

in December 1865, it found that most Southern states had elected former Confederate officials; former Vice President Alexander H. Stephens was even one of the new congressmen.

As a result, the Republican-dominated Congress barred the new members and began a power struggle with President Johnson. The Radicals dominated Congress and dealt harshly with the former Confederacy. To qualify for readmission to the Union, state constitutions had to be written to include the 13th and 14th amendments. Blacks, with military backing, were encouraged to vote, and some were elected to high office.

Thomas Nast caricatured Carl Schurz, Republican senator from Missouri from 1869 to 1875, as a "carpetbagger" who could not see the bigger carpetbag, the one containing his own faults. Schurz, a strong supporter of black rights, was a harsh critic of the Republican Reconstruction policy.

CARPETBAGGERS AND SCALAWAGS

Northerners went south to make their fortunes and profit from the area's misfortune. Carpetbaggers, as these men were called, were aided by "scalawags"—native Southerners who cooperated with their oppressors. Assisted by elected blacks, the men running the state governments passed heavy tax laws without proper bases. There was widespread land confiscation, much corruption, voter fraud, and large-scale social unrest.

Union troops remained in the South until 1877, when the last of the garrisons were withdrawn. By this time, native Southerners had reclaimed most of their state governments and had begun to pass the oppressive laws that restricted black civil rights until the 1960s. The Republican Party abandoned Southern blacks to their fate.

POLITICAL FORTUNES OF THE SOUTH

For the next 50 years, the South's political power was insignificant. Slaveholding men had been president of the United States for 49 years of the nation's first 72 years prior to 1861. In Congress 23 of the 36 speakers of the House had been Southern. The Supreme Court counted 20 of 35 justices as Southern-born.

The war changed the power structure. For the 50 years after 1865, none of the speakers of the House or presidents pro tem of the Senate came from the South. Only five of 26 Supreme Court justices were Southern-born. Presidents of the United States were Northerners until the 1912 election of Woodrow Wilson, who was born in Virginia.

In the early days of the republic, two divergent views were held of America's future. Thomas Jefferson held the agricultural view, looking toward yeoman farmers tilling their fields with minimum interference from cities, factories, and the federal government. Alexander Hamilton, on the other hand, held that a strong central government and strong manufacturing interests would enable the United States to grow into an economic superpower. To some, the Civil War settled the direction that America would take. The Northern military victory in 1865 insured that Jefferson's ideal of an agrarian nation gave way to Hamilton's ideal of the rise of an industrial power.

THE CIVIL WAR?

Although the term "Civil War" is generally accepted by the public as the name of the conflict in America from 1861 to 1865, the war has had other names. When the government began publishing the official records in the 1880s, it decided to use "War of the Rebellion" to denote the conflict. To Southerners, it was (and still is) the "War of Northern Aggression" or the "War for Southern Independence"—or to some, "the Late Unpleasantness." Some Yankees called it the "War for the Preservation of the Union" or the "War of Secession." Earlier this century, the term "War Between the States" was accepted as an alternate name. But "Civil War" continues to be the popular designation for the conflict.

UNION VETERANS

✴

*E*ven though the Federal army was huge, not all Northern men and boys joined the military. Most did not, and when the troops returned home in 1865, not everyone welcomed them with open arms. Many employers believed that army life corrupted the soldiers with alcohol, prostitutes, swearing, and general abrasiveness. Veterans found themselves out of jobs and discriminated against when they tried to find work. For the thousands of maimed ex-soldiers, life was even tougher.

THE GAR

As a result, the veterans banded together in fraternal and political organizations. The largest and most influential of these was the Grand Army of the Republic (GAR). Founded in 1866 by Benjamin F. Stephenson, John A. Logan, and Richard J. Oglesby, the GAR promoted veterans' benefits, aided needy soldiers and their widows, and encouraged public allegiance to the

Above: *In 1936 90-year-old Captain R. D. Parker played the drum in the final parade of the remaining members of the GAR in Washington.* Right: *These two former Union soldiers enjoyed a friendly game of cards at the 75th-anniversary encampment at Gettysburg in 1938.*

In this scene from the 1938 Memorial Day parade in New York City, surviving GAR members press forward, undaunted by age and infirmities. Relics of a bygone era, they were still, nevertheless, honored by their countrymen for their past deeds.

Veterans of the Hawkins Zouaves (9th New York Infantry) at the 1922 New York Memorial Day parade. The soldiers at the right are wearing the distinctive baggy trousers of the Zouave uniform.

VETERANS' PENSIONS

Returning Union veterans clamored for government assistance to offset the losses caused by the war. Thousands of men were maimed for life by loss of arms or legs, while thousands more were racked by debilitating diseases. Although Congress had passed a simple bill in 1862 to provide for such cases, it was not enough.

Congress tinkered with pension legislation for decades. An arrears bill passed in 1868 made disability awards retroactive to date of discharge. A second such bill was passed in 1879; a year later more than 130,000 new claims for pensions besieged the Pension Office.

One-third of Congress was composed of former veterans who sympathized with their less fortunate comrades. As a result, pension laws became more and more liberal—and open to fraud. Even the GAR pension committee admitted that the 1890 act "was calculated to place upon the pension rolls all survivors of the war whose conditions of health are not practically perfect." Between 1879 and 1924, veterans and their dependents received $5.7 trillion.

Former Confederate veterans received state-sponsored pensions for their services during the Civil War. The veterans are all gone, of course, but today a handful of offspring of Civil War veterans continue to draw compensation from the government.

government. The GAR organized local posts that used a system of ritual and secrecy. The posts were organized into departments, with a national convention each year. By 1890, membership totaled more than 400,000 veterans.

The GAR used its considerable political clout with effectiveness. All presidents through 1900 courted the GAR or risked its wrath. When President Grover Cleveland vetoed some pension legislation and had the nerve to suggest during his first term in office (1885–1889) returning captured Confederate battle flags to the South, the GAR withdrew its support, and he was defeated for reelection.

Among the accomplishments of the GAR was the establishment of Decoration (now Memorial) Day as a national holiday, the passage of liberal pension bills that benefitted all Union veterans and cost the government more

More than 17,000 Union soldiers are buried at Vicksburg National Cemetery in Vicksburg National Military Park in Mississippi. The Confederate soldiers are buried in a cemetery in the town of Vicksburg.

than $1 billion by 1900, patriotic exercises in public schools (including the adoption of the Pledge of Allegiance), and use of proper history textbooks in schools. The GAR conventions ceased in 1949, when only 16 members still lived. Albert Woolson, the last Union veteran, died in 1956.

OTHER UNION GROUPS

Another prominent group was the Military Order of the Loyal Legion of the United States, which was formed by a group of Union officers in April 1865. Membership was limited to former officers, their descendants, and their collateral descendants. The various state commanders eventually published more than 60 volumes of wartime reminiscences of their members and established a library in Philadelphia that is now the Civil War Library and Museum. MOLLUS continues to recruit new members and has shown increased membership in recent years.

Other Union groups included the Sons of Union Veterans, Daughters of Union Veterans, and the Union Veterans Legion. These organizations published a number of newspapers and magazines, the most prominent of which was the *National Tribune*, the unofficial voice of the GAR. This paper started as a monthly pension sheet in 1877, began weekly publication in 1881, and continues today as the *Stars and Stripes*. A host of other publications included the *Grand Army Review*, *Grand Army Scout and Soldiers Mail*, *American Tribune*, and *Blue and Gray*.

Reenacting Civil War battles and camp life has become a big business in America. A series of 125th anniversary battles (1986–1990) drew thousands of men and women from around the world to the battle sites. The 1988 Gettysburg reenactment involved more than 12,000 reenactors— infantry, cavalry, artillery, and civilians.

CONFEDERATE VETERANS

✦

*T*he postwar tribulations of former Confederate soldiers were similar to those suffered by their Yankee counterparts. And although Union veterans eventually received the largesse of pension benefits from Congress, their erstwhile foes were not totally forgotten. The former Confederate states eventually passed pension laws to aid impoverished and disabled Confederate veterans, and Congress passed pension legislation for Confederate veterans around 1930.

In 1889 representatives of several state veterans' groups met in New Orleans and established the United Confederate Veterans. Local posts were

In June 1917 Confederate veterans convened in Washington, D.C., for their annual reunion. A group from Texas, marching in one of the parades, proudly displayed both the American and Confederate flags.

called camps, which eventually totaled more than 1,800, with some 160,000 members overall. The UCV held annual meetings from 1890 to 1951, when only three members were able to attend. Pleasant Crump, the last Confederate veteran, died in 1951.

UCV camps functioned at the local level, lobbying for pensions for veterans and widows, raising money for monuments, and encouraging its view of the Civil War as opposed to the Northern view of the conflict. Former general Clement L. Evans, supported by UCV money, edited the 12-volume *Confederate Military History* in 1899.

The official voice of Southern veterans was the magazine *Confederate Veteran*, which was published from 1893 through 1932. This monthly magazine contained biographies, memoirs, obituaries, monument news, UCV news, and information on the South in general. Other Southern veterans' organizations included the Sons of Confederate Veterans and the United Daughters of the Confederacy, both still in existence and doing well.

In another scene from the June 1917 reunion, Virginia Confederates march with their old rifles, reproduction uniforms, and assistance from the United Daughters of the Confederacy. Note the veteran with an artificial leg on the left.

THE ULTIMATE SYMBOL OF REUNION

Joseph E. Johnston

During the Civil War, Major General William T. Sherman led the Union armies that advanced on and captured Atlanta in September 1864. Sherman's opponent, at least until he was relieved in July, was General Joseph E. Johnston. The two men had both been present at the battle of Bull Run (First Manassas), and their soldiers fired at each other in the waning days of the Vicksburg campaign, but they had never met prior to the 1864 Atlanta campaign.

Following the cessation of hostilities, the two opponents became cordial friends. Sherman died on February 14, 1891. During the funeral, his old friend Joe Johnston walked as an honorary pallbearer. It was pouring rain that day, but Johnston, in a show of tribute, stood bareheaded during the service. Younger men urged the old veteran to put his hat on and protect himself. Nonsense, replied the general. If the situation had been reversed, Sherman would not have put his hat on either. Johnston died of pneumonia on March 21.

William T. Sherman

CIVIL WAR TIME LINE

✯

1861

Blockade runner

Fort Sumter

(Lincoln's inauguration image top-left)

Lincoln's inauguration

JANUARY

9 Mississippi secedes from the Union
10 Florida secedes from the Union
11 Alabama secedes from the Union
19 Georgia secedes from the Union
26 Louisiana secedes from the Union
29 Kansas is admitted to the Union

FEBRUARY

1 Texas secedes from the Union
4 Secession states begin convention in Montgomery, Alabama
8 Montgomery convention adopts Constitution for a provisional Confederate government
18 Jefferson Davis inaugurated as provisional President of the Confederacy

MARCH

4 Abraham Lincoln inaugurated as president of the United States
6 Confederacy calls for 100,000 volunteers for the provisional army
11 Permanent Confederate Constitution adopted

APRIL

12 South Carolina militia opens fire on Fort Sumter in Charleston Harbor, South Carolina
13 Fort Sumter surrenders
15 Lincoln declares state of insurrection; calls for 75,000 military volunteers
17 Virginia State Convention passes secession ordinance
19 Lincoln calls for blockade of Southern ports

MAY

3 Lincoln calls for 42,000 three-year volunteers
6 Arkansas secedes from the Union
6 Tennessee secedes from the Union
13 Britain proclaims its neutrality
16 Confederate Congress authorizes recruiting of 400,000 volunteers
20 North Carolina secedes from the Union
20 Kentucky proclaims its neutrality
20 Confederate Congress votes to move capital to Richmond, Virginia
23 Citizens of Virginia vote to join the Confederacy
24 Federal troops occupy Alexandria, Virginia
28 Brigadier General Irvin McDowell appointed commander of Federal Department of Northeastern Virginia

JUNE

3 Battle of Philippi, western Virginia (Union victory)
10 Battle of Big Bethel, Virginia (Confederate victory)
11 Western Virginia organizes a pro-Union government

JULY

11 Battle of Rich Mountain, western Virginia (Union victory)

21 First Battle of Bull Run (Manassas), Virginia (Confederate victory)

27 Major General George B. McClellan replaces McDowell in command of Federal troops around Washington

AUGUST

10 Battle of Wilson's Creek, Missouri (Confederate victory)

SEPTEMBER

3 Confederate forces enter Kentucky

10 General Albert S. Johnston awarded command of Confederate armies in the West

11 Battle of Cheat Mountain, western Virginia (Union victory)

OCTOBER

21 Battle of Ball's Bluff, Virginia (Confederate victory)

NOVEMBER

1 McClellan named general in chief of Federal armies

6 Jefferson Davis elected to six-year term as President of the Confederacy

1862

JANUARY

19–20 Battle of Mill Springs, Kentucky (Union victory)

FEBRUARY

6 Federal capture of Fort Henry, Tennessee

8 Federal capture of Roanoke Island, North Carolina

15 Federal capture of Fort Donelson, Tennessee

22 Jefferson Davis inaugurated

25 Federals occupy Nashville, Tennessee

MARCH

7–8 Battle of Pea Ridge, Arkansas (Union victory)

9 Battle of the USS *Monitor* and the CSS *Merrimack*

11 Major General Henry Halleck named commander of all Federal troops in the West

11 McClellan removed as general in chief but remains as commander of the Army of the Potomac

13 Robert E. Lee is charged with the conduct of Confederate military operations

14 Federal capture of New Madrid, Missouri

17 McClellan begins Peninsula campaign

23 Battle of Kernstown, Virginia (Union victory); beginning of "Stonewall" Jackson's Shenandoah Valley campaign

28 Battle of La Glorietta Pass, New Mexico (Union victory)

APRIL

5 Federal siege of Yorktown, Virginia, begins

6–7 Battle of Shiloh, Tennessee (Union victory)

First Battle of Bull Run (Manassas)

Jefferson's inauguration

The Monitor *and the* Merrimack

Robert E. Lee

Ulysses S. Grant and his generals

Union occupation of Memphis

8   Federal capture of Island No. 10, Missouri

11   Federal capture of Fort Pulaski, Georgia

16   First Confederate Conscription Act; called for draft of men 18 to 35

25   Federal capture of New Orleans, Louisiana

MAY

3   Siege of Yorktown, Virginia, ends with Confederate Rebel retreat

5   Battle of Williamsburg, Virginia (Confederate victory)

8   Battle of McDowell, Virginia (Confederate victory)

12   Federals capture Baton Rouge, Louisiana

25   First battle of Winchester, Virginia (Confederate victory)

31–June 1   Battle of Fair Oaks (Seven Pines), Virginia (outcome inconclusive)

31   Robert E. Lee appointed to the command of the Confederate army he will soon rename the Army of Northern Virginia

JUNE

6   Federals occupy Memphis, Tennessee

8   Battle of Cross Keys, Virginia (Confederate victory)

9   Battle of Port Republic, Virginia (Confederate victory)

12–15   Confederate Brigadier General Jeb Stuart rides around Federal army

16   Battle of Secessionville, South Carolina

25   Battle of Oak Grove, Virginia, which begins the Seven Days' Campaign (each battle ultimately becoming a Confederate victory)

26   Battle of Mechanicsville, Virginia

27   Battle of Gaines' Mill, Virginia

27   General Braxton Bragg named commander of the Confederate Army of Tennessee

29   Battle of Savage's Station, Virginia

30   Battle of Frayser's Farm, Virginia

JULY

1   Battle of Malvern Hill, Virginia; end of the Seven Days' Campaign

1   Lincoln calls for 300,000 three-year volunteers

11   Halleck becomes general in chief of Federal armies

16   Major General Ulysses S. Grant named commander of Army of West Tennessee

AUGUST

4   Lincoln calls for 300,000 nine-months militia

9   Battle of Cedar Mountain, Virginia (Confederate victory)

28   Battle of Groveton, Virginia (Confederate victory)

28   Confederate Army of Tennessee, commanded by Braxton Bragg, begins campaign into Tennessee and Kentucky

29–30   Second Battle of Bull Run (Manassas), Virginia (Confederate victory)

SEPTEMBER

1 Battle of Chantilly, Virginia (Confederate victory)

4 Lee crosses the Potomac River into Maryland, beginning his first invasion of the North

5 McClellan resumes command of the Army of the Potomac

14 Battle of South Mountain, Maryland (Union victory)

15 "Stonewall" Jackson captures Harpers Ferry, western Virginia

17 Battle of Antietam (Sharpsburg), Maryland (Union victory)

19 Lee withdraws into Virginia

19 Battle of Iuka, Mississippi (Union victory)

22 Lincoln issues Preliminary Emancipation Proclamation

OCTOBER

3–4 Battle of Corinth, Mississippi (Union victory)

8 Battle of Perryville, Kentucky (outcome inconclusive)

NOVEMBER

1 Federals launch campaign for Vicksburg, Mississippi

7 Major General Ambrose Burnside replaces McClellan as commander of the Federal Army of the Potomac

DECEMBER

13 Battle of Fredericksburg, Virginia (Confederate victory)

27–29 Battle of Chickasaw Bayou, Mississippi (Confederate victory)

31–Jan. 2, 1863 Battle of Stones River (Murfreesboro), Tennessee (outcome inconclusive)

1863

JANUARY

1 Lincoln signs the Emancipation Proclamation

26 Major General Joseph Hooker replaces Burnside as commander of the Army of the Potomac

MARCH

3 Federal Congress passes the Conscription Act

APRIL

2 Bread riots begin in Richmond, Virginia

MAY

1 Battle of Port Gibson, Mississippi (Union victory)

1–4 Battle of Chancellorsville, Virginia (Confederate victory)

10 Death of "Stonewall" Jackson

12 Battle of Raymond, Mississippi (Union victory)

16 Battle of Champion's Hill, Mississippi (Union victory)

17 Battle of Big Black River Bridge, Mississippi (Union victory)

19 Federal attack on Vicksburg fails

21 Federals begin siege of Port Hudson, Mississippi

22 Second attack on Vicksburg fails; Federal siege of Vicksburg begins

JUNE

3 Lee begins his second invasion of the North

The Emancipation Proclamation

The siege of Vicksburg

General George B. McClellan

Pickett's Charge at Gettysburg

General Joseph E. Johnston

9 Battle of Brandy Station, Virginia (Union victory)

14–15 Second Battle of Winchester, Virginia (Confederate victory)

20 West Virginia becomes 35th state

28 Confederates capture York, Pennsylvania

28 Major General George G. Meade replaces Hooker as commander of the Federal Army of the Potomac

JULY

1–3 Battle of Gettysburg, Pennsylvania (Union victory)

4 Vicksburg, Mississippi, surrenders to the Federals

8 Federals capture Port Hudson; Mississippi River now completely under Federal control

13–16 New York City draft riots

14 Lee recrosses the Potomac River, ending his second and last invasion of the North

18 Battle of Fort Wagner, South Carolina

AUGUST

21 Confederate raiders under William Quantrill sack Lawrence, Kansas

SEPTEMBER

2 Federal troops occupy Knoxville, Tennessee

8 Battle of Sabine Pass, Texas (Confederate victory)

9 Federal troops occupy Chattanooga, Tennessee

19–20 Battle of Chickamauga, Georgia (Confederate victory)

23 Confederates begin siege of Chattanooga, Tennessee

OCTOBER

14 Battle of Bristoe Station, Virginia (Union victory)

16 Grant named commander of Federal forces in the West

27 Grant lifts siege of Chattanooga, Tennessee

NOVEMBER

19 Lincoln's Gettysburg Address

23–25 Battle of Chattanooga, Tennessee (Union victory)

26–December 1 Federal Mine Run Campaign, Virginia

29 Battle of Fort Sandars, Knoxville, Tennessee; Confederate forces driven from the state

DECEMBER

27 General Joseph Johnston replaces General Braxton Bragg as commander of the Confederate Army of Tennessee

1864

FEBRUARY

3 William T. Sherman begins Meridian Campaign in Mississippi

9 Mass escape of Federal officers from Libby Prison in Richmond, Virginia

20 Battle of Olustee, Florida (Confederate victory)

28–March 3 Federal cavalry raid on Richmond, Virginia, fails

MARCH

9 Grant promoted to rank of lieutenant general

10 Federals begin Red River campaign in Louisiana

12 Grant named general in chief of Federal armies

18 Major General William T. Sherman assumes command of Federal armies in the West

APRIL

12 Confederates capture Federal garrison at Fort Pillow, Tennessee; massacre black troops

17 Grant halts prisoner exchanges

MAY

4 Grant's Army of the Potomac crosses the Rapidan River into Virginia

5–6 Battle of the Wilderness, Virginia (outcome inconclusive)

7 Sherman begins Atlanta Campaign

8–18 Battle of Spotsylvania Court House, Virginia (outcome inconclusive)

11 Battle of Yellow Tavern, Virginia (Union victory)

12 Death of Jeb Stuart

14–15 Battle of Resaca, Georgia (Union victory)

15 Battle of New Market, Virginia (Confederate victory)

23–26 Battle of the North Anna River, Virginia (outcome inconclusive)

25–June 4 Federal Campaign of New Hope Church, Georgia (outcome inconclusive)

JUNE

1–3 Battle of Cold Harbor, Virginia (Confederate victory)

8 Lincoln nominated for a second term as President by Republicans

10 Battle of Brice's Crossroads, Mississippi (Confederate victory)

12 Battle of Trevilian Station, Virginia (Confederate victory)

15–18 Federal assault against Petersburg, Virginia, fails

18 Federal siege of Petersburg begins

19 Confederate raider Alabama sunk by USS *Kearsarge* off Cherbourg, France

22 Battle of Weldon Railroad, Virginia (Confederate victory)

27 Battle of Kennesaw Mountain, Georgia (Confederate victory)

JULY

6 Confederate Lieutenant General Jubal A. Early invades Maryland

9 Battle of Monocacy, Maryland (Confederate victory)

11–12 Early reaches outskirts of Washington but is forced to retreat

17 General John B. Hood replaces Johnston as commander of Army of Tennessee

20 Battle of Peachtree Creek, Georgia (Union victory)

22 Battle of Atlanta, Georgia (Union victory)

28 Battle of Ezra Church, Georgia (Union victory)

30 Battle of the Crater, Virginia (Confederate victory)

Fort Pillow massacre

Battle of Spotsylvania

Cartoon for 1864 election

Battle of Cedar Creek

Sherman's March to the Sea

AUGUST

5 Battle of Mobile Bay, Alabama (Union victory)

7 Major General Philip Sheridan assumes command of Federal troops in the Shenandoah Valley

21 Battle of Globe Tavern, Virginia (Union victory)

31 George McClellan nominated for President by Democratic party

31–September 1 Battle of Jonesborough, Georgia (Union victory)

SEPTEMBER

1 Confederates evacuate Atlanta, Georgia

2 Federals occupy Atlanta, Georgia

19 Third Battle of Winchester, Virginia (Union victory)

22 Battle of Fisher's Hill, Virginia (Union victory)

OCTOBER

5 Battle of Allatoona, Georgia (Union victory)

6 Federals begin destruction of Shenandoah Valley

19 Battle of Cedar Creek, Virginia (Union victory)

19 Confederate force from Canada raids St. Albans, Vermont

23 Battle of Westport, Missouri (Union victory)

27 Battle of Hatcher's Run, Virginia (Confederate victory)

31 Nevada admitted to the Union

NOVEMBER

8 Lincoln reelected President

15 Sherman begins March to the Sea after burning Atlanta

21 Confederate General John B. Hood begins Tennessee campaign

30 Battle of Franklin, Tennessee (Union victory)

DECEMBER

13 Federals capture Fort McAllister, Georgia; Sherman reaches the sea

15–16 Battle of Nashville, Tennessee (Union victory)

21 Federals occupy Savannah, Georgia

1865

JANUARY

13 Hood resigns command of the Army of Tennessee

15 Federals capture Fort Fisher, outside Wilmington, North Carolina, thereby closing the last Confederate port

19 Sherman marches into South Carolina

31 Federal Congress submits 13th Amendment abolishing slavery to states for ratification

FEBRUARY

1 Sherman begins the invasion of the Carolinas

3 Lincoln and Secretary of State William Seward meet with a Confederate delegation including Vice President Alexander Stephens, Assistant Secretary of War John Campbell, and Senator Robert M. T. Hunter; the conference fails to produce results

6	Robert E. Lee named general in chief of all Confederate armies
17	Federals occupy Columbia, South Carolina
18	Federals occupy Charleston, South Carolina
22	Federals occupy Wilmington, North Carolina
22	General Joseph Johnston reinstated as commander of the Confederate Army of Tennessee

MARCH

4	Lincoln inaugurated for his second term
13	Confederate Congress authorizes the use of slaves as troops
16	Battle of Averasboro, North Carolina (Union victory)
19	Battle of Bentonville, North Carolina (Union victory)
25	Battle of Fort Stedman, Virginia (Union victory)
28	Lincoln discusses terms for peace with Grant and Sherman

APRIL

1	Battle of Five Forks, Virginia (Union victory)
2	Petersburg, Virginia, falls to Federals
2	Confederate government flees Richmond
3	Federals occupy Richmond
4	Lincoln visits Richmond
6	Battle of Sayler's Creek, Virginia (Union victory)
7	Lee and Grant open discussions for surrender
9	Lee surrenders the Confederate Army of Northern Virginia at Appomattox Court House, Virginia
12	Federals capture Montgomery, Alabama
12	Federals occupy Mobile, Alabama
13	Federals occupy Raleigh, North Carolina
14	Federal flag raised over Fort Sumter
14	Lincoln shot by John Wilkes Booth
15	Lincoln dies and is succeeded by Andrew Johnson
18	Johnston and Sherman sign broad armistice agreement
21	President Johnson and his cabinet disapprove the Johnston-Sherman armistice
26	Johnston surrenders Army of Tennessee to Sherman near Durham Station, North Carolina
26	John Wilkes Booth killed by Federal troops
26	Confederate cabinet meets for last time at Charlotte, North Carolina

MAY

10	Jefferson Davis captured by Federal troops at Irwinsville, Georgia
10	President Johnson declares rebellion at an end; partially lifts blockade of Southern ports
12–13	Battle of Palmito Ranch, near Brownsville, Texas; last engagement of the war (Confederate victory)
23–24	Grand Review of Federal armies in Washington

The McLean house at Appomattox Court House

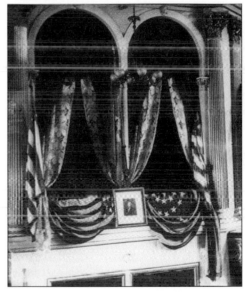

Lincoln's booth at Ford's Theatre

INDEX

Page numbers in italics refer to illustrations.

Abolitionists, 21–23, 26, *27,* 54.
Agriculture, 290–91; cotton (*see* Cotton); food crops, 66, 72, 236, 238–39; rice, 16–17; sugarcane, 17; tobacco, 16; wheat, 238, *239. See also* Plantation life.
Alabama, CSS, *160,* 161
Alabama State House, *37*
Alaska, 63
Albemarle, CSS, 169
Alcott, Louisa May, 271
Allegheny Arsenal, 274–75
Allison, Alexander, 228
Allison, Charles, 123
Ambulances, 81, *191, 197*
American Colonization Society, 21
American Red Cross, 269–70
Ammunition. *See* Warfare, technology of; Weapons manufacturing.
Amputations, *186,* 192. *See also* Medical care.
Anaconda Plan, 105
Anderson, Robert, 30–31, *224,* 225
Andersonville, prison at, 123, *126,* 127
Antietam, battle of, *44,* 90, 134, *269,* 274–275
Appomattox Court House, surrender at, 96, 101, 110, *280–81,* 283
Armies, burial of dead of, 196; camp life of, *142–44,* 145, *146–49;* cemeteries for, *296;* exchange of goods between, 145, 148; generals of, 87–101, *102–103* (*see also* Political generals; *specific generals*); and newspapers, 213; numbers of casualties of, 204–5; ordnance production for, 84–85 (*see also* Weapons manufacturing); pay of, 138, 234, 250; prisoners of, *see* Prisons; recruiting for, *32–34,* 35, *38, 56,* 133, 205, *243,* 244, *245,* 247; supply wagons of, *110;* uniforms of, *see* Uniforms. *See also specific battles;* Warfare, technology of.
Arsenals, women employed in, 274–75
Artists, 226–31. *See also specific artists.*
Association of Army and Navy Surgeons, 194
Atlanta, battle of, *48,* 49, 100, *107,* 285, 299
Atlanta, CSS, *158*
Auctions, slave, *10–11, 24, 26, 54*

Baker, Mrs. E. H., 256–57
Balloons, observation, 164–65, 170, *210*
Ball's Bluff, battle of, 234
"Barbara Frietchie" (Whittier), 275
Barnard, George N., 221–22
Baron de Kalb, USS, *152*
Barry, Major (Union), 140

Barton, Clara, *269–270*
Beauregard, Pierre G. T., 31, *53, 98,* 100, 225
Beecher, Henry Ward, *22*
Belle Isle, prison at, 126
Benjamin, Judah P., *64–65,* 75
Bickerdyke, Mary Ann Ball, *270*
Blacks, 21, 277; in Confederate army, *118–19,* 121, 243; elected to office, 291–92; in Federal army, *114–17,* 204; freed, *29, 252,* 285, *290,* 291; laws restricting civil rights of, 22, 291–92; living in North, 21–22, 247, 249; soldiers, massacres of, 119. *See also* Slavery.
Blaylock, Sarah, 266
Blockade, Federal, 58, *76,* 77, 160–61, 104; effect of, on Southern economy, 19, 57, 72, 74–75, 77, 109, 236–37
Bloody Angel battle, *97*
Bomb shelters, *176, 178, 179*
Bonaparte, Napoleon, *177*
Bonds, sale of, 68–69, 71, 286. *See also* Money.
Booth, John Wilkes, 282
Boston Harbor, *13*
Bounties, volunteer, 244–45, 247, 250
Boyd, Belle, *261*
Brady, Mathew B., *220–221,* 225
Bragg, Braxton, 100, 148, 258
Breckinridge, John C., 42, 61
Brown, John, 22, *23*
Brownell, Kady, *264*
Brown's Island, explosion at, 279
Buchanan, James, 30, *40–41,* 260
Buford, John, 204
Bugle, Union, *130*
Bull Run, battle of (First Manassas), 70, *86–87,* 88, 98, 106, 119, 140, 214, 260, 269, 299
Burnside, Ambrose E., 44, 57, *90,* 91, 177, 218
Burnside carbine, 165
Butler, Benjamin F., 46, 166

Cabinets, Presidential. *See* Davis, Jefferson; Lincoln, Abraham.
Calhoun, John C., 263
Cameron, Simon, 43, 62
Camp Chase, 123
Camp Morton, 123
Canadian recruits, 133
Cannon, 85, 166, *167–168, 180*
Carbines, 165, *167*
Carnegie, Andrew, *288*
Carte de visite photograph, 222–23
Carter, Jimmy, 277
Cashier, Albert (alias), 264

Casualties, numbers of, 204–5
Cedar Creek, battle of, 49, *229*
Chancellorsville, battle of, 93
Chandler, Zachariah, 59
Chaplains, military, *144*
Chapman, Conrad Wise, *147, 170, 230*–31
Charleston, burning of, 285
Charleston Harbor, *30,* 31
Chase, Salmon P., 43, 48, *63, 70,* 71, 240, 286
Chattanooga, battle of, 78, 95, 198
Chesnut, Mary, 31, 39, 69, *72*
Chevaux-de-frise obstacles, *178*
Chicago *Times,* 218
Chickamauga Creek, battle of, 100, *101,* 133, 197
Children recruits, 133, 168
Chimborazo Hospital, 198, 202, *203,* 273
Christian Commission, U.S., *201*
Civilian life, 233–53; displaced families, 236–37; effect of draft on, 242–43, 245, 247, 249–50; and election of 1864, 250–51; and food shortages, 234–37, 248, 252–53. *See also* Plantation life.
Civil rights, laws restricting, 22, 291–92
Civil War; alternative names for, 293; central issue of, 11, 36, 43; duration of, 128; economics of, 66–85, 71; end of, 252–53, 283; events leading up to, 11–39; important places of, *map 111;* legacy of, 281–99; reenactments of, *297*
Civil War Library and Museum, 297
Clarke, Amy, 266
Clem, Johnny, 133
Cleveland, Grover, 296
Cobb, Howell, 60, 118
Coffin, Charles, 227
Cold Harbor, battle of, 96
Colt, Samuel, 14; factory, *15*
Colt revolver, *167*
Columbia, burning of, 285
Combahee River, raid on, 277
Commodore Perry, USS, *153*
Communications, 133, 164, *169,* 257
Condor, CSS, 260
Confederacy, arms seized by, 38, 98, 160, 163; capital of, *37,* 52 (*see also* Richmond); Congress of, 53, *60,* 61, 68–69, 77, 113, 119, 203, 242–43; disagreement within, 39, 55; economy of, 19, 68–69, 138, 236–37, 285, 290–93; end of, 252–53; finances of, 68–69; food distribution of, 236; government of, 36, 53, 57, 64–65, 72, 108, 279; newspapers

Confederacy *(continued)*
of, 214; postwar, 290–93; president of, *see* Davis, Jefferson; principles of, 52, 54; rail system of, *see* Railroads; readmission of, to Union, 291; secession from Union by, 12, *16, 36*; ships seized by, 53; states of, *34*

Confederate army, 19, *38*, 55, 98, 108, 234, 235; soldiers of, 128, 133, 136–39, 141, 266–67; surrender of, 96, 101, 103, 110, *208, 280–81*; use of blacks by, *118–19*, 121, 243; war strategy of, 52, 108–10, 177

Confederate navy; blockade runners of, 77, 160–61; director of, 64–65

Confederate Ordnance Bureau, 85

Congress. *See* Confederacy, Congress of; Federal government, Congressional actions of.

Congress, USS, 158

Conkling, Roscoe, 14, 70

Contrabands, *114*

Cook, George S., 224–25

Cooke, Jay, 71

Cooke, John Esten, 231

Cooks, company, 145

Copperheads, *45*

Corps of Engineers, *169*

Corps of Topographical Engineers, *169*

Cotton, *14, 94, 25, 29, 216*; demise of, 72, 291; gin, *16*, 17, *18*; impact of war on, 74–75, 109; plantation, painting of, *66–67*; Southern dependence on, 17, *18–19*

Counterfeiting, money, 69

Cox's Mills, battle of, 162

Crane, William T., 209

"Crater, the," 177, 180

Crisis, 218

Crop lien system, 291

Cumberland, USS, 158

Cumberland River, Union control of, 80

Cushing, William, 169

Cushman, Pauline, 257, *258*

Custer, George A., *44*

Daguerre, Louis, 220

Dahlgren, John A., *167*, 171

Dahlgren gun, 165, *167*

Daughters of Union Veterans, 297

David, CSS, *171*

"David" torpedo boats, 171–72, *230*

Davis, Jefferson, 31, 36, 40, 50–52, 54–55, 57, 60–61, 87, 98–101, 103, 108–10, 113, 118, 127, 205, 233, 242, 248, 260, 263, 272; cabinet of, *64*, 65; cartoons of, *38, 49, 53, 55*;

Davis, Jefferson *(continued)*
executive mansion of, *50*; inauguration of, *37*, 82; wife of, *see* Davis, Varina Howell.

Davis, Theodore R., 209

Davis, Varina Howell, *51*, 108, *263*

Day, Francis, 265

Declaration of Secession, 36

Decoration Day, 296

DeLeon, David C., 194

Democratic party; cartoon depiction of, *52*; and Lincoln, 43, 46, 48, 56, 59; platform of, 251. *See also* Peace Democrats; War Democrats.

"Dictator" mortar, *168*

Dill, Benjamin F., 219

Dimmock, Charles H., 180

Dix, Dorothea, *268*

Douglass, Frederick, *27*, 29, 116–17

Draft, 53, 112–13, 236, 242–45, *246*, 247, 249

Drugs, production of, 197; substitutes for, 196–98. *See also* Medical care.

Drum, Union, *131*

Drummer boys, *133*

Durham Station, surrender at, 98

Eads, James B., 152–54

Early, Jubal, 49, 188, *229*, 267

Edmonds, Sarah Emma, 258, *259*

Edmondson, Belle, 261

Edwards, J. D., 224

Elections, of 1864, 250–51; of Jefferson Davis, 36; postwar, 102; wartime, 42, 46–49

Ellsworth, Elmer, 35

Elmira, prison at, *120, 122*

Emancipation Proclamation, 47, 59, 73

Enfield rifle, 163

Engineers, Corps of, *169*

England, 74–75, 163, 214

Enlistment, military. *See* Armies, recruiting for.

Enrollment Act of 1863, 112, 244–45

Ericsson, John, 156

Erie Canal, *12*

Europe, purchase of cotton by, 109

Evans, Clement L., 299

Farm workers, 236, 238, 284, 290, *290*, 291

Farragut, David, 160

Federal government, ban on slavery by, 24 (*see also* Slavery); centralization of power of, 56; Congressional actions of, 58–59, 70–71, 112, 114, 240–41, 244, 286–88, 291,

Federal government *(continued)*
296, 298; finances of, 70–71, 240–41, 286–87; media policy of, 209–10; Southern officials of, 292. *See also* Union; United States.

Ferryboats, *153*. *See also* Warfare, technology of.

Fitzpatrick, William, 265

Food. *See* Industry, food crops; Shortages, food.

Foote, Andrew H., 154

Foote, Henry S., 61

Forbes, Edwin, 209, 211, 234

Ford's Theatre, *282*

Fort Delaware, prison at, 123

Fort Donelson, battle of, *80*, 81, 89, 102, 152, 154, *229*

Fort Fisher, battle of, 157, 216–17

Fort Henry, battle of, 81, 89, 102, 154

Fort McAllister, battle of, 173

Fort Monroe, hospital at, *186*

Fort Pillow, battle of, *119*

Fort Sumter, battle of, *30–31*, 32, 36, *39*, 98, 225

Fort Wagner, battle of, 116, 117, *217*

Fraise, timber, *175*

Frank Leslie's Illustrated Newspaper, 55, *208–209*

Franklin, battle of, 100

Fredericksburg, battle of, *90–91*, *198*

Freedman's Bureau, 114

Frémont, John C., 48

Frietchie, Barbara, *275*

Galena, USS, *156–157*

Gardner, Alexander, 23, 45, 199, 205, 221, 285

Garrison, William Lloyd, *21*, 22

Gatling, Richard, *166*

Gatling gun, *166*

Gaul, Gilbert, 227–28

Gettysburg, battle of, 84, *92*, 93, *134, 185, 199*, 198 , 201, *204–205*, 229, *250*, 266; hospital at, *192*; reenactment of, *297*; veterans of, *294*

Goldsmith, Middleton, 193

Gorgas, Josiah, 85

Governors, states', 56–57

Grand Army of the Republic (GAR), 259, 264, 294–97

Grant, Ulysses S., 33, 47, 49, 80, 87, *92–95*, *97*, *102*, 103, *106*, 107, 117, 123, 157, 174, 177–81, 219, *229*, 283, 257, 270

Greenbacks, 71, 287. *See also* Money.

Greenhow, Rose O'Neal, *260*
Grenades, *173*
Guns. *See* Warfare, technology of.

H. L. Hunley, CSS, *170,* 172
Habeas corpus, suspension of, 52, 218
Halleck, Henry W., 90, 93, *95*
Hamilton, Alexander, 293
Hamlin, Hannibal, *43*
Hampton Roads, battle of, 158, *159*
Handguns, *167,* 190
Hardtack, 133, *134,* 138, *139*
Harpers Ferry, 22–23
Harper's Weekly, 208, 208–9, 226
Haupt, Herman, *78,* 79, 222
Haversack, *135*
Hawthorne, Julian, 34
Hawthorne, Nathaniel, 34
Hayes, Rutherford B., 35
Henry, Benjamin, 162
Henry, Patrick, 100
Henry rifles, 162
Hill, Benjamin H., *60,* 61
Hillen, John, 211
Hodgers, Jennie, 264
Hoge, Jane, 73
Holmes, Oliver Wendell, Jr., 135
Homer, Winslow, 209, 226–27
Homestead Act, 59, 241, 287–88
Hood, John Bell, *48,* 100–101
Hook, Frances, 265
Hooker, Joseph, *91,* 93
Horses, military use of, 81
Hospitals. *See* Medical care.
Hospital Sketches (Alcott), 271
Housatonic, USS, 170, *172*
Hunley, Horace L., 172
Hunter, Robert M. T., 65

Illustrated London News, 214, 216
Immigrants, 12, *33,* 46, *130,* 133, 239, 250
Indian soldiers, American, 204
Industry, banking, 241, 287 (*see also* Money); as ideal for nation, 293; manufacturing, 12, 14–16, 18, 53, 66, *84,* 85, 236, 239, 241, 274–75, 278–79, 284, 289; ordnance production, 84–85 (*see also* Weapons manufacturing); steel, 84
Inflation, 19, 138, 236–37
Intelligence. *See* Communications; Women, spies.
Intrepid balloon, 164, *165*
Invalid Corps, 188
Inventions. *See* Warfare, technology of.
Irish recruits, *33,* 46, *130,* 133
Ironclad ships. *See* Warfare, technology of.

Jackson, Thomas "Stonewall," 91, 261, 275
James Island, battle of, 117
James River Peninsula, campaign of, 89, 99, 103, 156
Jefferson, Thomas, 293
Johnson, Andrew, *58,* 277, 291
Johnson's Island, prison at, 123
Johnston, Joseph E., 96, 98–99, *100,* 101, 107, 118, *299*

Kansas, 23
Kearsarge, USS, 160, *161*
Kennesaw Mountain, battle of, *128–29*
Kentucky, 16, 34, 154
Knights of the Golden Circle (KGC), 44
Kurz, Louis, 228

Labor system, postwar Southern, 290–91
Lee, Harry "Light Horse", 103
Lee, Robert E., 47, 49, *64,* 87, 89–97, *91, 97, 99,* 101, *103,* 107, 110, 119, 174, 178, 180–81, 198, 214, 252, *280–81,* 283
Legal Tender Act, 59, 71, 240, 286–87
Lexington, battle of, 234
Libby Prison, *124,* 127, *224*
The Liberator journal, 21
Lillian, CSS, *215*
Lincoln, Abraham, 15, 20, 24, 30, 34, 35, 36, 39, 40–49, 52, 54, 58, 74, 78, 81, 87, 112, 153, 157, 196, 218, 233, 240, 241, 244, 262, 267, 275, 287; assassination of, 282; cabinet of, 62–63, *70,* 284; cartoons of, *49, 58;* as commander in chief, *44–45,* 46–47, 56, 88, 90–91, 93, 95, 102–4, 106, 174; and Congress, 58–59 (*see also* Federal government, Congressional actions of); elections of, 42, 48–49, *251;* political opposition to, 43–44, *45;* and Sanitary Commission, 73, 200
Lincoln, Mary Todd, 174, *262,* 282
Lincoln, Robert, 262
Lincoln, Willie, 262
Livermore, Mary, 32, 73
Logan, John A., 294
Longstreet, James, 216
Louisiana, 17, 27
Lovejoy, Rev. Elijah P., 22
Lovie, Henri, 209, 211
Lowe, Thaddeus, 164–65
Lumley, Arthur, 209–10

Mackenzie, Ranald, *33*
Maggots, medical use of, 198
Mallory, Stephen R., *64,* 65, 160
Manassas, first battle of. *See* Bull Run.
Manufacturing. *See* Industry.
Martial law, 58

Maryland, 34, 59, 108–9
Massachusetts, 54th Infantry Regiment, 115, *116–17*
Massachusetts Institute of Technology (MIT), *289*
Mayne, Frank (alias), 265
Mayo, Joseph, 248
McCallum, Daniel C., 81
McCaw, James B., 202–3
McClellan, George B., *44,* 46, *46,* 47, 49, 57, *88–89,* 89, 90, 99, 103, 106, 187, *251*
McCormick, Cyrus, *284*
McDowell, Irvin, 88, 106, 223
McLean, Wilmer, 283
McPherson, James B., 204
Meade, George G., 47, *92,* 93, 95, *96,* 107, 174, 177, 210–11
Medary, Samuel, 218
Medical care, 182–205; and camp diseases, 147–48, 187–88, 193–95, 204–5; evacuation of casualties, 197–98, *201;* examinations of troops, 186, 264; hospitals, *184–185, 187, 190–192,* 193–94, *195,* 198, 202, *203, 254–55,* 270, 272–73; knowledge of, 182, 193, 198; practioners of, 184–86, 188; and relief agencies, 73, 200–201; sanitation problems and, 186–87, 193; and shortages of supplies, 195–97; treatment for wounded, 192
Medical school, requirements of, 186
Meigs, Montgomery, 240
Memminger, Christopher G., *64,* 68–69, *279*
Memorial Day, 296
Memphis, battle of, *157, 216, 219*
Memphis *Appeal* newspaper, 219
Mendota, USS, *156*
Meredith, Minerva, 248
Merrimack, CSS, *150–51,* 154, 156, 158, *159. See also Virginia,* CSS.
Michigan, 131; 4th Infantry Regiment of, 131
Military Order of the Loyal Legion of the United States (MOLLUS), 297
Militia Draft Act, 244, 247
Milliken's Bend, battle of, 114
Mines, 169, 172–73
Minnesota, USS, 158–59
Missionary Ridge, battle of, 100
Mississippi, 263, 296
Mississippi River, battle for control of, 100, 104, 153–54, 157
Missouri, 34, 59
Mobile Bay, battle of, *157*
Money, Confederate, 68–69, 138, 237; Federal, 70–71, 240–41, 286–87
Monitor, USS, *150–51, 154–55,* 156, *159*
Moon, Lottie and Ginnie, 261

Moore, Samuel P., 194, 196–97, 202
Morgan, J. P., 288
Morrill Land Grant Act, 59, 288–89
Mosby, John, 188
"Mud March," Burnside's, 90–91
Musket, smoothbore, *167*, 190. *See also*
  Rifles.

Napoleonic strategy, 104, 177
Nashville, battle of, 101
Nast, Thomas, 24, 292
National Banking Act, 71, 287
New Orleans, 18–19; battle of, 267
News media, 207–31; army reaction to, 213;
  artists of, 209–14; censoring of, 218; inven-
  tions affecting, 207; newspapers, 208, *213*,
  214–19; photography, 138, 207, 213, 220–25;
  published artwork, 212–13; and veterans'
  organizations, 297, 299; weeklies, 208–10
New South, 290–93
New York Central railroad, 288
New York, *13, 33*, 208, 212, *249, 295;* 170th
  Infantry of, *130*
New York Herald, 212
New York Illustrated News, 208–9
New York *Journal of Commerce*, 218
New York *World*, 218
North Carolina, 57
North Star newspaper, 27
Nuns. *See* Women, nuns.
Nurses. *See* Women, nurses.

Observer newspaper, 22
Oglesby, Richard J., 294
Olmsted, Frederick Law, 200
Olustee, battle of, 117
O'Sullivan, Timothy, 199, 212, 221, 223

Peace Democrats, 43, 45
Pember, Phoebe Yates, 273
Pendleton, George H., *251*
Pennsylvania, 84
Pensions, veterans. *See* Veterans, pensions for.
Petersburg, battle of, 79, 96, 117, 119, *132*,
  166, 168, 173, 174, *175*, 176, 177, *178–80*,
  180, 181, *220*
Petersburg, prison at, *125*
Photography. *See* News media.
Pickens, Francis, *53*
Pickett's Charge, 93, 266
Pinkerton, Allan, *15, 256*
Pittsburgh, industry in, 84
Pittsburg Landing, battle of, 100
Plantation life, 24, *25, 26–29, 66–67. See also*
  Civilian life.
Pleasants, Henry, 177

Pledge of Allegiance, adoption of, 297
Political generals, 44, 46, 56
Politics, 40–65. *See also* Elections; *specific polit-
  ical parties.*
Pook, Samuel, 152
Pook Turtles, 152–53
Pope, John, 154
Population, 12, 16, 21, 24
Porter, David D., 100, 157
Porter, Felicia Grundy, *272*
Port Hudson, battle of, *157*
Pottawatomie Creek, 23
Powder monkeys, *168*
Preston, John S., 242
Prisons, Northern, *120–22*, 123, *125;* num-
  bers of deaths in, 204–5; Southern, 112,
  124–26, 127
Privateers, 53
Promontory Point, railroads converged at,
  287, 288

Quaker guns, *109*

Radical Republicans, 43, 48, 58–59, 291
Railroads; joining of cast and west, *287;* mili-
  tary photographer of, 222; as military tar-
  gets, *109;* nation's, *map 76;* Northern, 14,
  66, *78–79,* 81, 241; Southern, 18–19, 53, 57,
  82, 83, 236, 285
Railroad Act, 59, 288
Rams, 172
Rappahannock River, Union crossing of,
  90–91, 93
Reagan, John H., *64*
Reconstruction, Southern, 290–93
Recruiting practices. *See* Armies, recruiting
  for.
Redwood, Allen C., 230
Reed, Charles W., 228
Rees, Charles, 224
Relief agencies, 73, 200–201, 250, 268, 270,
  276. See also Veterans, organizations.
Republican party, 43, 46, 48, *52,* 59, 102, 241,
  286, 291, 292. *See also* Radical Republicans.
Rice, production of, 16–17
Richmond, 198, 202–3, 231, 272–73, 279;
  burning of, *223, 285;* food riot in, *218*
Richmond, battle of, 89, 96, 99, 103–4, 174,
  181
Riddle, A. J., 225
Rifles, *162–63, 167,* 190
Riots, 237, *248–249*
River combat. *See* Navies.
Roanoke Island, battle of, 213
Robert E. Lee, CSS, *74*
Robertson Hospital, 272–73

Rockefeller, John D., 288
Russell, Andrew J., 198, 222

St. Louis, USS, *152*
Salisbury Prison, 127
Sanitary Commission, U.S., 73, 200–201
Sanitation, camp, 186–87, 193
Savannah, battle of, 81
Schell, Frank H., 209, 213
Schools, 288, 297; medical, 186
Schurz, Carl, 46, *292*
Scott, Julian, *182–83,* 228
Scott, Winfield, 88, *104,* 105–7
Secession, Declaration of, 36
Semmes, Paul J., 205
Seth Thomas Clock Company, 12
Seven Pines, battle of, 99
Seward, William H., 43, *63*
Sewing kits, *145*
Seymour, Horatio, 56, 102
Sharecropping, 290–91
Sharpsburg, battle of, 90
Shaw, Robert G., 116–17, 217
Shenandoah, CSS, 160
Shenandoah Valley, battle of, 49, 180
Sheppard, William L., 231
Sheridan, Philip, 180–81, *229*
Sherman, William T., 12, *48,* 49, 66, 95–96,
  96, 100, *107,* 115, 210, 219, *222,* 270,
  278–79, 285, 299
Shiloh, battle of, 90, 95, 98, 100, 147
Shinplasters, 69
Ships. *See specific ships;* Warfare, technology of.
Shortages, coffee, 136–37, 145, 234; food,
  133–34, 136–38, 234–37, 248, 252–53;
  meat, 235; medical supplies, 195–97; salt,
  235; shoes, *136,* 199, *204,* 234; tea, 234
Sims, Frederick W., 83
Slater, Sarah, 261
Slavery, 11, 20, *28,* 36, 43, 55, 27–28; move-
  ment against, 21–23, 54; proclamation end-
  ing, 47, 59; Southern dependence on,
  16–17, 24, *25,* 26–29; uprisings against, 20,
  29. *See also* Blacks.; laws governing.
Soldiers. *See* Armies.
Sons of Confederate Veterans, 299
Sons of Union Veterans, 297
South Carolina, 12, 16–17, 36, 57
Southern Illustrated News, 214
Spencer carbine, *167*
Spies, women. *See* Women, spies.
Spotsylvania Court House, battle of, 92, 96,
  97
Springfield rifle, *163,* 284
Stanly, Edward, 59
Stanton, Edwin M., *62,* 218

Star of the West, USS, 31
Starvation. *See* Shortages, food.
Steel manufacturing, *14*
Stephens, Alexander H., 52, *53, 64,* 291
Stephenson, Benjamin F., 294
Stowe, Harriet Beecher, 20, 54
Strategies, war. *See* Armies; *specific battles; specific generals.*
Stuart, Jeb, *215*
Submarines. *See* Warfare, technology of.
Sugarcane, production of, 17
Sumner, Charles, *58,* 59
Supreme Court, U.S., 291–92
Surgery. *See* Medical care.
Sutlers, *144*
Sweetwater Factory, 278

Taney, Roger B., *42*
Taxation, 68–71, 241, 286, 292
Taylor, James E., 209
Technology. *See* Warfare, technology of.
Telegraph communications, 133, 164, 285
Thomas, George H., 101
Thompkins, Sally, *272*
Thompson, Frank (alias), 258–59
Thompson, Lucy, 266
Tobacco, production of, 16
Toombs, Robert A., 39, *53, 64*
Topographical Engineers, Corps of, *169*
Torpedo boats, *171,* 172, *230*
Torpedoes, *108,* 160–61, 169, 172–73
Trading with the Enemy Act, 196
Treasury notes, Federal, *71. See also* Money.
Tredegar Iron Works, *85*
Trench warfare, 174–81
Tubman, Harriet, *277*
Turner, Nat, *20,* 29
Turner, Richard, 124
Turner, Thomas P., *224*
Twenty-Negro Law, 243
Tycoons, postwar, 288

Uncle Tom's Cabin (Stowe), 20
Underground Railroad, *21,* 277
Uniforms, *36, 98, 193;* Confederate, *138, 149,* 194, *299;* Union, *35, 112, 140–41;* Zouave, *189, 295*
Union. *See also* Federal government; United States.; economy of, 70–71, 73, 240–41, 284, 288–89; first to secede from, 12, 16,

Union *(continued)*
36; Lincoln's goal for, 46; slave states in, 34, 59; states of, *34*
Union army, 47, 56, 81; animals used by, *80,* 81; blacks enlisted in, 27, 47, *114–17;* financing for, 70–71 (*see also* Federal government, finances of); medical examinations of, 186, 264; nuns with, 270–71; postwar, remaining in South, 292; soldiers of, 128–35, 140, 264–65; supplying civilians, *234–237;* Veteran Reserve Corps of, 188; victories of, 49, 81, 89–90; war strategy of, 102, 104–7, 153–54, 177; veterans of, *see* Veterans.
Union navy, 15, 204; on rivers, 81, 153–54; spy for, 256–57; at Vicksburg, 100
Union Veterans Legion, 297
United Confederate Veterans (UCV), 298–99
United Daughters of the Confederacy, 299
United States, opposing ideals for, 293; postwar changes in, 286–93; westward expansion of, 241, 287–88. *See also* Federal government; Union.
U.S. Christian Commission, *201*
U.S. Colored Troops, 117
U.S. Department of Agriculture, 59, 284
U.S. Medical Department, 184, 200
U.S. Military Railroad Service, 81
U.S. Sanitary Commission, 73, 200–201
U.S. Supreme Court, 291–92
U.S. Treasury Department, 70–71

Vallandigham, Clement L., 43, *44,* 45
Van Brunt, G. J., 158–59
Vanderbilt, Cornelius, *288*
Van Lew, Elizabeth, *257*
Velazquez, Loreta Janeta, *266,* 267
Veteran Reserve Corps, 188
Veterans, 297, 299; organizations, 294–99; parades for, *295, 298–299;* pensions for, 286, 296–98
Vicksburg, *208, 296*
Vicksburg, battle of, 81, 85, *94,* 95, 100, *157,* 299
Virginia, 16, 103; secession of, 35, 39; slave uprisings in, 20, 29. *See also* Harpers Ferry.
Virginia, CSS, 154–55. *See also Merrimack,* CSS.
Vizetelly, Frank, 214–17
Volunteers. *See* Relief agencies.

Wade, Benjamin F., *59*
Wadley, William M., 83
Walker, Leroy P., *64,* 65
Walker, Mary E., 275, *277*
War Democrats, 43, 59
Warfare, technology of, 150–81; advances in; balloons, 164–65, 170, *210;* communications, 133, 164, *169;* grenades, *173;* guns, *162–63,* 165–66, *167–68,* 170, 190, 289; ironclad ships, *152–61,* 289; mines, 169, 172–73; submarines, *170,* 172, 256–57; torpedo boats, *171,* 172, *230;* torpedoes, 108, 160–61, 169, 172–73; trench warfare, 174–81. *See also* Medical care.
Washington, battle of, 49, 188
Washington Artillery of New Orleans, *148*
Washington Square Hospital, *190*
Waud, Alfred, 209, *210,* 211, 237
Waud, William, 208–9, 212
Weapons manufacturing, 14–16, 18, 84–85, 163, 274–75, 279, 284. *See also* Warfare, technology of.
Welles, Gideon, 77
Whitman, Walt, 126, 142, 201
Whitney, Eli, 18
Whittier, John Greenleaf, 275
Whitworth rifle, 163
Wilderness, campaign, 96, *97,* 103, 130
Williams, Walter, 299
Williams rapid-fire gun, 170
Wilson, Fanny, 265
Wilson, James H., 219
Wilson Creek, battle of, 234
Winder Hospital, 198
Winter, surviving, 137, 146–48
Wirz, Henry, 123, *127*
Women, 254–79; commissioned by military, 272, 275, *277;* and food, *234–237,* 248; government employees, 279; joining soldiers at camp, *143;* laborers, *14, 274,* 275, 278–79; legends of, 275; letters of, 252–53; nuns, 270–71; nurses, *190–191, 200,* 203, 266, 268–70, *271,* 272, 277; reaction to war, *33,* 34–35, 130, *273,* 278 (*see also* Relief agencies); role of, 238–39, 254; soldiers, 264–67; spies, 256–61, 277

Yancey, William L., *61*

Zouave troops, 35, *91, 189, 295*